# Islam and Sustainable Development

*Do you not see how God strikes similitudes? A good word is as a good tree. Its roots are firm and its branches reach up into heaven. It gives forth its fruits in every season, by the leave of its Lord. And the similitude of a bad word is as a bad tree, uprooted from upon the earth, having no stability.*
(Quran: Ibrahim, 14:24–27)

*To my parents, who taught me to think of others and who were eager to see me as one who adds value to life.*

*To my wife Saheer Jallad, who devoted many hours in reviewing and commenting on the text and supported me throughout this journey.*

*To my family, Muath, Noor, Leena and Omar, who inspired me to start and complete this work. To my extended family, brothers and sisters, who always inspired to do to value the power of Now.*

*To all free thinkers and reflective practitioners who are leading transformation in the world.*

*To all the youth in the Tahrir Square in Egypt who enabled me to see the new worldviews.*

# Islam and Sustainable Development

## New Worldviews

ODEH RASHED AL-JAYYOUSI

GOWER

Published by
Gower Publishing Limited
Wey Court East
Union Road
Farnham
Surrey, GU9 7PT
England

Ashgate Publishing Company
Suite 420
101 Cherry Street
Burlington,
VT 05401-4405
USA

www.gowerpublishing.com

**British Library Cataloguing in Publication Data**
Al-Jayyousi, Odeh.
   Islam and sustainable development : new worldviews. --
   (Transformation and innovation)
   1. Sustainable development--Religious aspects--Islam.
   I. Title II. Series
   338.9'27'088297-dc23

   ISBN: 978-1-4094-2901-2 (hbk)
        978-1-4094-2902-9 (ebk)

**Library of Congress Cataloging-in-Publication Data**
Al-Jayyousi, Odeh Rashed.
  Islam and sustainable development : new worldviews / By Odeh Rashed Al-Jayyousi.
     p. cm.
   Includes index.
   ISBN 978-1-4094-2901-2 (hardback) -- ISBN 978-1-4094-2902-9 (ebook)
   1. Islam--Economic aspects. 2. Islam--Social aspects.
   3. Sustainable development. I. Title.
   BP173.75.A4183 2011
   297.2'7--dc23

                                                              2011048047

Printed and bound in Great Britain by the
MPG Books Group, UK

# Contents

# List of Figures

# List of Tables

# Acknowledgments

I wish to acknowledge the support and assistance from many who made this work possible. The review and comments I received from Khalil Jayousi, Khaldoun Jayousi, Ahmad Jayousi, Areen Jayousi, Deema Jayousi, Deena Jayousi, Al-Moayyed Assayed, Awni Bilal, Khalifa El-Jallad, Abed El-Jallad, Rami Daher, Ola Mallah, and Suha Murar are appreciated.

# Foreword

## His Royal Highness El Hassan Bin Talal of Jordan
Chairman, West Asia–North Africa Forum

In the current context of the 'Arab Spring', efforts emanating from within the West Asia–North Africa region to better understand, to inspire as well as to create proactive and home-grown approaches to development are required more than ever. With *Islam and Sustainable Development*, Professor Odeh Al-Jayyousi has made a positive move in that direction by attempting to demonstrate that some of the most cherished concepts and paradigms found in Islam are not only consistent with current notions of sustainable development, but may also be employed as a means to inspire others to participate more fully in the type of development that seeks to go beyond mere poverty reduction.

The author points out that Western models of development – while providing valuable references and starting points – should probably not be implemented 'as is' in Eastern contexts. While much development thinking has long been making this point, attempts to consolidate some of the specifics on how, exactly, development may be approached with greater efficacy and success in eastern and Islamic communities is a more recent phenomenon.

As an example from Jordan, a country with one of the most fragile and water-deficient ecosystems on the planet, I would like to mention that we are promoting approaches emphasising 'science, stewardship and tradition,' as a current form of the concept of '*Hima*.' This Arabic word literally means 'protected area', but carries layered connotations of meaning which support a community-based environmental resource management system. Valued as part of our knowledge heritage, the concept promotes acts of conservation and environmental protection that are intertwined with social justice. We believe that our region's rich tradition of Islamic ecological ethics can enable a platform for social investments locally that also provides ballast for and therefore greatly enhances, as opposed to threatens, all other types of investments – for example, green energy projects.

Development methodologists and theorists who anticipate or currently support development within the West Asia–North Africa region and who are seeking a language which will add inspirational value to technical approaches may find what they are looking for in this volume.

# Introduction
# Reflections and Personal
# Journey: In Search of Insight

The wave of democracy and Arab awakening in the Middle East / North Africa which started in Tunisia and Egypt in early 2011 paints new images of this part of the world. It also brings new hope and optimism that transformation and renewal is a natural and social law that needs to be harnessed to contribute to a new discourse and a new Dream. These unfolding events inform new rational imperatives for social innovation and help frame a new paradigm of sustainability that is rooted in the local soil, culture and ecology. The awakening in the Arab world was driven and motivated by the thirst for justice, dignity and sustainable development. This book is an attempt to set the scene for a new paradigm for sustainability that is informed by Islamic worldviews. The motto of the social movements, 'people wants to change the regime', is the first step in a long journey towards a sustainable human civilisation that is guided by a long-awaited justice (*adl*), inner/outer beauty (*ihsan*), social capital (*arham*) and a society without corruption (*fasad*). This book is about these four pillars of sustainability.

The story of this book started during my first trip to Yemen in 2004 during my professional career with IUCN – International Union for Conservation of Nature – as regional director in the Middle East. The seven years' work with IUCN in the Middle East opened my eyes to new perspectives of development and sustainability and in working with civil society, research institutions, donors and governments. In this first mission to Yemen, I encountered a personal experience that forced me to reflect on the future of development in the Arab region. While I was walking in the old city of Sanaa where one witnesses the early civilisations with limited interference of the modern world, the old market was full of life and dynamics unseen in any city. In a small shop with three steps below street level there was a camel with its eyes covered under a cloth and wandering in circles around a stone mill to grind seeds. When the camel finished this task the owner of the shop rewarded him with some vegetables. I was stunned by the multitude of images and thoughts that conquered my mind; this is the right analogy of our current development patterns in the Arab world. We have simply lost our compass, sight (*basar*) and insight (*baseera*). Yet, the developing world in the South is rewarded from various international aid agencies with programmes which in some cases may promote dependency and erode the human, social and the natural capitals.

This book is an attempt to uncover the mask on the eyes of reflective practitioners and public to rethink the current paradigm of development and sustainability. I do realise this is not an easy task but the deep experience I gained through my work in IUCN and also as an academic advisor (1997–2003) of the graduate programme in transformation management led by Professor Ronnie Lessem at Buckingham University opened new horizons for new domains of knowledge in social innovation and social change that inspired and transformed me. The seeds of this book stared after my mission to Yemen in 2004.

The last seven years of experience with IUCN shaped and deepened my awareness of sustainability especially in 2006 when there was a Thinkers' Meeting to revisit and debate the future of sustainability. This meeting urged me to contribute to this process from a cultural perspective as a voice from the South. The last section of this chapter relies on the publication of IUCN on transition to sustainability co-authored by W.M. Adams at Cambridge University and S. Jeanrenaud from IUCN (2008).

During my early days working with IUCN, I recall my brother-in-law, Adel Shaker, who was asking me about the geographical coverage of my region and I responded that it includes Iraq, Syria, Palestine, Iran, Pakistan and Afghanistan and the rest of Arab countries; his immediate response was 'you should quit the job ... who cares about fish, coral reefs or birds and endangered species if human lives are endangered? He added, 'There is no hope for environmental conservation in a region full of poverty, wealth and conflict.'

Being immersed in the work with civil society, donors, international organisations and governments in addressing the sustainability and governance issues in the Middle East enabled me to see new perspectives of development in action and the trickle down and trickle up effects of development. Also, having the chance to visit many countries across the globe from Switzerland, Monaco, Thailand, Mexico, Netherlands, Malaysia, Costa Rica, Senegal to South Africa, Yemen, Palestine, Oman, Iraq, Egypt, Bahrain, UAE, Pakistan, Lebanon, Syria,

India, Qatar and Saudi Arabia deepened and widened my understanding of how sustainable development is viewed from different perspectives and contexts. In this book I intend to synthesise my personal experience in all countries I visited with some reflections on how development is perceived and practised in different parts of the world.

Besides, I intend to contribute to help in bringing some insights on linkages between culture and development from my personal journey. This is also an attempt to describe some purposeful work that characterises many of development efforts in the Middle East. It is also an attempt to shed some light on attempts to embody the insight (*baseera*) and sight (*basar*) that makes the Middle East avoid entropy, inertia and stagnation.

Going back to my first trip to Yemen, I was puzzled by linking the text to context. Prophet Muhammad (peace be upon him and all prophets) praises Yemen saying that 'the faith is Yemeni and wisdom is Yemeni'. But how is it that we have lost these core values? One Yemeni journalist Nadia Al-Nasher from a Yemeni newspaper answered my question by saying: 'the wisdom was drowned and lost in the southern part of the Arabian Sea in Hadramout'. However, the current revival in the Middle East and North Africa proves that this wisdom was found and is vividly demonstrated by the resilient and determined requests from the people for reform, dignity and sustainable development.

In an effort to overcome this state of stagnation and decadence, I looked into the history of early civilisations in the Middle East and tried to understand the underlying reasons for the rise and fall of early civilisations like Sheba's (*Saba'*) civilisation in Yemen and in the rest of the world as outlined by Diamond (2005) in which he summarised key reasons for the collapse of nations which include an inability to realise and accept risk and an inability to act upon risk.

In 2009–2010, I was part of a global think-tank chaired by HRH Prince Al-Hassan bin Talal of Jordan called West Asia–North Africa (WANA) forum which aimed at developing a unifying regional vision for a sustainable future. I looked into the European Dream in search for a shared experience and common discourse that may develop a meta-narrative based on faith, reason and empathy to harness the wealth of the Middle East. This experience compelled me to rethink the regional unit of analysis so as to create a critical mass for a sustainable future. The debate was on how WANA can leapfrog by harnessing technology and building a regional infrastructure for transport like the Smart Green regional train system. My passion and interest was for localising technology in the region and rethinking the current unit of analysis for water/energy/food which are based on 'nation-state' boundaries. The evident examples of virtual water (water embedded in food), unemployment, energy and climate change challenges cannot be addressed within a nation-state context. A regional social contract among states needs to be developed as a rational imperative. The awakening in the Arab region will induce a new momentum when democratic institutions are mature and able to co-create and evolve a regional vision that promotes peace, freedom and sustainability. Sustainability requires a new regional science, new regional policy analysis and new units of analysis like an eco-region, a watershed, a river basin or a drainage basin that transcends the nation-state boundaries.

The financial crisis that began in 2008–9 compelled me to try to understand the underlying assumptions and root causes of the crisis and how Islamic finance may offer some ideas to the global financial crisis. Clinical economics, as presented by Sachs (2005), need to be applied to address the inequities between the North and the South. Scholars and economic experts were making references to Islamic finance as a means to provide a new paradigm to address the global spillover effects of the financial crisis. Besides, development experts were making strong cases of the paradoxes and the inverse proportionality between external aid to Africa and the decline of vital economic indicators. More money is spent, yet there is more poverty, a paradox that made me wonder about economic rationality and the theoretical underpinning of the development model and foreign aid. At the regional arena and its wealth, the wave of democracy in the Arab world revealed that leaders in Tunisia, Libya and Egypt own tens of billions of dollars while people are living under the poverty line. Had this money been invested in the region, it would have resulted in a new region that enjoys the same infrastructure and services found in any developed country in Europe or in the US. In this book, I argue that good governance (*adl*) is the cornerstone for a sustainable society.

This book consists of seven chapters and an epilogue. In Chapter 1, I review and critique the conventional concepts and approaches of sustainability so as to identify the missing elements in the Western model with its three pillars (economic, social and environmental). It was evident that the cultural and spiritual components are missing in the conventional model. Hence, I introduce a set of Islamic notions that will help to frame and develop a new model for sustainability. I argue that the current economic model has some blind spots and suffers from landscape amnesia and hence it fails people and nature, as is evident in the financial crisis, the poverty gap and climate change. Chapter 1 also addresses the pitfalls and shortcomings of the prevailing economic model that is based on growth and overconsumption and that is characterised by a huge gap between the rich and the poor, and by overconsumption, pollution and climate risks. I argue that we need a new model that promotes prosperity without overconsumption and pollution. The notions of balance, harmony, public interest, wisdom and living lightly on earth (*zuhd*) are introduced to help formulate a new model of sustainability.

Chapter 2 outlines a framework of a new model for sustainable development that is informed by Islamic local knowledge, spirituality and culture. The proposed framework for sustainability consists of four components: good governance (*adl*), excellence (*ihsan*), social capital (*arham*) and integrity without corruption (*fasad*). Each of the four components will be explained in the following chapters, starting from chapter 3 through to chapter 6. This four-dimensional model is linked to two domains or spheres, which are good life (*hayat tayebah*) and construction of the universe or earth (*emarat al ard*).

In Chapter 3, good governance, justice (*adl*) will be discussed which is the first dimension of the sustainability framework developed in Chapter 2. Also, land and property rights and economic justice in Islam are discussed from a legal perspective. The final section addresses fair trade and *hima* (protected areas) as a representation and application of justice in a globalised world.

In Chapter 4, the second pillar or dimension of the sustainability model, *ihsan*, is presented. *Ihsan* means inner beauty and consciousness. This concept implies the appreciation of beauty and harmony in the cosmos, nature and the communities of life. The degradation of aesthetic intelligence, I believe, is a result of the absence of the notion of *ihsan*. Learning to appreciate the outer beauty is a natural reflection of the inner beauty and the unity (*tawhid*) of both the inner and outer beauty is in essence the meaning of *ihsan*. Mecca as a model of a good city, and a good life will be discussed as a vision for the future.

In Chapter 5, the third dimension of the sustainability model will be presented which is the social capital (*arham*). Also, the Islamic social system is discussed which include the community (*ummah*), the family and the individual. In this chapter, a focus will be on the community since this domain captures the essence of collective action and choice. This value-based community is called a 'median community' (*ummah wassat*) which has a mandate to provide the common ground and common word for all people. The social capital (*arham*) encompasses the human and social dimension from an Islamic perspective. Moreover, trust fund (*waqf*) will be presented as a case study to support social cohesion and societal responsibility.

In Chapter 6, the fourth dimension of sustainability, the concept of pollution and corruption (*fasad*), will be discussed. Any deviation from the natural state (*fitra*) is viewed as pollution or corruption, or *fasad*. Hence, climate change from an Islamic perspective is a form of *fasad*. In this chapter, I argue that the unity of universe, humanity and destiny dictates the need for a transformational global leadership to address the potential threats of climate change. The global debate on climate change needs to be informed by Islamic discourse of trusteeship (*amanah*). Besides, a model to address the climate change is presented which include Green activism (*Jihad*), Green Innovation (*Ijtihad*) and Green lifestyle (*Zuhd*). The simple name of this model is Green JIZ which represents the response to climate change from an Islamic perspective.

In Chapter 7, education for sustainable development is presented from an Islamic perspective. This chapter is intended to critique and assess the current educational system which is devoid of cosmology and suffers from a lack of an ecological insight. The philosophy of Western education was influenced by the mechanistic Newtonian model which looks at nature as an opportunity for exploitation, not as a source for inspiration and innovation. This paradigm of education leads us to a state of 'nature-deficit disorder' and contributes to the current global challenges including consumerism, poverty and climate change. Transformative education that is informed and guided by Islamic worldviews and the unity (*tawhid*) of mind and soul, natural and social sciences and Today (*dunia*) and Hereafter will be proposed in this chapter. This transformative education will be the hope for a sustainable human civilisation.

In this book, I propose a new model for sustainable development which includes the spiritual and cultural components informed by Islamic perspectives. I will use the terminology '*Tayebah*' instead of the term 'sustainable' since the cultural implications of the term '*Tayebah*' means the intrinsic state of goodness which is inspired from local knowledge and Islamic culture. The Muslim world was plagued with a series of challenges that impeded its contribution to sustainability in the last century. The issues of political reform overshadowed the issues of sustainable development. After colonisation and the following era of independence, the Muslim world borrowed extensively from the Western models of developments along with their pitfalls. Hence, there is a need to rethink and reform the current thinking of sustainability and de-construct and re-construct a new model that is rooted in the local soil and culture of the Middle East. I will highlight the value of local knowledge, harmony and balance as key notions in Islam where every species is in a state of prayer '*Sujud and Tasbeeh*'. Celebrating the diversity and the beauty of life is part of being a player in the 'symphony of life'. This can be attained when the human is conscious of the blessings of the creator and lives the state of oneness (*tawhid*) with oneself, nature and the universe.

In this book, I argue that Islam is not simply a religion but rather a worldview and a way of life that organises relationships between humans and between humans and nature. This book is an attempt to contextualise some basic Islamic principles and notions in sustainable development in many domains from culture to economics, ecology and education.

# 1

# Sustainable Development Revisited

*The carbon cycle and Islam are both vital for life, however, both carbon and Islam are perceived as global threats to humanity and sustainability in the twenty-first century. Both concepts need to be de-constructed and re-constructed.*

(*The Author*)

## Overview

This chapter is intended to present some basic definitions and approaches of sustainability. Also, it aims to critique the current economic model which failed people, nature and economy. The argument is that the current market economy is not telling us the ecological truth and that GNP is not the right metrics to measure the heath and wealth of nations. The chapter describes the pitfalls and shortcomings of the prevailing economic model that is based on growth and overconsumption and that is characterised by huge gap between the rich and the poor, overconsumption, pollution and climate risks.

The chapter sets the scene for the need for a new model that promotes prosperity without overconsumption and pollution. It is about living lightly on earth (*zuhd*). This chapter also introduces key Islamic concepts to set the scene for Chapter 2 which outlines the framework of a new model for sustainable development informed by Islamic local knowledge, spirituality and culture.

## Objectives

The main objectives of this chapter are outlined below:

1.  Review the evolutions and terminology of sustainable development.

2.  Critique the current market-based economic model.

3.  Discuss the foundations of sustainable development.

4.  Assess the adequacy and reasonableness of the conventional model of sustainable development.

5.  Introduce the basic concepts of sustainability from an Islamic perspective.

## Sustainable Development – Revisited

I started this chapter on 25 September 2010 in Bahrain where I was listening to the UN General Assembly on Millennium Development Goals (MDGs) and the level of meeting the targets. Watching BBC and Al-Jazeera International revealed interesting facts. One BBC commentator was stating that the UN building was so majestic but the actions and results of 192 nations did not meet expectations. Questionable fund effectiveness, lack of incentives for private sector and a limited role for civil society and poor governance are key issues that limit the effective attainment of MDGs targets. There is a lot of concern and scepticism that 2015 will come and still the world will be lagging behind meeting many targets for the MDGs.

## The Evolution of the Concept of Sustainable Development

The concept and challenges of sustainability were addressed in many studies like the *World Conservation Strategy* published by IUCN, WWF and UNEP in 1980, and its successor *Caring for the Earth* in 1991, and in the report of the World Commission on Environment and Development (WCED) in 1987. It was discussed at United Nations conferences in Stockholm in 1972, Rio in 1992 and Johannesburg in 2002 (Adams, 2009).

The key question is 'Are we moving towards a sustainable future considering the poverty trap, human dignity deficit, HIV and ecological degradation?' Are we having the right balance between all capitals (natural, social, human, manufactured and financial)? The current global trade suggests that we are outsourcing China to feed and provide goods to billions of people worldwide. The global governance is dysfunctional as was evident in Copenhagen climate talks in 2009. We are using the natural capital of China through the use of virtual energy, water and food, and the question is how much time does it take to maintain the status quo?

Detailed analysis of the ecological, economic and social vital statistics reveals that the current economic development model is failing people, nature and the economy. There are ecological and land-use amnesia and blind spots in the current economic model, a reason it fails to tell us ecological truth.

Specifically, the term 'sustainable development' was used in 1987 by the Brundtland Commission and has become a widely used notion in many disciplines like, transport, water, housing and tourism. The term meant the ability to 'meet the needs of the present without comprising the ability of future generations to meet their own needs'.

In the 1970s, the term sustainability was used to describe an economy in equilibrium with basic ecological support systems. The three key components of sustainable development include environmental, economic and social dimensions as depicted in Figure 1.1. However, other models viewed the environment (natural capital) as the overall foundation of life-support systems that underpin our social capital and financial capital as shown in Figure 1.2.

The following is a review of the basic definitions of sustainable development. Sustainability means different things to different people yet it appears to unite them under a shared target. The purpose of this review is to help identify gaps in these definitions so as to help formulate a new model for sustainability. The concept of sustainable development will be explored below after which key elements of the definitions will be discussed based on the work of Rijsberman (2000):

1.  The Brundtland Commission defines sustainable development as 'a development that fulfills the needs of the present generation, without compromising the ability of the future generations to fulfill their need' (WCED, 1987, p. 43). An important element in this definition is the fulfilment of the needs of the present generation on the one hand and of the needs of future generations on the other.

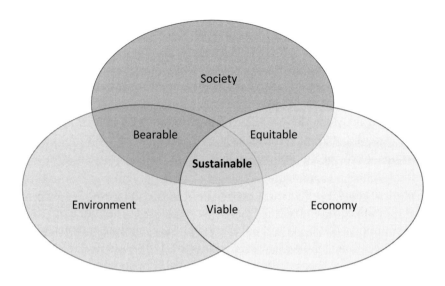

**Figure 1.1      Scheme of sustainable development (IUCN, 2006)**

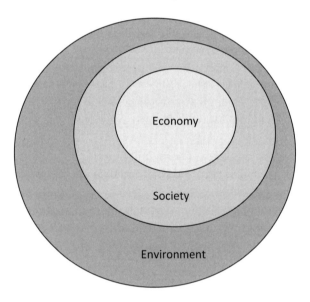

**Figure 1.2      A representation of sustainability showing how both economy and society are constrained by environmental limits**

2.      The International Union for Conservation of Nature (IUCN) defines the term as: 'Sustainable development means improving the quality of life while living within the carrying capacity of supporting ecosystems' (World Conservation Union et al., 1991). This definition is broader than the one of the Brundtland Commission. It is evident that

this definition includes important elements like the improvement of the quality of life and the carrying capacity of supporting ecosystems. The 'improvement of the quality of life' in this definition seems more ambitious than the 'fulfillment of needs' in the Brundtland definition. Improving of the quality of life' can be interpreted as equal to fulfilling needs to a higher degree: the quality of life can be thought of as the amount in which people's needs are fulfilled.

3. According to Mostert (1998), sustainability implies that the supply of 'natural capital' is maintained'. He stated that the sustainable development should meet the following conditions:

- the use of renewable sources – such as water – should not exceed the rate of renewal;

- the use of non-renewable resources – such as fossil fuels – should be such that they will not be exhausted before alternative sources are available;

- fundamental ecological processes and structures should be maintained.

This definition addresses the carrying capacity of supporting systems and the maintenance of the integrity of the system which is referred to as the prevention of system degradation.

Based on the above definitions, we can frame and construct four approaches to sustainable development based on people, environment, norms and values as depicted in Figure 1.3. The combinations and relationships between the four components (people/environment/norms/values) form four approaches for understanding sustainable development. These are as follows:

a) Carrying capacity approach which is based on being aware of the carrying capacity of environment which is referred to in Islam as balance (*Mizan*).

b) Ratio approach which is based on an evaluation of a present situation under certain criteria and objectives including physical and human factors which is referred to from an Islamic perspective as beauty (*Ihsan*).

c)     Socio-approach which takes into account people's interests and opinions in policy formulation and decision-making which is referred to as *Arham* which refers to the human social capital and connectivity.

d)     Eco-approach which focuses on the intrinsic value of nature and the ecosystem services which is referred to as *Tasbeeh* since all species are in a state of prayers (*Tasbeeh*).

Figure 1.3 outlines key sustainability concepts and the corresponding Islamic concepts associated in the four approaches to sustainable development.

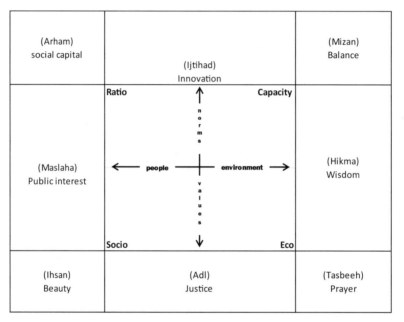

**Figure 1.3     Terms associated to the various aspects and approaches of sustainability: Rijsberman (2000) and Al Jayyousi (2008)**

It should be mentioned that we need to look at sustainability as a process, not as a project or a product since in the real world we deal with complex problems that need multiple solutions and perspectives and that is why the various approaches and notions of sustainability (*Tayyebah*) may offer multiples views and solutions to the same problem.

The key concepts associated with sustainable development from an Islamic perspective as depicted in Figure 1.4 include:

1.  Wisdom (*hikma*): this represents the purposeful pursuit of acquiring and embodying wisdom from all nations. This cross-fertilisation of knowledge is a critical element in transforming societies to value-based eco-communities that embrace sustainability as a way of life.

2.  Justice (*adl*): this implies the good governance in its broad sense which is the core of a sustainable rule that is based on rights.

3.  Public interest (*maslaha*): this notion refers to a consensus reached by a community on what constitutes 'good' for all. This represents a ruling and a principle for defining collective goods.

4.  Innovation (*ijtihad*): this refers to applying diligence and intellectual capital to solve current and emerging problems. It is also about reinventing new tools and methods to make a transition to sustainable development.

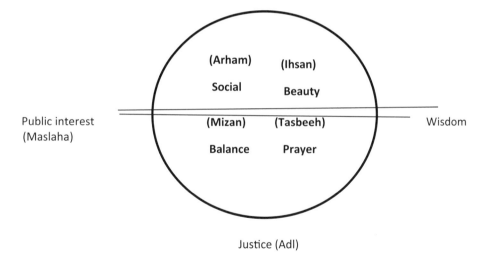

Justice (Adl)

**Figure 1.4    Key Islamic terms related to sustainability**

Moreover, the combination of each pair of the above concepts yields a set of notions that inform sustainability. Specifically, beauty (*ihsan*) is the trade-off between innovation (*ijtihad*) and wisdom (*hikma*). The other concepts *Tasbeeh*,

*Mizan and Arham*, are the trade-offs resulting from (wisdom-justice), (justice-public interest) and (public interest-innovation) respectively as illustrated in Figure 1.4. These concepts will be discussed in detail in the following chapters.

## Sustainability Principles: Lessons from Ecology and Thermodynamics

In the 1960s and 1970s, the planet was viewed as 'Spaceship Earth', as articulated by Kenneth Boulding and Barbara Ward (Ward, 1966). The challenge we had is that population growth follows geometric series while natural resources follow a mathematical series.

The imagined clash between development and conservation of nature was reconciled by the term 'sustainable development' but this concept meant many things and the concept lacks quantified indicators and metrics. However, the key notion of taking attention of both intra-generational equity (between rich and poor now) and intergenerational equity (between present and future generations) is the cornerstone for a sustainable future.

As argued by Adams (2008), faith in 'business as usual' to deliver the changes needed owes more to the hopes of those with wealth and power than to a coherent analysis of the state of the environment or the needs of the global poor. We face the risks of tipping points and irreversible changes in the environment and in its capacity to support and sustain human life in all its dimensions. This state of imbalance and pollution is referred to as '*fasad*' in Islam which is attributed to human-made actions.

Mainstream sustainable development, according to Adams (2008), encompasses a series of ideas such as ecological modernisation and market environmentalism that promise to steer the world towards sustainability in ways that do not demand too many dramatic changes, and that do not upset the comfortable, the rich or the powerful.

Transforming society and the world's economy to a sustainable basis presents the most significant challenge to the twenty-first century. This challenge is unprecedented in scope. Its context is the planet as a whole. It requires a fundamental shift in consciousness as well as in action. It calls for a fresh vision, a new approach for shaping a new reality. The following principles are based on the work of Ben-Eli (2005).

## THE FIRST PRINCIPLE: NATURAL STATE (*FITRA*) PRINCIPLE

*Contain entropy and ensure that the flow of resources, through and within the economy, is as nearly non-declining (mizan) as is permitted by physical laws.*

This principle implies a number of policy and operational implications which include (a) striving for highest resource productivity, (b) amplifying performance with each cycle of use, (c) employing 'income' rather than 'capital' sources where applicable and continuously recycling non-regenerative resources, (d) affecting an unbroken, closed-loop flow of matter and energy in a planetary productive infrastructure, (e) controlling leakages and avoiding stagnation, misplaced concentrations or random diffusion of chemical elements during cycles of use, and (f) establishing a service, 'performance leasing' orientation for managing durable goods.

## THE SECOND PRINCIPLE: ACCOUNT FOR ECOSYSTEM SERVICES (*MIZAN*) PRINCIPLE

*Adopt an appropriate accounting system, fully aligned with the planet's ecological processes and reflecting true, comprehensive biospheric pricing to guide the economy.*

This principle implies a set of policy options such as (a) employing a comprehensive concept of wealth related to the simultaneous enhancement of five key forms of capital (natural, human, social, manufactured and financial), (b) aligning the world's economy with nature's regeneration capacity and incorporate critical 'externalities' in all cost and benefit accounts, (c) embodying a measure of well-being and human development in economic calculations, (d) designing regulation and taxation policies to accentuate desirable and eliminating adverse outcomes, optimising the whole.

## THE THIRD PRINCIPLE: RESPECT ALL COMMUNITIES OF LIFE (*UMAM*) PRINCIPLE

*Ensure that the essential diversity of all forms of life in the Biosphere is maintained.*

A set of policy and operational implications can be devised which (a) harvest species only to regeneration capacity, (b) assume a responsible stewardship for our planet's web of biological diversity, (c) shape land-use patterns to reduce human encroachment on other forms of life and enhance biological diversity in areas of human habitat, and (4) conserve the variety of existing gene pool.

## THE FOURTH PRINCIPLE: PROMOTE THE ROLE OF A TRUSTEE (*UMMAH WASSAT*) GLOBAL COMMUNITY

> *Maximise degrees of freedom and potential self-realisation of all humans without any individual or group, adversely affecting others.*

Based on the above principle a set of policy and operational implications can be identified. These include (a) fostering tolerance as a cornerstone of social interactions, (b) enshrining human rights within a framework of planetary citizenship like the Earth Charter, (c) providing for good governance, (d) ensuring equitable access to life nurturing support, and (e) establishing cooperation as a basis for managing global issues and planetary resources.

## THE FIFTH PRINCIPLE: UNDERSTAND THE SYMPHONY OF LIFE (*TASBEEH* AND *SUJOOD*) PRINCIPLE

> *Recognise the seamless, dynamic continuum of wisdom, love, and energy that links the outer reaches of the cosmos with our solar system, our planet and its biosphere including all humans, with our internal metabolic systems.*

The above principle may inform a number of policy actions. These include (a) acknowledging the transcendent mystery (*ghayb*) that underlies existence, (b) seeking to understand and fulfil humanity's unique function in Universe (*taskheer and istikhlaf*), (c) honouring the Earth with its intricate ecology of which humans are an integral part (*ummam amthalokom*), (d) fostering compassion and an inclusive, comprehensive perspective in the underlying intention, motivation and actual implementation of human endeavours, and (e) linking inner transformation (*dameer*) of individuals to transformations in the social collective (*taghyeer*), laying foundations for emergence of a new planetary consciousness.

## THE FIVE PRINCIPLES AS AN INTEGRATED WHOLE: UNITY WITHIN DIVERSITY

Deeper reflection on the concept of sustainability and the five core principles which together prescribe it reveals that the spiritual dimension, the spiritual principle, is fundamental to the quality and coherence of the whole. As a guiding principle, Islamic values and thought form the foundation and underpins the spiritual dimension. Islam, viewed as a worldview and a way of life, evokes the soul-focused integration of mind and heart in realisation of the essential oneness (*tawhid*) at the centre of being.

By anchoring the essence of human motivation and intention as framed in Islam as 'the construction of Earth' (*Emmarat al ard*) and stewardship (*istikhlaf*), the spiritual principle acts as the causal root which sets the tone for the whole. It drives the integration of the four principles, those related to the material, economic, life and social domains. It integrates in a balanced way to evolve a value-based and objective community (*ummah wasat*); it can infuse a common purpose, provide a common foundation and stimulate common resolve.

A balanced and full integration of all five principles is essential, however, for conceptualising and realising sustainability as a state. The whole set has to be integrated into a single unity in which the five principles come together as one. The five domains underlying the principles interact and co-define one another to contribute to define what constitutes a good life (*Hayat Tayebah*).

Good life (*Hayat Tayebah*) and the pursuit of happiness in Islam have little to do material accumulation and consumption. In a consumer-based credit society the media promotes the illusion that the more one consumes the more he attains happiness. This illusion which the media promotes through the manipulation of minds creates a lot of consumer products and shift 'wants' to 'needs'. The media also helps to promote universally accepted ethos, standards and norms in a globalised world and globalised minds which are risky to cultural and biological diversity.

Good life (*Hayat Tayebah*), from an Islamic perspective, has to do with the positive role of the human to construct and add-value to life (*Emarat al Ard*) and to be a witness and a trustee and to leave a good legacy. Euro-centric or US-centric views of what constitutes a good life differ from the basic Islamic notions of simplicity or sufficiency (*Zuhd*) and using local resources and knowledge to attain a people-centred development as the model developed in Egypt by Ibrahim abu El Aish.

## The State of the Environment

This section argues that our economic development model has many blind spots when it comes to nature conservation. Besides, humans suffer from landscape and species amnesia. We tend to worry about our financial capital but are not aware of or less concerned with our social and natural capital.

The notion of *natural state 'fitra'*, or the balance in nature, is a key concept in Islamic worldview. This implies that everything on earth is in balance (*qadar*) and there is sufficient food and resources, if distributional equity and justice exist. Islamic thought states that if conditions of equity are met, no scarcity of resources will exist. Islam views the current global ecological crisis as a problem of ethics and equity.

The current Western development paradigm is founded on consumerism. What makes things worse is that the global media promotes overconsumption as a means to pursue happiness. The scale and speed of consumption was referred to as 'great acceleration' shows increasing trends in water, food, energy use. Reports about the 'state of the world', ecological footprints and the metrics of the World Wide Fund for Nature's 'Living Planet Index' (LPI), show the level of the ecological crisis as estimated in 1998 and 2008 (MEA, 2005). Statistics of global population, urban population and consumption, the level of international telecommunications, motor vehicles all show steep rises in the second half of the twentieth century. As documented by Adams (2008), Table 1.1 shows the salient impacts of the current human development patterns on biosphere.

Statistics show that a 16-fold growth in energy use in the twentieth century was associated with sulphur dioxide emissions twice natural emissions – nitric oxide, carbon, dioxide, methane emissions all far above background levels – and the release of manufactured chemicals such as chlorofluorocarbons (Crutzen, 2002). The Intergovernmental Panel on Climate Change (IPCC) *Fourth Assessment Report* (2007) found that 11 of the 12 years 1996–2006 were among the 10 warmest years in the instrumental record, which began in 1850.

The question remains whether we can attain prosperity without growth and without having an economy based on fossil oil. Transformation to a sustainable future requires reducing consumption (*zuhd*) and redirecting consumption to less destructive forms (*ihsan*) and learning from ecology as detailed by Kiuchi

**Table 1.1     Human impacts on the biosphere**

- Between 1970 and 2003, the 'Living Planet Index' fell by about 30 per cent. The terrestrial index (695 species) fell by 31 per cent, the marine index (274 species) by 27 per cent and the freshwater index (344 species) by 29 per cent.
- Three-quarters of the habitable surface of the earth has been disturbed by human activity.
- Human activities have increased previous 'background' extinction rates by between 100 and 10,000 times.
- 40 per cent of potential terrestrial net primary production was used directly by human activities, co-opted or forgone as a result of those activities.
- Fertiliser made from industrially produced ammonia sustains roughly 40 per cent of the human population and comprises 40–60 per cent of the nitrogen in the human body.
- Industrial fish-harvesting techniques, such as trawling, and pollution of productive shallow seas and areas of living diversity such as coral reefs and seamounts has led to a transformation of the ecology of the oceans to an extent that even marine scientists have only recently begun to appreciate.
- The population of large predatory fish is now less than 10 per cent of pre-industrial levels.
- More than 2 million people globally die prematurely every year due to outdoor and indoor air pollution.
- Per capita availability of freshwater is declining globally, and contaminated water remains the single greatest environmental cause of human sickness and death.

and Shireman (2002). This implies a transformation towards a low-carbon society or a green economy. The 'Factor 10 Club' founded in France in 1994 by Friedrich Schmidt-Bleek, whose goal is to dematerialise the economies of the industrialised countries tenfold on the average within 30 to 50 years, is an example for a transition to sustainability (Hawken et al., 1999).

There is a growing interest in ideas of 'de-growth' (*zuhd*) or downscaling (Latouche, 2004). De-growth is a term created by radical critics of growth theory. The transformation to clean energy is imperative in light of the fact that the energy peak oil is being reached and the era of cheap hydrocarbons is coming to an end. High energy prices will drive changes in the technology and human behaviour. The WRI estimates that 30 per cent of greenhouse gas emissions come from deforestation, agriculture and forestry. The value of economic services is to be mainstreamed in development thinking. In 2006, $52 billion was invested in renewable energy sources worldwide (WWI, 2008). Investing in ecosystems through natural solutions (*fitra* solutions) provides immense opportunities to secure a sustainable future. In a nutshell, the current global state of environment provides evidence that the current development model is unsustainable. In essence, the climate change risk is an indicator of a market failure. It is imperative to look for an alternative model to ensure a sustainable future for people and nature.

At the social front, according to Sachs (2005), every day about 20,000 people perish because of extreme poverty. Everyday 7,500 young adults die because of AIDS. Since 11 September 2001, the United States has engaged in a war on terror, but neglected the deeper causes of global instability. The $450 billion that the United States spent in 2001 on the military will never buy peace if it continues to spend about one thirtieth of that, just $15 billion, to address the plight of the world poorest of the poor. The $15 billion represents 15 cents on every $100 of US gross national product. The share of US GNP devoted to helping the poor has declined for decades, and is a tiny fraction of what the US has promised.

As argued by Sachs (2005), official development assistance (ODA) is the largest source of external funding and is critical to the achievement of the development goals and targets of the Millennium Declaration. The consensus among the developed world is to devote 0.7 per cent of GDP as ODA. In 2002, aid was $53 billion, just 0.2 per cent of rich-world GNP. If rich countries met the target, aid would reach $175 billion per year, equal to 0.7 per cent of the $25 trillion rich-world GNP in 2002. For the US, foreign aid would rise from around $15 billion per year in 2004 (0.14 per cent of GNP) to around $75 billion (0.7 per cent of US GNP). The poverty trap and the recipe to end poverty were articulated by Sachs (2005). The remedy is about political will and commitment to allocate sufficient (0.5 per cent of global GNP) resources from North to South.

The idea that decades of formal 'development' have created a world where all countries are experiencing economic growth and gains in quality of life (let alone all people in those countries) is an illusion. Less than 10 per cent of the world's gross national product (GNP) stems from low-income countries (World Bank, 2000). Average annual income is less than $300 per head in Burundi, Cambodia, Chad, the Democratic Republic of Congo, the Central African Republic, Eritrea, Ethiopia, Malawi, Mali, Nepal, Niger, Nigeria, Rwanda, Sierra Leone, Tanzania and the Yemen Republic. Many, although not all, of these poorest countries are in Africa, and many are also suffering the destruction brought by civil or international war (for example, Sudan, Sierra Leone, Liberia, Democratic Republic of Congo). The share of global wealth enjoyed by the world's poorest countries, and by the world's poorest people in all countries, is low and falling.

In September 2000, the United Nations Millennium Summit agreed on eight Millennium Development Goals, with 18 targets and 48 indicators as yardsticks for measuring improvements in people's lives. And the good news is that there has been substantial progress in poverty reduction: the proportion of people subsisting on less than a dollar a day globally halved between 1981 and 2001, and for the first time in human history, the absolute number of people living at this level fell. But that still left 21.3 per cent of the world's population living in extreme poverty, some 1.1 billion people. Poverty gains have been concentrated in Asia, especially China. Indeed, if China is excluded, the number of people living on less than a dollar a day has actually increased, growing from 836 million to 841 million between 1981 and 2004. This increase in the number of the poor was most marked in Africa, where the number living at this level rose from 164 million to 314 million between 1981 and 2001, 46 per cent of the population.

It is argued that the current concern for sustainable development needs to be replaced with a new and broader concern for 'environmental sustainability and justice (*adl*)'. This must embrace both the familiar concerns for intra-generational justice (justice for the poor now) and inter-generational justice (justice for those yet unborn), and also justice with respect to other species. Justice (*Adl*) from an Islamic perspective is the cornerstone for good governance and a sustainable civilisation.

There is a worrying tendency in international debates as argued by Adams (2008) to use arguments about efficiency to pursue policies aimed at sustainability onto the poor. The cost-effectiveness too often trumps justice, whether it is plans to control human use of forests or to promote the growing of biofuels. Thus enthusiasm for REDD (reduced deforestation and degradation) is partly driven by arguments that it is simply cheaper to reduce carbon loss from developing world forests and farmlands than by interfering with the high-value economies (and lifestyles) of developed countries. It is no part of a justice agenda to let the world's poor be paid the low rate for carbon to deal with the consequences of a world economy that so strongly favours the rich. Actions to tackle climate change are unlikely to be uniform and thus responses to climate change have justice implications.

## The Need to Rethink Sustainable Development

The following presents a set of arguments pertaining to why we need to rethink development and sustainability based on new metrics of measuring sustainability, the pitfalls of using GNP as a sole indicator for sustainability and the cost of economic growth on our natural capital:

1. *No metrics to measure sustainability:* One of the challenges of sustainability as revealed in the global statistics is the lack of objective and realistic metrics and indicators to measure sustainability. Besides, the conventional framework or mental model for sustainability where the social, economic and ecological domains are viewed as overlapped circles as shown in Figure 1.1 makes the implicit assumption that we can make trade-offs between the three domains. This perception resulted in irreversible losses in ecosystem services which represents our natural capital. Another conceptual model (as depicted in Figure 1.2) sees the three domains (ecology, society and economics) as three circles which share the same centre with the largest domain as the natural capital and the smallest one is the financial capital. This means that our natural capital underpins our social and financial capitals.

2. *Addressing poverty and natural conservation:* The trickle-down effects of international aid need to be assessed to ensure that the local poor benefits. It is interesting to note that of the $350 billion spent by the US Government in developing countries, 90 per cent goes to people above median incomes – this is essentially a subsidy to the middle class. Public policies and aid need to move beyond cash transfer which often involves a translation to a Western-style modernity, industrial, urban, democratic and capitalist to a context and a culture that is not congruent with local norms and values.

3. *Thinking beyond GNP as a measure of the health and wealth of nations:* The twentieth-century fixation with GNP, as argued by Korten (1995), as a measure of human development is flawed. Developed countries do not provide good models for a transition to sustainability as articulated by Adams (2008): they are the least sustainable on earth. Their levels of consumption are the chief drivers of anthropogenic climate change and biodiversity loss; their economies draw poor communities in the developing world communities into systems of production and exchange, but even where they generate wealth they do not stimulate equity. High quality of life and high scores on measures of human development are not necessarily associated with high GNP per capita: as argued by Fanelli (2007), Cuba offers

an interesting challenge to the notion that rich countries show the way towards sustainability. An analysis of the Global Footprint Network of ecological footprints of 93 nations over the last 30 years shows Cuba alone on the path to sustainability.

Cultural wealth, not least of indigenous peoples, is rarely measured, but is critically important to human welfare. Islam represents the local knowledge and the cultural wealth that needs to harnessed to convey a new model for sustainability and mercy for all humankind (*rahma lel alameen*). As argued by Korten (1995), the major portion of what shows up as growth in GNP is a result of:

a)    shifting activities for the non-money social economy of household and community to the money economy with the consequent erosion of social capital;

b)    depleting natural resources stocks such as forests, fisheries and oil and mineral reserves at far above their recovery rates;

c)    counting as income the costs of defending ourselves against the consequences of growth, such as disposing of waste, cleaning up toxic dumps and oil spills, providing health care for victims of environmentally caused illnesses, rebuilding after floods resulting from human activities such as deforestation, and financing pollution-control devices.

The trade-off between the economic, social and environmental domains often results in sub-optimal solutions that need a negotiated agreement among different stakeholders, as illustrated in the case of managing the Azraq wetland in Jordan.

---

**AZRAQ OASIS IN JORDAN: ALLOCATION OF WATER USES AMONG COMPETING USERS**

The Azraq Oasis is a wetland site located in eastern Jordanian desert. It is an outstanding example of an oasis wetland in an arid region with a unique ecosystem wetland and immense biological, cultural and socioeconomic value. It lies on the heart of the Azraq Basin with an area of approximately 12710 km²; the oasis supports a rich and varied aquatic fauna and flora that are very rare in the region. It is also important for migratory birds, with up to a million birds utilise the area during migration, forming one of the most unique ecosystems in the world.

The oasis is under severe pressure and ecosystems are in the far stage of degradation. The main cause of the destruction of the Azraq Oasis in the last twenty years is the overexploitation of its groundwater for various water uses. During the 1970s and after, agricultural activities began to ignite in the Azraq area, leading to high extraction levels, 3 times more than the safe sustainable yield.

However, the gap between water supply and demand widened, water uses were much exceeding the safe yield, which is currently about 24 MCM, in percentages it's around 260% more than the safe yield, while the over-extraction is -38.5 MCM as documented in the Ministry of Environment; Environmental Profile of Jordan, 2006. This water deficit was due more than one reason; the inter-basin transfer between Azraq and Amman, inappropriate agricultural patterns and illegal wells. As a result for water over-extraction, the Azraq wetland was at risk and it lost its biodiversity and touristic attraction. Many competing users from domestic, farming, environment and industry are competing to secure their fair share but a question was raised; what is the fair and reasonable share, and how can we develop a platform to enable users to see facts and risks and to change their perceptions about how can we achieve sustainable development.

## Rethinking Sustainability: An Islamic Worldview

Nomani and Rahnema (1994) and Chapra (2008) outlined a set of concepts for the Islamic economic system and meaning of money from in Islam. This chapter relies on their work.

The cornerstone of Islamic belief is oneness or unity (*tawhid*) of the Creator, oneness of human origin and oneness of human destiny. Since sustainability is guided by norms and values, the following are some basic concepts in Islam that will help define and frame sustainability in a broader sense.

### UNITY OF ORIGIN AND DESTINY

According to the Islamic view, God has created the universe for the benefit of all human beings. God has made the resources of this earth available to humans who have the responsibility to conserve and utilise them in a rational manner. God has given humans the necessary abilities to understand the universe, nature and life. Humans are viewed as trustees and stewards who are responsible to respect the natural laws and ensure justice (*adl*) and sustainability (*tayebah*) approaches to harness natural resources. All human endeavours and acts are forms of worship of God. There is no disconnect between the spiritual and the secular or this life and Hereafter. This unity of time and belief inspires the human to celebrate the diversity of life and to proceed continually in his (her) pursuit to discover, understand, live and enjoy this world.

The Islamic worldview and perspective of the origin and the unity of humanity are simple and clear. Islam views all human beings as children of Adam. As human beings, they are all equal and are part of a global family who should know each other and share knowledge. Thus, the present day situation in which the poor countries are heavily indebted to the rich countries is not in conformity with the Islamic vision. Social, economic and environmental justice are universal human ethics that must be respected by all. The Islamic economic model is based on communal equity and encourages individual innovation (*ijtihad*) but with certain checks and balances to define the limits and degree of government invention that would prevent the building up of concentration of economic power.

Islam teaches that there is a purpose for this creation and humans are accountable. Humans have responsibility and trust (*amanah*) as the vicegerent of God and they are accountable to God for all actions on the Day of Judgement. Thus, Islam prescribes a strong system of accountability at all levels. This is true at the international level as in the case of the climate change debate. The present situation in which certain powerful nations and global corporations are not accountable to anyone in this world is not congruent with the Islamic worldview. Islam envisages a world in which everyone with authority is accountable for his actions. Also, Islam teaches that all species, human and natural resources must be safeguarded against waste, depletion and destruction.

## ISLAMIC ECONOMIC MODEL

The basic underlying conventional economic theory is the assumption that humans are rational and are utility maximisers. This implies that human beings are inherently selfish and that their primary concern is to derive maximum utility; this in turn will yield a positive utility for the society as a whole. In other words, in capitalism the individualistic human behaviour of individuals and nations is not only rationalised but also encouraged. Hence, at the individual level, an individualistic attitude that shows little concern for the betterment of people and nature may be seen as acceptable and reasonable. At the national plane, it is considered perfectly legitimate both for individuals and nations to adopt policies which serve self-interest.

Islam, however, recognises the dual nature of human beings. Human beings are selfish as well as altruistic. It does, however, encourage human balance between needs and wants. Also, Islam seeks to control human selfishness and enhance human altruistic motives to help the community of life at large as part of social responsibility.

On the other hand, the capitalist economic model places a very high value on material accumulation and links it as a means to pursue happiness. The capitalist approach to life had accelerated over-consumption, pollution, depletion of non-renewable natural resources, deforestation and ecological imbalances which contribute to climate change as articulated by Hussain (2007).

Islam treats material possessions as means not ends and as secondary to the moral and spiritual development of the human and social capital. It does encourage enterprise and effort to increase one's material well-being within good (*tayebah*) means so as to be rewarded in the Hereafter (Day of Judgement). This change in the focus of human striving introduces a balanced approach to economic development in terms of time and space. The Islamic approach urges to embody and adopt restraints in the human endeavour to manage wealth or material consumption. This is referred to as de-growth (*zuhd*).

The colonial era had resulted in excessive exploitation of many countries and degraded their natural, human and social capital. The governments and private sector in the industrialised West have a responsibility to restore and rehabilitate the damage resulted in degradation of the developing world. The current inequity is a result of decades of colonial use of natural and human capital. In the same context, the environmental justice (*adl*) in the global climate debate should consider the historical and moral responsibility of the industrialised world towards the poor South.

Islam prescribes a free market based on supply and demand. At the same time, it ensures that the economic power is not accumulated with few people. Islam prohibits interest on capital and thus it promotes purposeful investment and ethical work to achieve progress of society. The general rule in Islamic investment is that whoever wants to earn a profit must assume risk as well. Islam views a society where an individual is productive and independent. It recognises the need of each individual to actualise his potential abilities. Thus, it sees a society where a maximum number of people are independent in their earning and living. This is also one of the implications of belief in One God as the sustainer of the entire universe. The messenger of God indicated codes of conduct to ensure harmony between humans and nature. Traditionally, the Muslim societies have placed a low value on wage-labour. Instead, they have always encouraged forms of self-employment through what is referred to as (*mudarabah*). The Islamic economy would encourage such forms of people-centred development where local people harness their local resources to achieve local benefits.

Islamic ethos encourages the introduction of new technology and innovation (*ijtihad*). Moreover, it urges the industrialists to bear the cost of the dislocation or economic hardship created by the introduction of new technology based on the concept of 'no harm'(*darar* principle). Moreover, once the economy is organised on the principle of worker ownership, the benefits of new technology would automatically spread over to the whole economy.

Since Islamic economy does not allow interest on loan capital, all probability interest-free business credit will not be available on a large scale. Consequently, the question of limited liability of the shareholders in a joint stock company would lose much of its relevance. This in turn will limit market vulnerabilities and failures. Also, the Islamic economy discourages monopoly to ensure genuine competition and fair trade.

In an Islamic economic model, the issue of demand creation through media and advertisement would not take place in a remarkable manner as in the capitalist model. The fact that there is no interest will result in a condition that the constraints on the expansion of investment will be removed. The economy is likely to settle at full employment or near full employment level. The business organisations will have a lesser compulsion to create demand artificially through advertisements. In sum, Islam seems to prefer a society where the ownership of resources is widely dispersed. Islam would also like to maintain a high level of effective demand so that the resources remain fully employed. To achieve that end the Islamic economy has a mechanism of transferring wealth from the rich to the poor. It has made obligatory on everyone who owns a certain minimum of wealth to pay a fixed sum as *zakah* for the expenditure on the welfare of the poor and the needy. Besides, it encourages sharing resources through charity (*infaq*). Besides, the Islamic law of inheritance also contributes to the dispersion of wealth on a wide scale. Thus, Islam visualises transfer of sufficient purchasing power to the poor so as to keep the effective demand high enough for sustaining human dignity and combating poverty of the one billion poor in the bottom of the economic ladder. Islamic economic model had devised a set of strategies to address poverty. These include:

a)      a focus on human development, self-mastery and on quality education and capacity building;

b)      promotion of small-scale and people-centred development;

c)      sharing of profit and loss in finance and investment;

d)      good governance (*adl*) as a key to address the root cause of poverty;

e)      cooperation between different countries on the basis of equity participation in joint ventures;

f)      establishment of trust or endowment funds (*waqf*) to support community needs in all domains of life;

g)      social security at the local level through the collection and distribution of *zakah*.

## ISLAMIC CONCEPT OF MONEY

As compared to capitalism, Islam treats money as a medium of exchange but not as a commodity. Money becomes useful only when it is exchanged into a real asset or when it is used to buy a service. Therefore, money cannot be sold or bought on credit. The economic model of Islam, by prohibiting interest, takes care of the problems of unemployment, inflation, foreign exchange volatility, business cycles and excessive depletion of natural resources.

The banking system in an Islamic economy is based on the concept of sharing profit as well as loss. The general principle is that those who want to earn a return on their savings should also be willing to assume a risk. The banks will have to share the loss of the enterprise as well if they wish to obtain a return on their capital.

The consumer behaviour in the capitalist economies is explained in terms of the sovereignty of consumers. It is contended that one is free to buy anything one likes. Consumers are excessively influenced by the credit-card mentality, media and advertisements. The temptation to buy new things is promoted as a social value which rates the pursuit of novelty very highly. The consumers are persuaded to pursue happiness through accumulation of goods which they may not have sufficient time to utilise.

The effect of such an attitude is that the people living in developed countries, who are barely 25 per cent of the globe's population, consume 15 times as much paper, 10 times as much steel and 12 times as much energy as the remaining 75 per cent of people in the world. It is obvious that the resources of the world are just not sufficient to afford the same lifestyle for everyone on this earth. There is a great need for restraint. But the capitalist system does not have sufficient mechanisms to restrain people from wasteful consumption. Instead, its banks, media, business corporations and governments all have a vested interest in encouraging consumption so that a high level of investment is sustained.

## SIMPLE LIVING (*ZUHD*)

The kind of economy that seems to be in harmony with the Islamic ethos is a low-consumption economy. This in turn will minimise the ecological footprints and help to transform societies into a low-carbon economy. The Islamic approach would require individuals to use the resource as intensively as possible and not to replace them until they have truly outlived their utility as outlined by Al-Jayyousi (2009). The prophet (peace be upon him) placed a very high premium on simple living and discouraged people from luxuries. Islam visualises an egalitarian society where relative differences in socio-economic conditions will be a lot less than what we observe in the capitalist societies. The Islamic view of life would require that those who can afford to have a higher material standard should voluntarily forego some of their comforts and help others improve their economic lot so as to enjoy a similar life style. It is only after most of the people have acquired a comparable living standard that the society as a whole should move to a higher socio-economic level.

The value system of Islam supports the above consumption pattern. An Islamic society that is founded and informed by God consciousness (*taqwa*) is considered a good community. *Taqwa* comprises a cluster of values like justice (*adl*), benevolence (*ihsan*) and benevolent spending in the cause of God (*infaq*). *Taqwa* channels the energies of the people away from acquisitiveness to a sustained effort aimed at spiritual self-enrichment and ecological and social awareness. Islam visualises an economy where the resources are conserved rather than depleted and consumed away. In the context of the present time, the Islamic approach would require a close cooperation among all the countries of the world to harness and conserve new renewable resources of the earth.

Despite this, it cannot be denied that a number of countries in the South have made serious efforts to build the economic infrastructure necessary for development. But the essential question remains as to why these efforts have not been able to achieve a breakthrough. The reasons seem to be primarily more social and political rather than economic as outlined below:

a)     The roots of this underdevelopment are deeply embedded in the philosophy of development which these countries have pursued. Development, according to the prevalent theories, means increase in the physical stock of capital and infrastructure. The GNP has been the focus of all development effort regardless of the consideration how it is increased and who benefits from such an increase. In the process the Islamic countries and many developing countries have ignored their human, social and natural capitals.

b)     The poor people of these countries do not have access to the resources of their country. The number of landless labourers is very high. Even those who happen to have a piece of land do not have access to finance, technology, water supply, market, fertiliser and pesticides. Therefore, they sell off this land and prefer to become labourers again.

c)     There is a rampant corruption (*fasad*) in many developing countries. Corruption takes place to keep the people deprived of resources. A favourite class is groomed by means of licences, permits and other privileges at the expense of the poor.

## SOCIETAL RESPONSIBILITY

The local community at the neighbourhood level constitutes the core of economic solidarity and social cohesion. *Zakat* and *Infaq* (sharing resources) refer to spending on others and on the social needs of the community merely to seek God's pleasure. The pre-Islamic Arabs were also aware of charity. But Islam has broadened the concept of charity in a number of ways. Firstly, it has made obligatory a bare minimum of social spending (called *zakah*) on all those who have a surplus over and above their needs. Second, in its broader meaning, *infaq* covers expenditure on one's own family as well which is not so in the case of charity. Third, Islam recognises the right of the poor and the needy to receive a share from the wealth of the rich. Forth, *infaq* has to be purely for the sake of God who has promised reward in the hereafter. *Infaq* in the Islamic sense is a mechanism to nourish one's spirituality. The Quran has laid down *infaq* as a condition to achieve success and prosperity (*falah*). Fulfilling the covenants towards people and nature leads to *falah*. This means to honour personal commitments to the community and nature. This implies that polluting the environment is against achieving *falah* and efforts to harness natural resources are essential conditions to achieve *falah*.

In sum, the Islamic worldview sees the entire world has been created by God for the benefit of all human beings as discussed in Al-Jayyousi (2001). There is, thus, a great need for all the peoples of the world to consult and cooperate with one another while pursuing economic policies which might adversely affect others. Global, regional and local governance need to be mindful of the moral and rational imperatives to achieve world peace and prosperity. The above concepts in the economic and social system in Islam provide the foundations for sustainability and good life (*hayat tayebah*).

## References

Abouleish, I. (2005). *Sekem: A Sustainable Community in Egyptian Desert*. Floris. University of Michigan, USA.

Adams, W.M. and Jeanrenaud, S.J. (2009). *Transition to Sustainability*. World Conservation Union.

Al-Jayyousi, O.R. (2001). 'Islamic water management and the Dublin Statement', in Faruqui, N., Biswas, A. and Bino, M. (eds), *Water Management in Islam*, United Nations University Press, Tokyo, pp. 33–8.

Al-Jayyousi, Odeh. (2008). The State of Ecosystems and Progress of Societies. Proceedings of the International Conference on Statistics, Knowledge and Policy: Measuring and fostering the progress of societies. OECD.

Al-Jayyousi, Odeh. (2009). 'Islamic Values and Rural Sustainable Development'. *Rural 21 Journal*. Vol. 41, Issue 3.

Ben-Eli, Micjael. (2005). *Sustainability: The Five Principles – A New Framework*. NY, USA: The Cybertec Consulting Group, Inc.

Boulding, Kenneth E. (1966). 'The Economics of the Coming Spaceship Earth', in Jarrett, H. (ed.), *Environmental Quality in a Growing Economy*, Resources for the Future, Baltimore, MD: Johns Hopkins University Press, pp. 3–14.

Capra, F. (2002). *The Hidden Connection: A Science for Sustainable Living*. NY: Doubleday.

Carson, R. (2002). *Silent Spring*. Boston: Mariner.

Chapra, U. (2008). *Islam and Economic Development*. New Delhi: Adam.

Crutzen, P. J (2000). Geology of Mankind. Nature, 415, p. 23.

Fanelli, Daniele. (2007) 'World failing on sustainable development', *New Scientist*, 2624.

Habermas, J. (1985). *The Theory of Communicative Action*. Boston: Beacon Press.

Hussain, Muzammal. (2007). *Islam and Climate Change: Perspectives and Engagements*. UK. Weblink: www.lineonweb.org.uk/Resources/reading.htm (accessed in Jan. 10, 2011).

Hawken, P., Lovins, A. and Lovins, L. (1999). *Natural Capitalism*. CO, USA: Rocky Mountains Institute.

International Panel on Climate Change (IPCC) 2007. Special Report on IPCC-Renewable Energy sources and Climate Change Mitigation: Working Group III.

Kiuchi, T. and Shireman, W. (2002). *What We Learned in the Rainforest: Business Lessons from Nature*. San Francisco: Berrett-Koehler Publications Inc.

Korten, D.C. (1995). *When Corporations Rule the World*. San Francisco: Berrett-Koehler Publishers, Kumaian Press.

Korten, D. (2009). *Agenda for New Economy*. San Francisco: Berret Koehler.

Latouche, Serge. (2004). 'De-Growth Economics: Why Less Should Be so Much More', *Le Monde Diplomatique*, November 2004.

Lessem, R. and Palsule, S. (1997). *Managing in Four Worlds*. Oxford: Blackwell.

Lessem, R. and Schieffer, A. (2009). *Transformation Management: Towards the Integral Enterprise*. Farnham: Gower Publishing.

Meadows, D. (1993). *Beyond the Limits: Confronting Global Collap*se. Vermont: Chelsen, Green.

Meadows, D. et al. (1979). *The Limits to Growth*. NY: Macmillan.

Millennium Ecosystem Assessment (MEA). (2005). *Ecosystems and Human Well-Being*. Washington, DC: Synthesis, Island Press.

Mostert, E. (1998). A Framework for Conflict Resolution, *Water International*, Dec. 1998, 206-215.

Nomani, F. and Rahnema, A. (1994). *Islamic Economic*. London: Zed Books.

Rijsberman, M. (2000). *Sustainable Water Management*, Delft, issue number 85, Netherlands.

Sachs, J. (2005). *End of Poverty*. NY: The Penguin Press.

Sardar, Z. (1987). *The Future of Muslim Civilisation*. London: Mansell.

Schumacher, E.F. (1994). *Small is Beautiful: Economics as if People Mattered*. London: Abacus.

Sen, A. (1999). *Development as Freedom*. NY: Anchor.

Smith, A. (2003). *The Wealth of Nations*. NY: Penguin.

Soros, G. (1999). *The Crisis of Global Financial Capitalism*. NY: Little, Brown.

Soros, G. (2000). *Open Society*. NY: Little, Brown.

UNEP. (1995). *Global Biodiversity Assessment*. UNEP.

UNEP (2007). *Global Environment Outlook (GEO)*. GEO Year Book, UNEP.

Ward, B. (1966). *Spaceship Earth*. New York: University of Columbia Press.

WCED. (1987). *Report of the World Commission on Environment and Development*. Oxford University Press. Worldwatch Institute (WWI). (2008). *State of the World 2008: Innovations for a Sustainable Economy*. Washington.

World Bank (2000). World Development Report: Attacking Poverty, Empowerment, and Security, Washington, DC. USA.

Yunus, M. (2008). *Creating a World Without Poverty*. NY: Public Affairs.

# 2

# A Framework for Sustainable Development: Islamic Worldviews

## Summary

This chapter is intended to frame an enlightened Islamic discourse to address global environmental issues. Islam, as a way of life, is seen as the mercy to all humanity that can provide some remedies and insights to the global debate on poverty, finance, human well-being, progress, sustainable development and good life (*hayat tayebah*). The essence of knowledge, role of human and the environment in Islam will be presented. A framework for sustainability which represents four components, good governance (*adl*), excellence (*ihsan*), social capital (*arham*) and integrity and no corruption (*fasad*) will be outlined.

## Objectives

1. Frame and devise new notions for sustainability that are informed by Islam.

2. Develop a holistic understanding for development from an Islamic perspective.

3. Mainstream spiritual and cultural dimensions in sustainability.

4. Define broader perspectives of sustainability and stewardship from an Islamic perspective.

## Introduction

*The pursuit of happiness and gratification in Islam is attained through being a steward and a trustee (khalifah) and in being in harmony with self, universe and ecology. It is about being part and celebrating the symphony of life (tasbeeh).*

*(The Author)*

The twenty-first century is characterised by a number of global economic (financial crisis of 2008), security (9/11), social (HIV-AIDS) and environmental challenges (climate change) that shape and define the discourse and agenda of the West with respect to the developing world and specifically the Islamic world. This chapter will shed some light on the global environmental challenges and how Islam can contribute to explaining and providing insights to address these challenges. Metrics for measuring sustainable development and progress of societies will be outlined. Also, since sustainability is linked to the notion of good life (*hayat tayebah*), an attempt to define what constitutes a good life will be discussed.

Between 1700 and 1980, 1.2 billion hectares of agricultural land were gained at the expense of a roughly equal amount of forest (Richards, 1990). Such conversion involves loss of species and biological diversity which in turn limits the provision of ecosystem services. The problem is further magnified due to pollution as a result of land use and ecosystem changes.

The conversion of natural areas to agriculture has brought benefits in terms of food production, but it has come at a cost of lost species and changes in ecosystem functions. Part of the problem is that the benefits of agriculture are commercial, whereas the benefits of species diversity do not show up in the form of financial forms. The challenge is that economic approaches are faced with the question of what are the benefits of conservation and what are the economic value of ecosystem services and species. There is a critical need to explain why biodiversity needs to be conserved and what does this mean to the progress of society. This requires that economists need to understand ecology and its ecosystem services and also ecologists need to be mindful of the economic valuation and the mental model of economists.

Sachs and Reids (2006) argue for the need to invest in ecological infrastructure in poor countries and establish a periodic assessment of the benefits that people obtain from ecosystems. The main conclusions of Millennium Ecosystem Assessment (MEA) are (1) environmental degradation is a major barrier to the achievement of the Millennium Development Goals; out of 24 ecosystem services, only the productivity of 4 had been enhanced over the last 50 years; more that 70 per cent of the 1.1 billion poor people surviving on less than $1 per day live in rural areas, where they are directly dependant on ecosystem services; (2) investing in environmental assets and equitable strategies are vital to achieve national goals for relief from poverty, hunger and disease; (3) reaching environmental goals requires progress in eradicating poverty.

Major changes are needed in consumption patterns and education paradigms to ensure a sustainable future (Al-Jayyousi, 2001, 2008). Also, there is a need to rethink notions of green economy and clean technology, Green Fund (based on *waqf*) for mainstreaming environment in national development strategies and periodic assessments of MEA and higher prices for exploiting ecosystems could reverse the degradation of ecosystems services over the next 50 years.

The concept of sustainable development (*tayebah* development) and the future of sustainability were debated at the International Union for Conservation of Nature (IUCN) so as to evolve a new paradigm (IUCN, 2006). Zaidi (1981) argues that the ecological crisis is actually a moral crisis and he demonstrates why the ecological crisis warrants an ethic grounded in a religious matrix that acknowledges a law with divine principles. He concludes by stating that faith in Islam translates into action, through what he terms 'the process of decision-action' as contextualised in Quran's faith and good action (*eman* and *amal saleh*).

Ban (1999) argues that human history is determined by the environment and human behaviours. As a result of the last ice age, a once-verdant Garden of Eden was transformed into the barren deserts of today's North Africa and the Middle East, while Europe's glacier cover was to be gradually replaced by thick, fertile forests. I believe that it is enlightening to reflect of the fate of the early hydraulic civilisations' where the over-exploitation of natural capital resulted in collapse of hydraulic civilisations along the Nile, Euphrates and Jordan rivers.

Foltz et al. (2003) contributed to Harvard Divinity School publication which attempted to reinterpret Islam from an environmental perspective. This literature focused on the notion of 'vice regency' and made a correlation of the Islamic understanding of 'justice' with ecological concerns. Erdur (1997) demonstrates how the American environmental movement began as a radical critique of Western modernity and was subsequently absorbed into it. I argue that there is a need to deconstruct and rethink the fundamental underpinnings of the Western economic model after the financial crisis of 2008–09 so as to evolve an Islamic environmental worldview that is in harmony with ecology, society and culture.

Foltz (2000) noted that the majority of Muslim scholars are more focused on social rather than environmental injustices. He stressed the need to revitalise the Islamic tradition of rational intelligence (*aql*) as a positive force for addressing the global environmental crises. It is critical, I believe, that both value and aesthetic rationality (*ihsan*) are informed by economic rationality (*aql*) to ensure sustainability and progress.

Nasr (1992) argues that religion has both an ethical and intellectual component. He suggests that the environmental crisis can only be cured through the spiritual healing of humankind. He also critiqued Darwin's evolutionary ideas and argued that any environmental understanding founded in Islam must include the notion of transcendence, a correspondence between the microcosm and macrocosm. This will entail, I think, a transformative education that will develop a story for the creation of universe and human based on an Islamic value system and perspectives as informed from ideology, epistemology and norms and values. Islam sees the role of the individual as a value-and knowledge creator, a steward, witness and a reformer who strives to contribute to progress and good life (*hayat tayebah*) (Al-Jayyousi, 2008). To be able to achieve this, we must establish development models informed and transformed by both culture and ecology.

Islam should be viewed not only as a religion but also as a way of life, a worldview, a holistic culture and a vision of a just and equitable society and human civilisation. Islam also provides new perspectives for discovering and explaining the root causes for the current environmental, economic and social crises as manifested in climate change, HIV, poverty and human security. Specifically, the Islamic perspective is that social, economic and political problems manifested in global poverty, financial crisis and climate change are indications of market failure. Besides, Islam views the root cause of global warming and ecological crisis are attributed to the absence or lack of human stewardship and the deviation and departure from 'natural state' or (*fitra*).

This chapter will focus on how Islam views the notion of sustainability, as a good indication for progress. I argue that Islam should be viewed not as merely a religion but as a worldview and a way of life to address the current global problems including the ecological crises. To address the notion of sustainability in a broader term, I intend to look at the three pillars of sustainability, that is, ecological, social and economic. Progress of societies and sustainability will be framed and defined with respect to five pillars: natural (ecosystems and renewable energy), social, human, financial and manufactured (technology) capitals.

The following section will address the value and significance of incorporating our natural capital to measure sustainability and progress of societies. It also seeks to shed some light on the linkages and synergy between ecology and culture when framing a new paradigm for sustainability.

## Our Natural Capital – Learning from Ecology and Culture

The mental model that captures how humans conceptualise the linkages between ecology, economics and society determines how we view new notions and domains of sustainability. The conventional model for sustainability used to see the three spheres of sustainability, that is, ecology, economics and society as three overlapping domains as shown in Figure 1.1 (p. 12). This implied that the three components have equal weights and thus we can make trade-offs using market mechanisms and pricing techniques to offset ecological damage. Recently, there was a new model which sees the three domains as three contained circles with the same centre as shown in Figure 1.2 (p. 12). The larger circle is the natural capital (ecology); the second smaller circle is the social capital, and the smallest circle is the financial capital. This model has the following simple implications and meanings:

a)  Nature and ecosystem services underpin all other capitals. Hence, progress means that ensuring the life, functioning and resilience of our nature is maintained.

b)  We need to invest in nature to ensure sustainability and progress since we cannot invest on a dead planet.

c)  Progress should entail the careful consideration of all five capitals.

d)  Technology and energy are key components in defining sustainability and progress.

e)  We can envision Islam as the 4th larger virtual axis (which means spirituality) that shapes and unifies all capitals.

The linkages between ecology and culture are evident in the rich use of metaphors and analogies in Islamic culture. Both sources of knowledge in Islam, Quran and *Hadith*, promote reflection on the cosmos, nature and human creation. Signs (*ayat*) of the Creator are evident in both the text (Quran) and in the Creation of God in nature, cosmos and human.

The Islamic notion of humankind's stewardship of the earth entails a profound responsibility. Other living species are also considered by the Quran to be 'peoples or communities' (*umam*; Sura 6:38). The creation itself, in all its myriad diversity and complexity, may be thought of as a vast universe of 'signs' of God's power, wisdom, beneficence and majesty. Islam is not a new religion but a continuity of Abraham's message. Believing in Islam entails a belief in all prophets including Moses and Jesus. Islam is keen to enable humanity to see this notion of 'unity' within 'diversity' through promoting dialogue and wisdom sharing between cultures.

Quran teaches that the whole creation is in a state of prayers (*tasbeeh* and *sujood*), which I call symphony of life in which all creations praise God by its very being (Sura 59:24). According to the Quran, the creation of the cosmos is a greater reality than the creation of humankind (Sura 40:57). Islam does view the earth to be subservient to humankind but it should be administered and utilised responsibly. Prophet Muhammad said, 'When doomsday comes, if someone has a palm shoot in his hand he should plant it'. It is illuminating to reflect on this notion of harnessing every single positive bit of energy to green the planet and to invest in nature as part of serving God through environmental stewardship. This example is a good indication for the emphasis on Islam on positive action, hope, and optimism for dealing with ecological risks including climate change, pollution, desertification and de-forestation. This positive call 'to plant' (*fal yaghresha*) should be harnessed to form coalition for a green activism (or Green Jihad), adopt a green economy, and to establish people-centred development.

In Islam, the Quran contains many metaphors that link human evolution, history and nature. Conceptualising society as an ecosystem (not a machine based on Newtonian physics) informs and enlightens the mind and soul to be aligned with new worldviews and mindsets that resonate with ecology and culture. In an attempt to link environment and culture, Islam draws analogies and metaphors between human and ecology to illustrate notions of renewal, value, learning, succession and innovation.

As articulated by Kiuchi and Shireman (2002), nature is a source of knowledge, a research and development lab with 3.8 billion years of product development. Societies can get inspirations and information from culture and ecology. A society founded on information – one whose lifestyle and ideas reflect the idea that knowledge and design are the root source of value – is where the emerging economies in the South should be heading. Seeing unity within diversity among disciplines and themes of ecology and culture can open new possibilities for harnessing the best of the five capitals.

In a knowledge economy, businesses and societies run not just on fossil fuels and raw materials but also on ideas, information and inspiration; they begin more and more to resemble the creative systems of nature – systems like the prairie, the coral reef and the rainforest. The patterns and cycles of rainforest, for example, can inform us how phases we see in nature can evolve towards more creative, value creating and life affirming patterns. The heavy emphasis of the industrial economy on replication tends to cultivate false beliefs about the source of value. According to the machine model of business and society, it is natural to think we create value by taking in resources so as to develop products along with pollution and waste.

As we leave the machine economy behind and cultivate a living economy that is informed and reformed by ecology and culture, we discover new drivers for societal and human transformation. For example, diversity promotes sustainability simply because *diversity is choice*. The more diverse the organisms in an ecosystem, the more types of resources are available to deal with a challenge, the greater the likelihood of success.

Broadly speaking, in the cultures of the North and West, in Europe, industrialised America and Asia, material affluence is vast. Yet the loss of connection to community, and the alienation it brings with it, can erode our own foundations and undermine our culture's capacity to sustain itself. In the cultures of the South and East, parts of Middle East, Latin America, Africa and Asia, we are reminded of the value of faith, human connection and empathy.

Living systems, such as the water cycle, are regulated by such limiting factors as seasons, weather, sun and soil, each of which is governed by feedback loops. Feedback in nature is continual. Such elements as carbon, oxygen and nitrogen are constantly being recycled. Societies and business may not only be informed by nature but also reformed by nature and culture. The Arabic language and the Islamic term to describe this: visible (*thaher*) is contextualised through nature and invisible (*batin*) through culture and belief system. This duality of the Seen (*thaher*) and the Unseen (*batin*) explains the substance and form of the underlying reality of progress and sustainability.

A sustainable society, community or ecology needs an accurate balance sheet that reflects the status of the ecosystem services and enhances the flow of financial, manufactured, human, social and natural capital. The current economic metrics do not account for the value and benefit for the ecosystem services. The key to sustainability according to Hawken et al. (1999) is to seek that all forms of capitals (financial and manufactured, natural, human, social and human) are as prudently stewarded. It is believed that the next revolution then, after the industrial and digital revolution, is an ecological one. The key implications and requirements for this ecological revolution include increased resource productivity, enhancement of flow and service and reduction or elimination of waste. Reducing and eliminating the very idea of waste, can be accomplished by redesigning industrial systems on biological lines. This serves to change the nature of industrial processes and materials, enabling the newly sustainable society to maintain and develop a constant use of materials in continuous closed circles. This entails a new perception of value, a shift from the acquisition of goods to the purchase of services, whereby quality, utility and performance is continually sought to promote natural and social well-being.

## Ecosystems and Sustainability

The end of the millennium witnessed three *independent* processes, that is, the information technology revolution, the economic crisis of capitalism and the emergence of cultural social movements, such as human rights, feminism and environmentalism. Castells and Blackwall (2000) argued that the interaction between these processes, and the reactions they triggered, brought into being a new dominant social structure, the network society; a new economy, the informational/global economy; and a new culture. The logic embedded in this economy and society underlies all institutions in an interdependent world.

The progress of these new network societies should ensure a balanced use of all capitals including human, natural capital, social capital, financial and manufactured (technology). Measuring and defining (or redefining) progress of societies relies mainly on a societal embodiment of a dream that integrates the four capitals. The aim of this chapter is to evolve and revive a culturally based notion for the progress of societies that have resonance to norms and values of Islam. Paradoxically, Islam is currently viewed as a threat rather than a remedy or cure from the fragmentation of knowledge, matter and spirit and human and the community. In this chapter, I am arguing that Islam should be detached and analysed out of the realm of the separation of Church and state and the Western narrative of secularisation of science and knowledge. In today's global crises which include human health, poverty, finance and ecology, Islam can offer a fresh and renewed model for a redefinition of progress of societies. This is attained through the articulation of what constitutes a good life (*hayat tayebeh*) and also is part of a larger process of civic renewal (Al-Jayyousi, 2008).

In liberal economic theory, happiness was already an economic measurement used interchangeably with utility as well as general welfare. Economists attempt to quantify happiness through measurements in consumption and profits. The underlying assumption is that when societies consume more of a product it means they generate happiness. It is this equating of high consumption levels with happiness that has been challenged by proponents of gross national happiness (GNH). GNH depends on a series of subjective judgements about well-being to address the limitations of gross domestic product (GDP).

However, gross domestic product (GDP), remains the dominant indicator of national performance for most developed countries. Measuring progress covers a wide range of attributes which include health, social and spiritual dimensions. A number of experts challenge the GNP as an adequate measure for assessing the progress of societies (Korten, 1995). As a result, genuine progress indicator (GPI) and happy planet index (HPI) were developed as a refined version of GDP to address other dimensions like the state of environment and other social and health aspects.

The GPI is an index that intends to reflect the sustainable economic welfare. The formulation of GPI was based on the basics of GDP but modified to address the value of household and community work, and deducts the costs of commuting, pollution, land degradation and industrial accidents. However, the GPI does not account for either the accumulation or decline of human capital (health, skills, knowledge and experience) or social capital as sound and stable institutions and supportive communities.

The GPI advocates argue that the GDP commands such overwhelming attention that needs to be replaced by a similar, single measure, which is underpinned by considerations of sustainability. On the other hand, other indices include the Happy Planet Index (HPI) which is a measure that shows the ecological efficiency with which human well-being is delivered. The index is built from three different indicators, two of which are objective: life expectancy, ecological footprints and people's well-being or 'life satisfaction'. Human Development Index (HDI) is another index developed in 1990 and consists of three elements: standard of living, life expectancy and knowledge.

In sum, all what these measures attempt to do is to ensure that markets tell us the ecological and social truth.

## Islam and Redefinition of Progress

It is enlightening to realise the historical role of Islamic culture and worldviews in promoting coexistence, socialisation of knowledge and dialogue between cultures. Ibn Khaldoun in his *Mukadimmah* presented a social theory for explaining the rise and fall of nations during the Muslim rule in Spain and North Africa. He developed a theory of economic cycles which is an inter-temporal analysis of socio-economic and political changes. He also outlined the societal transformation from nomadic (*badawah*) to urban (*madaneyah*). Ibn Khaldoun argued that it is the sociological make-up of society which holds the secret to economic growth and decline.

An understanding of the interaction between demographic, technological and institutional factors would provide fundamental insights into societal evolution. Also, of special significance is the notion of *assabiyah* (group solidarity, group consciousness) that Ibn Khaldoun introduced to explain social cohesion. *Assabiyah* is a group feeling and energy that emerges from the unity of social, economic and political interests. The existing social solidarity is both conducive in providing economic activities that provide further impetus for social binding and synergy.

Islam looks upon the challenges of the twenty-first century as a crisis of values. It realises the need to re-examine the foundations on which the entire structure of society is built. The crisis in economic, ecological and political relations is the natural outcome of values and institutions that characterise modern civilisation. It is believed that through a thorough understanding of the social values of Islam, set in the context of sustainable development, value-oriented communities can develop (and transform) a creative and innovative approach to the challenges confronting humanity today. Paradoxically, the dominant worldview as framed in the media industry paints and projects

Islam as a potential global threat. My intent in this book is to transform this misconception and to present Islam as a source of emancipation, remedy and mercy for humanity (*rahma lel alameen*) and a way to redefine good life and progress of societies.

Islam as a way of life covers all aspects of human life. It regulates the relationships between God, Human and Nature. It is based on the recognition of the unity of the Creator and of human's submission to His will. Everything originates from the One God, and everyone is responsible to Him. Human is viewed as a trustee (*khalifah*) and a witness (*shahed*). Human role and responsibility is to ensure that all resources, physical and human, are utilised in a reasonable, equitable and sustainable manner.

Islam teaches that nature is created by *Allah* for the benefit of humans. The relationship between humans and nature is based on harmony, since all creatures obey the laws (*sunan*) of *Allah*. Humans are urged to explore and utilise the natural resources in a sustainable manner. It is through submission to the Will of *Allah* that peace is brought about. Harmonisation of a human's will with the Will of *Allah* leads to a responsible and balanced life. Every human activity is given a transcendent dimension; it becomes sacred, meaningful and goal-centred. Islam does not approve the useless cutting of trees and bushes. Humans can use their fruits but they haves not the right to destroy them. Nor does Islam allow waste among even lifeless things, to the extent that it disapproves of wasteful use of water, even if there is no scarcity of water. Its vowed purpose is to avoid waste in every conceivable form and to make the best use of all resources.

Humans have been endowed with countless powers and faculties. They possess intellect and wisdom to achieve balance in this universe. Their very life and success depends on the proper use of these powers. *Allah* has also provided humans with all those means and resources to make their natural faculties function and to achieve the fulfilment of their needs. The environment and surroundings contain resources that are harnessed for humans. Quran teaches that human beings from all faiths and nations should cooperate and exchange knowledge and wisdom (*hikmah*) to establish a better and prosperous life. The proper use of human's powers implies the attainment of benefits to public or what is referred to as 'construction of the world' (*emmart al kawn*). Every other use of resources which results in waste or destruction is wrong and unreasonable. I argue that the Western model which is based on market economy and consumerism as a means for the pursuit of happiness had failed people, nature and economy. It failed people since we live in a world where there are one billion people who live in extreme poverty and that the top 200 wealthy people have more income that 2.5 billion inhabitants. It failed nature since we are experiencing species extinction, loss of forests and the global warming. It failed economic development since it created an artificial meaning for development and progress that resulted in collapse of financial markets and promoted arms race and became addicted to oil.

Hence, there is a need to rethink the current western development model and evolve a new model inspired from Islamic culture. In an effort to shed some light on how Islam as a way of life sets a framework for sustainable development and the meaning of a good life and sufficiency (*Zuhd*), I will discuss a framework for a sustainable development inspired from Islamic values which looks at the key ingredients of the foundations of good life and progress. These include justice (*adl*), excellence (*ihsan*), family-community values (*arham*) and limit of corruption (*no fasad*).

To address the notion sustainable development and progress, I intend to introduce a set of concepts extracted and synthesised from Islam to contextualise these notions. This framework, as depicted in Figure 2.1, comprises a core circle which represents good life (*hayat tayebah*) and a larger circle which represents the notion of construction of earth (*emaret al-ard or al-kwan*). The four components which constitute progress are outlined below:

- Justice (a*dl or mizan*) which corresponds to cosmic, ecological, human justice and harmony in the Universe. Hence, good and ethical governance is the cornerstone for attaining and sustaining progress and thus good life (*hayat tayebah*).

- Excellence (*ihsan*) which means inner beauty, excellence and conscious evolution of individuals, organisations and society (*ummah*). This also entails the continuous improvement and value and knowledge creation for all humanity.

- Family-community values (*arham*) which refers to the social networks from family to neighbourhood and the global human community at large. Islam teaches that all people were created from different nations so as to be able to achieve 'social learning and intelligence' (*le ta'arafu*).

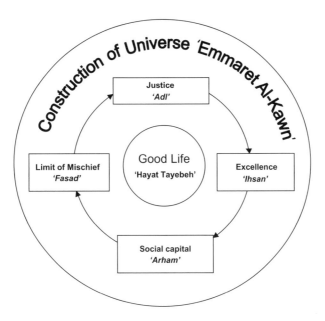

**Figure 2.1**   **A model for sustainable development based on Islamic worldviews**

- Limit mischief and corruption (*fasad*) which is an indication for the deviation from natural state (*fitra*) and the balance that was created by God. This imbalance was attributed to human activities that do not consider ecological and ethical values. These notions from Islam can constitute new parameters for progress of societies. Transforming Islam to a knowledge-based and diverse worldview will help both our ecosystems and the global community.

The Islamic value system establishes clear relationship between finite, mortal human beings and the infinite Divine, the secular and the sacred. Oneness (*tawhid*) or unity of God and submission of human to the Creator are the foundations in the Islamic belief.

Hence, humans are created to play the role of a witness and steward. Islam, as a way of life expects human beings to conserve the environment, since the environment is God's creation. The creation of this earth and all its natural resources is a sign of God's wisdom, mercy and power. The environment contains God's creatures which Islam teaches that these species resemble human communities and also deserve protection (*hima*). Besides, Islam promotes the notion of good (*khair*) and protecting environment is viewed as good.

It should be noted that the schism between the spiritual and the 'scientific' was imported into the Muslim world when the material, industrial culture was introduced, effectively separating the political system from the traditions of the community. This had a devastating effect on the indigenous culture and the environment and its biota.

Despite the fact that Islam's attitude in the theoretical environmental debate is evident and documented, many parts of the Muslim world are currently witnessing a cultural environmental divergence. This was attributed to the fast introduction of the industrial age to these countries without regard to local value systems. Hence, Islamic values and industrial values need to be re-examined to ensure a value system that fits current realities and contexts that is informed and inspired by Islamic worldviews and values. It is imperative for all Muslim scholars to purposefully apply innovation (*ijtihad*) and seek sustainable solutions for people and nature that transcend the existing economic model.

The Western model of economic development with its free market economies, political, economic and social institutions created a number of externalities and environmental costs. In the name of development, local and indigenous people are deprived of their rights in the developing world. Rights and natural resources of local people are taken away and substituted by needs that are defined by the west. As argued by Sardar (2006), no matter how you define and redefine development, how you rework it and rethink it, it just does not fit non-Western countries; and when it is imposed on them, it fragments, dislocates and destroys societies based on traditional worldviews.

The high cost and irreversible environmental costs of the market-based economic model is evident. It is argued that markets do not tell us the ecological truth and that risks from climate change and global financial crises are evidence of the market failure. Redefining the basic notion of 'what constitutes a good life' and how to pursue happiness are critical in understanding sustainability from an Islamic perspective. The notion of progress and pursuit of happiness (or *hayat tayebah*) from an Islamic perspective is about adding value to life through good deeds and knowledge as part of human role in the *construction* of universe (*imarat al kawn*), helping others, bringing up good children, and also about living lightly on earth (*zuhd*) and elimination of waste and overconsumption (*israf*). The Islamic dream is not linked to accumulation of wealth and living in luxury but rather on conserving the human, social and natural capitals which are considered as necessities (*darurat*).

A key pitfall of the Western models of development undermines communal existence by suppressing tradition, breaking up rural communities by promoting urban development, increasing insecurity by displacing traditional agriculture and debt finance. What turns development into sustainable development, is the principle that it should meet the needs of the present generation without compromising the ability of future generations to meet their own needs and also to ensure inter-generational equity. It is insightful to know that life-enhancing tradition has always been about preserving resources. Hence, Islamic values, local knowledge and practices can be viewed as a model for sustainability, progress and good life (*hayat tayebah*). Islam represents the cultural authenticity which means deep respect for norms, language, beliefs, knowledge systems and arts and crafts of all people – the very factors which provide richness and meaning to people's lives.

The following is a brief outline on how Islam looks at sustainability and progress as manifested in the three pillars of sustainability (environment, social and economic).

## A. THE ENVIRONMENT AND SPIRITUALITY

The most interesting feature of the Islamic worldview is that it presents an interactive and integrated outlook. Therefore, a contemporary understanding of the notion of public interest (*maslaha*) may lead to a theoretical understanding of sustainability in its broader terms. Islam represents the natural state (*fitra*) or the intrinsic state of goodness. The natural state  implies a full harmony with nature, people and the built environment. It also means a full realisation and consciousness of the role of the human as a trustee and a witness (*Khalifa-singular*). It also enables the human to adhere and appreciate all forms of reform and enlightenment that are inspired by Islam.

Islam offers an eco-cosmic meta-narrative of the origin of universe and human beings. The story is simple and compelling. The earth is created for the benefit of human beings. Humans are trustees (*khulafa-plural*) to make sure that all resources are used in a sustainable manner. Islam views the potential risks of climate change as a problem of absence of human trusteeship which is referred to as mischief (*fasad*). Islam looks at species as nations (*umam*) like humankind. Reading Quran informs the mind and the soul that our natural capital and social capital are interconnected and interdependent.

Islam teaches that species including plants and wildlife are in a state of prayers (*tasbeeh*). The harm of any species means that we are disrupting the symphony of life and silencing worshipers. Quran elevates and deepens the notion of aesthetic intelligence, bio-mimicry and learning from nature. Both Quran and nature contain many signs (*ayat*) that demonstrate and offer insights and guidance to nurture naturalistic intelligence, innovation and learning. The notion of *ihsan* means the inner beauty, continuous improvement and heightened consciousness. *Ihsan* is a key concept in Islam which is the driver and fuel for human stewardship, responsibility and excellence. *Zuhd* means living lightly on earth which is an Islamic concept that promotes conservation and rational use of resources. *Waqf* is endowment-fund-resourced by civil society and private sector as an economic tool to ensure socio-economic and environmental security and also as a vehicle to contextualise the notion of corporate social responsibility (CSR) and a value-based organisation. Ghazi bin Mohammad, Reza Shah-Kazemi and Aftab Ahmad (2010) outlined the key elements of environment in Islam as summarised in the following section. The Islamic perspective of concept of cosmos, the creation of Earth, the source of knowledge and the relationship of humans and nature are outlined in Quran and *Hadith* as guiding principles.

### Creation as a reflection of Truth

The created environment is not just a random form, but rather a reflection of the Truth, which is one of the Divine names. Indeed, the environment manifests and reflects a number of the Divine Names and Qualities. These qualities are made known to us by the Creator's own description of Himself in the Quran. Four of these Divine Names are given in the following verse:

> *He is the First and the Last, the Outward and the Inward.*
> *(Al-Hadid, 57:3)*

Moreover, God (Allah) is informing us that the environment is a reflection of the Name the Seen (Al-Thaher). This is confirmed by the following verse:

> *Unto God belong the East and the West. So wherever you turn, there is the face of God.*
> *(Al-Baqara, 2:115)*

## Human is responsible and accountable

The notion that the natural environment is sacred and everything and change in the universe is known to God instils in the heart and mind of a believer utmost respect towards nature.

> '... not a leaf falleth but He knoweth it.'
>
> (Al-An'am, 6:59)

The above verse conveys a simple message that a believer must be fully aware of his activity and knowledge and ponder the consequences of everything he does as he interacts with the environment. God is active in His creation now and He knows every detail.

> '... Thou can't see no fault in the Beneficent One's creation.'
>
> (Al-Mulk, 67:3)

## Nature as a book of signs

The natural phenomena of the environment are referred to as *'ayat'* (signs). This is the same word used to describe the verses of the Quran. This shows us that the environment can be viewed as a cosmic Quran (*kitab manthor*) which corresponds to the verses of the Quran. By just observing, or being in nature, we should be able to gain some profound knowledge or insight into the workings of the cosmos, about the Creator and about ourselves. Many chapter headings in Quran indicate the importance of the natural world, such as: 'Thunder', 'The Star', 'The Moon', 'The Sun', 'Dawn', 'Morning' 'Hours', 'The Sand Dunes', 'Smoke', 'The Winds', 'Iron', 'The Ants', 'The Bees', 'The Spider', 'Cattle', 'The Elephant' and 'The Fig'. This constant reference to the phenomena of virgin nature invites people to contemplate, to meditate, to reflect on the signs of virgin nature as being expressions of the Divine creativity, and thus of being holy in their very substance.

In these verses, God links His signs in the environment with His signs within ourselves. This means that the Divine Metacosm is reflected in both the microcosm which is Man and the macrocosm which is the universe. In other words, Man is like a small world, and the universe is like a large Man, and by recognising the signs in either world we can come to know the Truth of God, for His signs are both within us and within the world.

*We shall show them Our signs on the horizons and in their own souls
until it becomes clear to them that He is the Truth.*

*(Fussilat, 41:53)*

And:

*And in the earth are signs for those whose faith is sure. And (also) in
yourselves. Can ye then not see?*

*(Al-Dhariyat,51:20–21)*

## Everything in nature praises God

The symphony of life that exists in mountains, seas, trees, sun, moon, stars
and all living creatures. Humans thus need to be aware of the origin, beauty,
function and mystery of everything in creation. The Holy Quran proceeds to
provide an existential key to this understanding.

*Do you not see that everything that is in the heavens and the earth
praises God and the birds with wings outspread of each He knoweth the
worship and the praise.*

*(Al-Nur,24:41)*

*The seven Heavens and the Earth and all that they contain glorifies
Him in praise; yet you understand not their praise.*

*(Al-Isra' 17:44)*

Moreover, all life-affirming patterns in nature are a form of praise to God.
There is more than just existential praise of God in nature. There is praise that
is active, aware and deliberate. God gives us insight into this in the following
verse about bees:

*Your Lord has revealed unto the bee: make your home in the mountains,
and on the trees, and the trellises which they erect then eat from every
fruit and follow humbly the ways of your Lord. There comes forth from
their bellies a drink of diverse hues, wherein is a cure for mankind.*

*(Al-Nahl, 16:68–9)*

## Knowledge creation through social networking

The diversity of life and cultures is a source of sharing wisdom and co-creation and evolving new consciousness (*taqwa*) for God as stated in the Holy Quran:

> *O mankind! We have indeed created you from male and female, and made you nations and tribes that you may come to know one another. Truly the noblest of you in the sight of God is the most pious (atqa) among you. Truly God is 'Knower, Aware'.*
>
> *(Al-Hujurat, 49:13)*

It should be noted that all creatures form interactive communities ('*umam*', singular: '*umma*') much like ourselves. God says in the Holy Quran:

> *There is not an animal on earth nor a flying creature with wings which do not form communities (umam) analogous to you.*
>
> *(Al-An'am, 6:38)*

Each community of life-like species is an 'umma' in a divinely-willed community of beings. Each species has its 'community' like ourselves, and this in itself should be a powerful warning to us to respect, cherish and empathise with nature and all its creatures.

One of the implications of a truly Quranic awareness of the natural world is that the loss of any kind of species, any kind of creature is an indication that humans are not fulfilling their stewardship (*amanah* and *istikhlaf*).

## Human as a trustee

Human beings are after all only mere stewards, and not owners.

Man's rights and responsibilities towards the environment are summarised by the Quranic word *khalifa* (viceroy, representative, steward). The earth is made subservient to human beings, and it provides for humans with benefits. However, this subservience must be contextualised in the light of what has already been said about everything in nature being created by God, being full of the presence of His Qualities, being in constant praise and glorification of God, and being aware of God. The earth being made subservient to humans does not mean that humans are free to do all that they please without care, or that they are free to upset the balance of nature. God makes this clear in Quran:

> He created human, teaching him the coherent speech. The sun and the moon follow a reckoning, and the grass and the trees prostrate. And He has raised the heaven and set up the balance, (declaring) that you should not contravene with regard to the balance. And observe the measure with justice and do not skimp the balance. And the earth, He placed it for (all) creatures. In it are fruits and date-palms with sheaths, and grain with husk, and fragrant herb. So which of your Lord's favours will you deny?
>
> (Al-Rahman, 55:3–13)

### Corruption due to human action can be reversible

Islam sees humankind's inward corruption is not only reflected in the world's outward corruption, it is its actual cause. This is the real reason why no amount of scientific environmental action can fully work without spiritual renewal. This particular insight is lacking in most of the environmental views and actions. Environmentalists think they know the world and can save it without knowing and saving themselves first. Inner renewal (*ihsan*) is a prerequisite for achieving the genuine construction of earth (*emart al ard*) and attaining and living a good life (*hayat tayebah*).

The extravagant and wasteful lifestyles of more and more people can only mean a plundering and destruction of the earth. Our current consumerism lifestyle is a recipe for destruction of ecosystems and species. To live in such a manner throws the environment out of balance and means that others will live a life of misery and poverty. Unaware of the intricate relationship among the phenomena of the world, modern man looks upon them as separate, individual entities, which can then be manipulated without regard to other entities. In the name of achieving development and growth for the sake of growth, we destroy mountains, but build islands; wipe out forests, but fill the seas with poison and waste; eliminate wild animals, but clone pets; kill off birds, and make junkyards in the sky; make landfills of junk in the ground, but deplete the earth for its treasures; desertify the plains, but build golf courses in the desert.

Nature reacts to the spiritual corruption of human and the consequences are severe floods. droughts, species extinction, habitat destruction, climate change and desertification.

> *Corruption has appeared on earth and at sea because of what the hands of people have wrought; in order that God may make them taste the consequences of their actions; so that they might return (that is: so that they might return to God).*
>
> *(Al-Rum, 30:41)*

Our 'hands' (which is a reflection of mindsets and mode of economic development) have literally corrupted the 'earth and sea' and now we are to 'taste' the consequences of our actions in order to evolve a new consciousness and realise the need to return to God; and return to that natural equilibrium (*fitra*).

## Transforming the human self is a prerequiste for development and progress

Naturalistic intelligence can be attained by being mindful of the sacredness of the environment, the praise that all things hymn to their Lord, and both the outward and inward signs of God. This remembrance will alter the way we perceive things, and this of course will impact our actions.

> *Truly God will not change the condition of a people until they change the condition of their own souls.*
>
> *(Al-Ra'd,13:11).*

Islam views the struggle to achieve self-mastery and living lightly on earth (*zuhd*) as a form of inner *jihad*. The struggle to break our bad habits and to align our very selves with a purer and simpler ways of living can only be achieved through the alignment with the code of conduct of Islam (*sebghat allah*). Islam teaches that attaining self-mastery can be realised by being humble and practising simplicity, contentment, resisting endless desires and then remembering God. These new attitude in lifestyle will 'reduce' our carbon footprints and will minimise future risks of global warming.

## The metaphor of good discourse as a good flourishing tree

Islam, as a mercy to humanity, stresses the notion of communicating a good word to others that emphasises hope and optimism that the future can be bright of we change our mental models. The Quran uses the metaphor of a good word and as a good tree:

*Do you not see how God strikes similitudes? A good word is as a good tree. Its roots are firm and its branches reach up into heaven. It gives forth its fruits in every season, by the leave of its Lord. And the similitude of a bad word is as a bad tree, uprooted from upon the earth, having no stability.*

(Ibrahim, 14:24–7).

For all the above principles on the environmental stewardship based on Quran, we can develop a holistic approach for sustainability which is multidimensional and all-encompassing of cosmos, nature and human as shown in Table 2.1.

**Table 2.1      Principles and implications of sustainability of Islam**

| Principle | Implication to sustainability |
|---|---|
| Creation is a reflection of Truth | Spirituality underpins development |
| Human is responsible | Purposeful human action is needed |
| Nature as the Book of signs | Nurturing naturalistic intelligence |
| Everything praises God | Mainstreaming harmony and reconciliation |
| Knowledge creation through social interaction | Diversity of cultures is of value to cross-fertilisation of knowledge |
| Human as a trustee | Human capital is key to sustainability |
| Human–cosmos linkages | Nurturing eco-cosmic intelligence |
| Corruption and the role of human | Regaining balance through negative feedback. |
| Transform human self | Change of self as part of resilience |
| Good word is a good tree | Universal discourse for nurturing peace |

## B. THE SOCIAL DIMENSION

> Islam was not only successful due to its warfare and social system, but also due to the fact that people saw in Islam a 'civilizing force' in addition to its spiritual benefits.   Islam provided the habitat and enabling environment to nurture creativity and to harness the potential of people out of which arose a new human civilization.

Losing the social compass, from an Islamic worldview, means the lack or absence of embodiment of the teachings of Islam (as a code of reference). This will result in a state of both ecological degradation (*fasad*) and human and social alienation (*taktee arham*). The second pillar of sustainability is the realisation of the human and social dimension of development. The notion of equity, social justice (*adl*), public participation (*shura*) and the deep concern for future generation are cornerstones in Islam. The role of *Ummah* as a community of practice is to set standards for ethical codes of conduct and also to create new knowledge based on attaining public good and public interest.

Within the framework of the Islamic way of development, material and spiritual aspects of life are complementary. To be able to live the good life, we have to make the best use of the material resources of our world. Talking about development without considering the spiritual side of people is meaningless; development must preserve the essence of our humanity. Among the dynamic principles of social life, Islam has particularly emphasised the optimal utilisation of resources and their equitable use and distribution to achieve human prosperity by the promotion of all human relationships on the basis of rights and justice (*adl*). Care for the poor and the marginalised through sharing resources and financial contribution of charity (*zakat*) and trust fund (*waqf*) are key concepts in Islam that need to be harnessed through institutional innovation (*ijtihad*) and reform of governance.

## C. THE ECONOMIC DIMENSION

The current global financial crisis along with poverty, HIV-AIDS and climate change challenges compel and incite a dire need for a new economic model that address these global challenges. There is a need to critique and rethink the underpinning assumptions of the current market economy that looks at human, nature and culture as a commodity. The main pitfalls of the existing market model are that it discounts the future and is based on compound interest rate and a banking system that encourages loans and over-consumption. When looking at the benefit-cost analysis of climate change, the interest rate (how much we discount the future) will justify the rationality of taking preventive action. In other words, the more the future was discounted the more it made economic sense for climate change impacts to take place.

Islamic economics prohibits the compound interest which is the basic concept of the Western banking system. Also, Islam provides regulatory framework that ensures the development projects are in the interest for the wider community, not for few individuals. Islam also provides a framework for valuing and weighting interest and value that transcends humans to species and natural resources and future generations.

The fundamental concept in Islamic economics is that it prohibits usury (*riba*) and does not discount the future which implies that fossil oil at the present is not discounted in the future and hence Islam limits overuse of fossil oil and hence contributes to limit $CO_2$ emissions which causes climate change. Unlike the existing banking system which encourages loans and mega-projects that exploits our natural capital. Islam encourages small-scale development which will result in lessening the distance that goods are transported and hence lowering of greenhouse gas emissions and the ecological footprints in the business sector.

Rutledge (2006) studied the relationship between Islam and oil. Linking 'oil' with 'Islam' illuminates a number of domains including the economic model based on market-led policies, overconsumption and commercial banking investment based on compound interest. It should be mentioned that Rutledge (2006) from Norway revealed a number of observations and findings as outlined below. These include:

### Islam as a new socio-economic model

The emergence of Islam in the Arabian Peninsula about 1,400 ago was in a society of urban merchant families which were surrounded by a periphery of nomadic Bedouin herdsmen, a tribal society which was at the same time both conservative and egalitarian. Hence, Islam as a monotheistic religion was an efficient way to ideologically unite different factions of a complex society. As a consequence, the movement had, from the outset, certain clear economic and social implications. On the one hand, Islam has elements of both a capitalist and socialist system, with its emphasis on individual responsibility, private property and the private accumulation of wealth through trade and productive work. To this extent, it represented the interests of the urban merchant class. On the other hand, Islam also emphasises social justice, the sharing of wealth and welfare with the poorer parts of society. Compassion for the poor is a central element in the faith. In this way it also represents the interests of the rural and urban poor, the voiceless and the marginalised.

### Islam as a new worldview for enlightenment and renewal

Noreng (2006) also emphasised the extent to which Islam had developed the idea that Islam did not recognise any separation of the worldly from the godly. Islam is more than a religion. It is a new worldview, a way of life, code of conduct and transformation of individual and society aiming to human civic civilisation and society. Hence, social and communal solidarity (*takaful* and *tarahum*) is key in Islam as it forms a social contract whereby the rich do not exploit their advantage through the consumption of luxuries so long as the latter still lack the basic necessities of life. Islam does recognise and accepts the existence of rich individuals in society under the condition they contribute to social and economic development in many forms of helping the poor through various forms of charity like *zakat*, *sadaka* and *waqf*.

## Islam and living lightly of earth (zuhd)

Islam outlines a social contract that call for the prohibition of over-consumption (*israf*) as part of the ethical code of conduct. This is practised by having Zakat (paying to poor part of income equal to 2.5 per cent of annual cash balance). The Arabic word *riba* has often been translated as 'usury', but today most Islamic sources define it as 'interest', that is, the charging of any fixed amount of money over and above the capital sum loaned (except, perhaps, for an allowance for price inflation). The prohibition of this form of income is consistent with that strand of socio-economic thought in Islam which accepts the accumulation of wealth through personal effort while rejecting a purely rentier type of economic activity.

These notions inspired from Islam invite and urge us to rethink energy policy for the twenty-first century. We need to be mindful that oil reserves are non-renewable energy resources. The problem of how rapidly this non-renewable resource should be used up and (depleted) has been troubling economists since the early 1930s. However, there is no denying the fact that, for a given country, there is a finite time horizon for the life of its oil reserves as some argue that we already reached the era of peak oil. Consequently, extracting and consuming (or selling) the oil today is to deny the benefit of doing so to future generations. Equity (*adl*) is a key concept in Islam for good governance and intergenerational equity. In theory, strict adherence to Islam's prohibition of *riba* (interest) would rule out the use of 'discounting' when making choices about present versus future consumption. Discounting implies attaching a lower value to a certain activity.

Since Islam prohibits *riba*, that is, charging interest, such a discounting procedure would be forbidden in a strict and literal interpretation of Islam, with the result that an Islamic economic regime which was comparing a future sum of wealth with the same sum today would, in effect, use a zero discount (interest) rate. Which is to say that, contrary to Western economics, Muslims should put exactly the same value on future wealth as on present wealth, provided of course that both are measured in 'real' terms – after allowing for anticipated price inflation.

The relevance of this to oil depletion policy implies that an oil producer has two basic options: to extract the oil now or to preserve the oil for future extraction. For the Western economist, who discounts the future oil sales with a rate of interest, it will usually be preferable to extract the oil earlier rather than later. Muslim economists, on the other hand, should not be indifferent about when the extraction takes place. Moreover, if they choose immediate, value-maximising extraction, this would probably lead to wealth creation well beyond the basic needs of the society and thus, inevitably, to over-consumption (*israf*) and wasteful expenditure.

Historically, between 1985 and 1986, the Middle Eastern and North African OPEC countries increased oil output from 9.96 million to 12.4 million barrel per day. As a result, the price of the Gulf oil export immediately fell from $27.53 per barrel to $12.95 per barrel. During the 1990s they continued to increase oil output and when Venezuela too increased production in 1998, there was another sudden collapse in the price of the Gulf oil export blend to $12.16 per barrel in 1998.

The public policy implications from these policy options are divergent. At one domain, there is no inconsistency between a desire to leave more oil in the ground for future generations (or invest in renewable energy) and one seeking a major increase in the oil price (and current welfare). The only problem with such a policy is that, over time, a very high oil price might encourage the development of substitutes for petroleum which has been happening since 2007.

Since 2008, while we are witnessing a global financial crisis along with climate change risks, Islamic economics in its profit-sharing and absence of usury provides sound constraints to prevent borrowers from running into un-payable debts whilst encouraging wealth to be distributed evenly. This in turn will help to contribute to a low-carbon and a green economy that is reformed and transformed by Islamic worldviews.

## Conclusions

Islamic civilisation and culture redefine the notion of good life (*hayat tayebah*) according to their notions like *zuhd* which means sufficiency and living lightly on earth and *ihsan* which means inner beauty and excellence. The Western life styles and standard of living and consumption patterns produce high ecological footprints in terms of consumption of food, energy and goods. Through global trade we are outsourcing development and environmental costs across borders to India, China and other parts of the world. The scale and intensity of ecological degradation (which Islam refers to as *fasad*) in the last five decades is unsurpassed in the history of humanity.

There is a need for a macro-shift in our worldviews; a rethinking of the fundamentals of the Western economic model to ensure a humanistic and sustainable model that resonate with culture and ensures balance (*mizan*), social equity (*adl*) and respects harmony between nature, people and markets. Above all, what is needed is a new and fresh look at Islam as a source of global peace, prosperity, inspiration, restoration and equilibrium (*fitra*) between society, markets and nature.

In sum, Islam offers new worldviews and perspectives for defining good life and sustainable civilisation that is based on social justice and quality of life rather than unlimited individual accumulation of wealth. Hence, what becomes important in the new Islamic vision is personal transformation of a balanced and harmonious human (*annafsu al motmaennah*) rather than a consumer who strives for material accumulation. Simply said, the Islamic model or paradigm is focused on expanding human empathy not territory.

For Muslims, prosperity and progress imply that humans are to be free and to have access to rich and diverse relations with others (*le taarafu*) or what I call socialisation of knowledge among all cultures worldwide. The new Islamic model focuses more on attaining a good life (*hayat tayebah*), quality of life and interdependence. It is critical to synthesise and combine all the above Islamic notions so as to develop new metrics beyond GDP to foster a sustainable human civilisation that is based on happiness, family values, social learning, universal peace (*rahama lel alameen*), green and clean economy.

In conclusion, modern physics and relativity theory informed us with the 4th dimension, time, which transcended the classical Newtonian physics. Islam, I believe, can provide the 5th dimension for seeing new worldviews and perspectives of life, like progress, justice, peace and sustainability for both humans and nature. We all have a responsibility to evolve and co-create new models for progress of humanity through purposeful efforts that enhance deep understanding and interpretation of cosmos, culture and ecology.

## References

Al-Jayyousi, O.R. (2001). 'Islamic water management and the Dublin Statement', in Faruqui, N., Biswas, A. and Bino, M. (eds), *Water Management in Islam*, United Nations University Press, Tokyo, pp. 33–8.

Al-Jayyousi, Odeh. (2008). 'The State of Ecosystems and Progress of Societies', in *Statistics, Knowledge and Policy: Measuring and Fostering the Progress of Societies*. OECD.

Ban, E.G. (1999). *The Constant Feud: Forest vs. Desert*. New York, NY: Gefen.

Castells, M. (1996). *Rise of a Network Society*. Oxford: Blackwell.

Chapra, U. (2008). *Islam and Economic Development*. New Delhi: Adam.

Erdur, Oguz. (1997). 'Reappropriating the "Green": Islamist Environmentalism.' *New Perspectives on Turkey*, 17 (Fall): 151–66.

Foltz, Richard. (2000). 'Is There an Islamic Environmentalism?'. *Environmental Ethics*, 22, no. 4: 63–72.

Foltz, Richard C., Baharuddin, Azizan and Denny, Frederick M. (eds). (2003). *Islam and Ecology: A Bestowed Trust*. Cambridge, MA: Center for the Study of World Religions, Harvard Divinity School, Distributed by Harvard University Press.

Hawken, P., Lovins, A. and Lovins, L. (1999). *Natural Capitalism*. CO, USA: Rocky Mountains Institute.

Kiuchi, T. and Shireman, W. (2002). *What We Learned in the Rainforest: Business Lessons from Nature*. San Francisco: Berrett-Koehler Publications Inc.

Korten, D.C. (1995). *When Corporations Rule the World*. San Francisco: Berrett-Koehler Publishers, Kumaian Press.

Lessem, R. and Palsule, S. (1997). *Managing in Four Worlds*. Oxford: Blackwell.

Lessem, R. and Schieffer, A. (2009). *Transformation Management: Towards the Integral Enterprise*. Farnham: Gower Publishing.

Millennium Ecosystem Assessment (MEA). (2005). *Ecosystems and Human Well-Being*. Washington, DC: Synthesis, Island Press.

Muhammad, Ghazi bin, Shah-Kazemi, Reza and Ahmad, Aftab. (2010). *The Holy Quran and the Environment*. The Royal Aal Al-Bayt Institute for Islamic Thought. Jordan.

Nasr, Seyyed Hossein. (1992). 'Islam and the Environmental Crisis', in Rockefeller, Steven C. and Elder, John C. (eds), *Spirit and Nature*, Boston: Beacon Press, 83–108.

Nomani, F. and Rahnema, A. (1994). *Islamic Economic*. London: Zed Books.

Richards, J. (1990). 'Land Transformation', in Turner, B., Clark, H., Kates, R., Richards, J., Mathews, J. and Meyer, W. (eds), *The Earth as Transformed by Human Action*. Cambridge: Cambridge University Press, pp. 163–78.

Norreng (2006). *Crude Power*. London: I.B. Tauris Publishing.

Rutledge, Ian. (2006). *Addicted to Oil: America's Relentless Drive for Energy Security*. New Yok: I.B. Tauris.

Sachs, J. and Reids, D. (2006). 'Investments towards Sustainable Development'. *Science*, 312 (2776): 1002.

Sardar, Z. (1987). *The Future of Muslim Civilization*. London: Mansell.

The World Conservation Union – IUCN. (2006). *The Future of Sustainability*. Gland, Switzerland.

Zaidi, Iqtidar H. (1981). 'On the Ethics of Man's Interaction with the Environment: An Islamic Approach'. *Environmental Ethics*, 3, no. 1 (Spring): 35–47.

# 3

# Good Governance and Justice (*Adl*)

## Summary

This chapter intends to shed some light on the key component of the sustainability model which is *adl*. This concept has many dimensions which include justice in the three domains of social, economic and environment. It addresses the notion on land and property rights, the essence and framework for social and economic justice in Islam. The final section addresses Fairtrade and *Hima* (protected areas) as a representation and application of justice in a globalised world that promotes people-centred development and equity.

## Objectives

The main objectives of this chapter are:

1. Introduce the key concepts on land and property rights in Islam and its significance to right-based approaches in natural resource management.

2. Define the key concepts of justice and its implications for sustainable development.

3. Discuss the Fairtrade in light of Islamic values and its value in a globalised world.

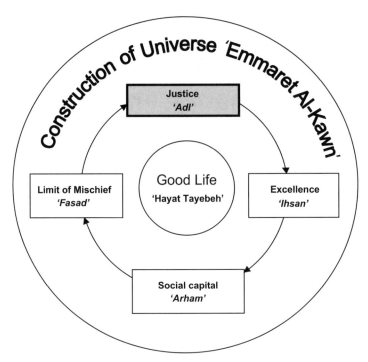

**Figure 3.1    A model for sustainable development based on Islamic worldviews – Justice (*Adl*)**

## Background: Good Governance and Justice (*Adl*)

Historians and medieval Arab and Persian kings articulated popular sayings that they attributed to the Greek philosopher Aristotle (322 BCE) and to Ardashir (ruled 224–241 CE), the founder of the Persian Sasanian dynasty. This narrative emphasises the ways that leaders ought to organise societies to facilitate political stability, order and economic prosperity. They are also part of wisdom literature (*hikma*) which illuminates the social and cultural context of the structure and norms of a society and the perception of equity and justice. The saying reads:

> *The world is a garden (bustan),*
> *And the fence of it is the dynasty (dawla);*
> *The dynasty is authority (sultan),*
> *And through its customs (sunna) are kept alive;*
> *The customs (sunna) are a way of governing (siyasa),*
> *That is implemented by the sovereign (malik);*
> *The sovereign (malik) is a shepherd (raie),*

This chapter is based on the work of Normani et al. (1995), Ali (1989), Ishaque (1983), Khalid (2002) and Khan (1994). The meaning of justice in Arabic is '*adalah*'. Also, the word 'justice' has several meanings. It may refer to conformity to the law and the quality or fact of being just. In essence, law is about ensuring justice and justice is synonymous with morality. Ideas of justice have been formulated by legal thinkers in different ways. A group of them defined justice in two domains; that is, distributive and corrective. Distributive justice addresses equality and the fair division of social benefits and burden among members of a community. Distributive justice then serves to secure a balance among the members of society. Corrective justice seeks to restore equality. In a just system of law, we shall expect to find on the one hand, rules aiming to address equality of distribution, and on the other, specific rules relating to the application of corrective justice by the courts. In short, justice demands that equality, freedom and other basic rights.

Islam articulated and framed an absolute standard of justice as they are based upon the revelation and the fundamental principles of law. Islam teaches that love is fundamentally for Allah, the Creator of the whole universe. The essence of love and brotherhood in Islam leads to attain good for the whole universe including people and nature. Love, in Islam therefore, leads to the conscious appreciation of good and a hatred of evil, but not the evil doer. This is the distinctive feature of Islamic justice.

In Surah al-Nisa, Allah (SWT) commands to the effect:

> *O ye who believe. Stand out firmly for justice, as witnesses to Allah, even as against yourselves, or your parent, or your kin, and whether it be (against) rich or poor. For Allah can best protect both. Follow no the lusts (of your hearts), lest ye swerve, and if ye distort (justice) or decline to do justice, verily Allah is well acquainted with all that ye do.*

Justice is Allah's attribute, and to stand firm for justice is to be witness to Allah (SWT), even if it is detrimental to our own interests or to the interests of those who are near and dear to us. Islamic justice is something higher than the formal justice of Roman law or any other human law. It is even penetrative than the subtler justice in the speculation of the Greek philosophers. It searches the innermost motives, because we are to act as in the presence of Allah (SWT), to whom all things, acts and motives are known.

Quran demands all to fulfil all trusts (*amanat*) by giving everyone his due and judge impartially between people. Justice is linked to a sacred trust, a duty imposed upon human to be sincere and honest. According to Razi and other commentators, the word 'trusts' in the plural, comprises all sorts of trust which has to fulfil, most important among them being 'justice' and that people in authority should not judge according to their whims but in strict conformity with the ethical code of Islam.

Everyone is responsible and accountable for his (her) actions. Abdullah bin Umar reported the prophet (peace be upon him) as saying:

> *Each of you is a shepherd and each of you is responsible for his flock. The Imam who is over the people is a shepherd and is responsible for his flock; a man is a shepherd in charge of the inhabitants of his household and he is responsible for his flock; a woman is a shepherdess in charge of her husband's house and children and she is responsible for them; a man's slave is a shepherd is charge of his master's property and he is responsible for it. So each of you is a shepherd and each of you is responsible for his flock. (Bukhari and Muslim)*

This notion of trusteeship which is based on justice is, in fact, the bond which holds family, organisations and society together and transforms it into one community (*ummah*). The Quran commands to the effect:

> *O ye who believe, stand out firmly for Allah, as witnesses to fair dealing, and let not the hatred of others to you swerve to wrong and depart from justice. Be just; that is next to piety and fear Allah for Allah is well-acquainted with all that ye do.*

Justice in Islam is a sacred concept that a believer and a community must abide by despite the fact it may be detrimental to our own interests of those who are near and dear to us. The concept of justice is far higher than the so-called distributive and corrective justice, the natural justice, the formal justice or any other man-made law.

## THE MEANING OF SOCIAL JUSTICE

Plato in his writing on social justice speaks of justice in terms of services and functions which the individual performs with regard to state. With this theory in view, social justice has been defined in Greek political theory as the 'principle of a society, consisting of different types of men who have combined under the impulse of their need for one another, and by their combination in one society, and their concentration on their separate functions, have made a whole which is perfect because it is the product and image of the whole of the human mind'.

In contrast, in Islam, the state is not a deity to be worshipped but a social organisation subject to the guidance of the Divine Law. In an Islamic society, humans are not combined merely under the impulse of their need for one another. They are combined as collective whole to look after one another and be responsible for the welfare of the whole. In sum, social justice may thus be defined as the following:

1.    to treat (wo)man as an individual with liberty and equality as his/her birth right;

2.    to provide a human with equal opportunities of developing his/her personality so that he/she is better fitted to fill the situation to which he is entitled;

3.    to regulate human relation with society for the benefit of all members of society.

Islam lays down certain basic moral principles which are the guidelines for human action as documented by Izzi Deen (1990) and Faruqui et al. (2001). In the twenty-first century, we are witnessing a new knowledge economy with global corporations that conduct business in new ways that required new social, political and economic institutions. Islam encourages the search for new knowledge and advancement of these institutions to address current needs.

Islamic ideology can be characterised as a middle ground between extremes of capitalism and communism. While upholding the dignity and freedom of the individual, it stands firmly for social justice in its all-embracing supranational settings. The task before human society is to keep on advancing within the moral limits and thus ensure for itself an evolutionary progress with universal justice. As articulated by Iqbal (1934) in which he asserts that life is a process of progressive creation that requires each generation to solve its own problems.

## OWNERSHIP AND PROPERTY RIGHTS IN ISLAM

Islam with its coverage of over 57 Muslim majority countries, the estimated 1.2 billion Muslims comprise a fifth of the world's population. Sardar (1987) argued that due to the cultural diversity in Islam and the influence of modern and secular concepts, Islam must be revisited and analysed to harness its potential role in the enlightenment of twenty-first century in all domains of life.

The concept of dual ownership between human being and God is one of the key characteristics of the Islamic model as documented by Normani and Rahnema (1994), Ali (1989), Ishaque (1983), Khalid (2002) and Khan (1994). Islam protects the personal right to own and consider it as a sacred right. Yet, from an Islamic perspective, human ownership is in fact a matter of trusteeship, whereby we have temporary authority to benefit from property. The Islamic property rights framework conceives land as a sacred trust but promotes individual ownership. This section argues that Islamic rulings related to land may support land rights initiatives in Muslim societies and has implications for sustainable development and good governance. In Islam, property relationships are considered social relations, which under Islamic law are called *mu'amalat* (as distinct from *ibadat*, matters relating to worship). Also, concepts of consultation (*shura*) and justice (*adl*) are well embedded in Islamic consciousness and governance.

All Muslim scholars had a consensus that property rights are one of the five essential values of Islamic law which must be protected. The Prophet Muhammad (peace be upon him) emphasised the importance of property rights in his farewell pilgrimage by declaring the following:

> Nothing shall be legitimate to a Muslim which belongs to a fellow
> Muslim unless it was given freely and willingly.

Private property rights are well established but constructed as a sacred trust based on the doctrine of unity (*tawhid*), stewardship (*khalifa*) and trust (*amana*). Property and land are temporally utilised by humans as a trust from God as the Owner (*Al Malek*) and Sustainer (*Al Hafeth*).

Islamic property rights are conditional that property is not used wastefully or in a way that will deprive others of their property rights as discussed by Forni (2005). The Quran mandates respect for property rights of all persons regardless of religious faith. All members of the community, Muslims and non-Muslims, enjoy the similar property rights. The divine ownership is coupled with Quranic references that all of humanity benefits from nature's resources. The state assumes land 'ownership' on behalf of God but for the benefit of the community. Islamic property rights incorporate a redistributive element, which is evident in institutions such as the endowment (*waqf*) and charity (*zakat*). Historical review of the traditional civil society shows that institutions such as the endowment funds (*waqf*) were key components in social responsibility which contributed to support public institutions, infrastructure, social development, public health, water supply, conservation and education as documented by Al-Jayyousi (2007, 2008).

Land management principles which are derived from Islamic law can be understood from the perspective of public interest (*maslaha*). Protection of property interests, as part of the essentials (*daruriyyat*) of Islamic order, is subject to a public interest consideration as a matter of priority. Islam promotes small-scale, human-centred development that benefits the local communities. It is argued that the current Western market-based model of development resulted in environmental challenges, like, climate change, pollution, urbanisation and overuse of resources. These challenges are the constraints of sustainable development and hence a new model of development. Hence, alternative small-scale, decentralised models of development that benefits the poor were advocated by Yunus (2008) and Korten (1995, 2009).

The Quranic view holds that everything on the earth was created for humankind as God's bounty (*ni'amah*) to be exercised with care as a trusteeship (*amana*). Islamic law had developed a set of policies, approaches and guidelines to promote sustainability like protected area (*hima*), revival of barren land (*mawwat land*) and endowment (*waqf*). There are a large number of institutions and mechanisms to foster environmental protection. In contrast to classical Islamic theory in which all land is held in trust for the benefit of the community, water rights over individual lands were bought and sold during the Ottoman period, and this continues to this day.

The concept of property rights in Islamic economics has implications far beyond the material domain as it lays stress on responsibility, poverty alleviation and redistribution. Islamic doctrines engage with entitlement to land rights for a broad range of beneficiaries including women, children, landless and minorities. The Islamic emphasis on obligations regarding philanthropy, fairness and poverty alleviation are influential in land rights argumentation based on a holistic, authentic, moral, ethical and legal land rights code.

Under Islamic theory, the state in land management is seen as supervising land which is ultimately belonging to God. Thus, the state is mandated to administer land, efficiently and fairly, in accordance with God's laws and ethical and moral principles. An Islamic framework gives states wide leeway in promoting security of tenure and access to land.

Islam is considered by Muslims to be a holistic worldview and complete way of life. It should be noted that in many domains, Islamic land principles and practices run parallel or are similar to contemporary international codes, norms and standards. This implies that Islamic worldviews inform and bring new insight to Western views and even offer an alternative paradigm. Though there is limited application of the Islamic worldviews in finance and social policy, still the set of Islamic principles, mechanisms and processes can provide legitimate and durable solutions for a sustainable human civilisation.

## ISLAMIC PARADIGM VERSUS OTHER WORLDVIEWS

Islam proposes a new worldview to life which is purposeful, rational and adaptive as articulated by Al-Jayyousi (2007, 2008). Hammoudeh (2011) developed a model called I-theory which stresses the notion of justice, unity and excellence. Transformation of current development model to one that captures the cultural dimension is critical to cope and address the global challenges by promoting local solutions as documented by the work of Abouleish (2005) and Lessem et al. (1997, 1999). The Islamic view emphasises the ethical underpinnings of the socio-economic order and the synthesis of the material with the spiritual. From the concept of the unity of God flows the concept of unity and brotherhood of humanity. The foundations of Islamic ideology rest upon justice, reason, empathy and faith.

Islam holds a balanced view towards property ownership compared to both capitalism and communism. At one extreme, capitalism is driven by the profit motive and the absolute right of private ownership. The underlying principles and drive in capitalism are based on the notion of profit seeking outlook, regardless of social consequences. It is argued that capitalism to some extent is a soulless institution which is driven by profit and growth and lacks the inner impulse for social justice.

At the other extreme stands communism which takes the view that private ownership is the source of all exploitations. Hence, it makes people vest all instruments of production in the hands of the state and abolishes private property. In such an organised society, the individuals are reduced to be mere instruments and tools of a planning process. This results in the loss of individual's identity and innovation. However, over the decades, capitalism has evolved and adapted to be more workable and more acceptable principles that attempt to balance the role of markets and governments. Rodinson (1973) commented that we now live in a world of mixed capitalism, with a great deal of state regulation, social security and state investment in education, housing and public in what has been defined as social capital. Most capitalist countries take for granted the state's role in promoting economic growth and the maximising of public welfare.

To the extent that modern capitalism lays emphasis on human freedom and social welfare, it is not contrary to the Islamic socio-economic ideology. Islam recognises individual initiative and the right of personal ownership and the diversity in human capabilities and hence the differences in earnings and ownership. To address disparities between the rich and the poor, Islam has institutionalised social security through charity (*zakat*) and trust funds (*waqf*). However, all property ownerships are subjected to moral responsibility towards society as a whole. The right of ownership is thus conceived as a trust to be exercised within the framework of its social function. The upholder of Quranic values would look with strong disfavour upon the hoarding of wealth and encourage their productive use. Undue profiteering is as emphatically disapproved as is ostentatious extravagance, while modest living (*zuhd*), the prompt payment of fair wages and spending for charity is encouraged.

Islam stipulates that individuals should not neglect living well in this world. One should work hard and earn as much as possible by fair and lawful means. He (she) should fulfil his (her) obligations to society. One must abstain from sinful acts which include unjustified personal enrichment, unfair dealings, fraud, falsehood and corruption. Wealth and property are not to be squandered purely for personal enjoyment. Instead, it must be increased by economic use such as by embarking on trading through mutual consent, not by exploiting other nations and raging wars for control of resources. Islam enforces the rules of morality in ownership of property, in his earning and spending. Usury (*riba*) is forbidden, extravagance is denounced and moderation is enjoined.

The Islamic ethos on the subject is best illustrated by the Quranic injunction that wealth should not circulate only amongst the rich. Within the Islamic framework, the right of property ownership must be conceived as a trust to be exercised within the framework of its social function and subjected to moral responsibility towards society as a whole.

## Principles for Understanding Islam as a Universal Worldview

Islam is a universal faith which is simple and easy to understand and rationalise. It is based on three fundamental principles which are *tawhid* (unity), *khilafah* (vicegerency) and *adalah* (justice). These principles not only frame the Islamic worldview, they also constitute the fountainhead of the intent of Islamic law (*maqasid*) as outlined by Chapra (1970, 1992, 2008). The following is an overview of the meaning and significance of these three fundamental principles which is based on the work of Chapra (1992).

### TAWHID (UNITY OR ONENESS)

The foundation of the Islamic faith is *tawhid* (oneness and Unity of God). Everything else logically emanates from the notion of *tawhid*. It means that the universe has been consciously designed and created by the Supreme Being, who is One and Unique, and did not come into existence by chance or accident (Quran, 3:191, 38:27 and 23:15). Everything created by God has a purpose which gives meaning and significance to the existence of the universe, of which Human is part. After creating the universe, the Supreme Being (God) is continuously and actively involved in its affairs (Quran, 10:3 and 32:5) and is aware of and deeply concerned with even the minutest details (Quran 31:16 and 67:14).

### KHILAFAH (TRUSTEESHIP)

The human being in his *khilafah* or vicegerent on earth (Quran, 2:30, 6:165, 35:39, 38:28 and 57:7 has been endowed with all the spiritual and mental characteristics, as well as material resources, to enable him (her) to live up to his mission effectively. Within the terms of reference of his (her) *khilafah* he (she) is free, and also able to think and reason, to choose between right and wrong, fair and unfair, and to change the conditions of his (her) life, his (her) society and the course of history, if he (she) so wishes. Human is by nature good and noble (Quran, 15:29, 30:30 and 95:4) and is capable of preserving his (her) goodness and nobility and rising to the challenges before him if he (she) receives proper education and guidance and is properly motivated. Since human is good by nature, he (she) feels psychologically happy and satisfied only as long as he (she) stays in, or moves closer to, his inner nature, and feels unhappy and miserable when he (she) deviates from it.

The resources with which God has endowed this world are not unlimited. They are sufficient to cater for the well-being of all, if used 'efficiently' and equitably'. The human being is free to choose between the alternative uses of these resources. However, since any individual is not the only one who is a *khalifah* and there are millions of other human beings who are *khalifahs* like him and who are his brothers and equals, one of his real tests lies in utilising the God-given resources in such an 'efficient' and 'equitable' manner that the well-being and prosperity (*falah*) of all is ensured.

The concepts of *tawhid* and *khilafah* are inherently in conflict with the concepts of 'born sinner'. The concept of original sin is also in conflict with God's attributes of God as the Most Merciful and the Most Compassionate. It would be impossible for Him to do so, given that He is a Loving and Forgiving God and has all conceivable good attributes (Quran, 7:180)

Islam has a different view for understanding human behaviour and history. The Western view sees human lives are determined by material forces of history (Marx), or conditioned by psychological (Freud), instinctive (Lorenz) and environmental (Pavlov, Watson and Skinner) influences. This leads to the verdict in step with Skinner, that 'individual freedom is a myth'. Determinism and human responsibility cannot be reconciled with each other. Determinism negates human responsibility for the prevailing conditions and for the inefficient and inequitable distribution of resources.

At the other extreme to the determinists is Sartre's existentialism which claims that there is no God, Man is 'condemned to be free' and there is no limit to his freedom except that he is not free to cease being free. But for Sartre, this freedom is absolute – everything is permitted. There is no ultimate meaning or purpose inherent in human life. There is no transcendent or objective values set for human beings, neither laws of God. Human beings are 'abandoned' in the world to look after themselves completely. The only foundation for values is human freedom, and there can be no external or objective justification for the values anyone chooses to adopt. Such a concept of absolute freedom can only lead to the capitalist notions of laissez-faire and value neutrality.

The Islamic worldview is in sharp contrast with these ideas, the concept of *khilafah* (*trusteeship*) raises human beings to an honourable and dignified status in the universe (Quran, 17:70) and provides the life of both man and woman with a meaning and a mission. The meaning is provided by the conviction that they have not been created in vain (Quran 3:192 and 23:115), but rather to fulfil a mission. Their mission is an act in accordance with Divine tenets in spite of being free. This is what is implied by worship (*ibadah*) (Quran, 51:56) in the Islamic sense, an inviolable imperative of which is fulfilling one's obligations toward other human beings (*huquq al-ibad*), to promote their well-being and to actualise the intent of law (*maqasid*). No wonder that Islam, like some other great religions, places a greater emphasis on duties than on rights. The fundamental wisdom behind this is that if duties are fulfilled by everyone, self-interest is automatically held within bounds and the rights of all are undoubtedly safeguarded.

Success in this mission requires spiritual uplift through total commitment to the Creator, who is the Wise, the Just, the Benevolent and the Loving God, and to the Guidance provided by Him. Human beings must submit to none but Him, to no other values but His, and to live for no other mission but His. They are responsible to Him for all their deeds in this world. They are, however, accountable only for their own actions (Quran 6:164, 17:15 and 35:18) and not for the actions of other, past or present, except to the extent to which they are themselves the ultimate cause. Even though they are destined to die (Quran, 3:185, 4:78 and 29:57), their life is not confined to this world alone, which is a place of trial and test and hence temporary. Their real reference point is the Hereafter, where they will be rewarded or punished in accordance with how they have discharged their responsibilities in this world. They can never succeed in escaping their accountability before God. Their life is thus not 'destined to extinction in the vast death of the solar system', and the whole temple of man's achievement will not be 'buried beneath the debris of a universe in ruins', as Bertrand Russell pessimistically expected.

The concept of *khilafah* has a number of implications, or corollaries as outlined by Chapra (1970, 1992, 2008) as summarised below.

## Universal brotherhood

*Khilafah* implies the fundamental unity and brotherhood of humankind. Everyone is a *Khalifah* and not any single privileged person, or members of a particular race or group or country. This makes the social equality and dignity of all human beings, white or black, high or low, a cardinal element of the Islamic faith. The criteria of determining the human's worth are not race, family or wealth but rather faith and service to humanity. The prophet, may the peace and blessings of God be on him, said categorically: 'All human beings are dependents of God and the most beloved of them before Him are those who are the best His dependents.'

Within the framework of this concept of brotherhood, the right attitude towards other human beings is not 'might is right', struggle to serve only one's own 'self-interest', or 'survival of the fittest', but rather mutual sacrifice and cooperation to fulfil the basic needs of all, to develop the entire human potential and to enrich human life. Competition is hence to be encouraged to the extent to which it is healthy, raises efficiency and helps promote human well-being.

### Resources are a Trust (Amanah)

Since all resources at the disposal of human beings have been provided by God, human as *khalifah* is not their primary owner. He is just a trustee (*amin*). While this trusteeship (*amanah*) does not mean 'a negation of private property', it does carry a number of very important implications which create a revolutionary difference in the concept of private ownership of resources in Islam and other economic systems.

Firstly, the resources are for the benefit of all and not just a few (Qura'n, 2: 29). They must be utilised equitably for the well-being of all. Secondly, everyone must acquire resources rightfully, in a manner indicated by the Quran and the *Sunnah*. Acting otherwise constitutes a violation of the terms of *khilafah*. Thirdly, even the resources so acquired, should not be disposed of except in accordance with the terms of the trust, which are the well-being not only of one's own self and family but also that of the community at large. Fourthly, no one is authorised to destroy or waste the God given resources. Doing so has been equated by the Quran with the spreading of *fasad* (mischief and corruption), which God abhors (Quran, 2:205). Accordingly, when Abu-Bakr, the first Caliph, sent Yazid ibn Abu Sufyan on a war assignment, he exhorted him not to kill indiscriminately or to destroy vegetation or animal life even in enemy territory. If this is not allowed even in war and other territory, there is no question of its being allowed in peacetime and home territory.

### Humble Life Style (Zuhd)

The only life style that suits the *khalifah* of God is one that is humble. It should not reflect arrogance and grandeur. Such life styles lead to extravagance and waste and result in unnecessary pressure on resources, reducing a society's ability to satisfy the needs of all. They also promote unethical ways of earning and generate inequalities of income beyond the normal distribution that is warranted by differences in skill, initiative, effort and risk. They also erode the feeling of equality and weaken the bonds of brotherhood that are an essential characteristic of a Muslim society (*ummah*). Since human beings are the *khalifas* of God, they are subservient to none but Him. Serfdom of any kind, irrespective of whether it is social, political or economics is, therefore, alien to the teachings of Islam. The Quran states that one of the primary objectives of Islam is to release humankind from the burdens and chains that have been imposed upon them (Quran 7:157).

Accordingly, no one, not even the state, has the right to abrogate this freedom and to subject human life to any kind of constraints. It is this teaching which prompted Omar, the second Caliph to ask: 'Since when have you enslaved people although they were given birth as free individuals by their mothers?'

This does not imply that human beings are free to do anything that they want. They are subject to the *Shari'ah*, which aims at achieving the well-being and harmony between humans and nature. They are thus free only within the bounds of the social responsibility as specified by the *Shari'ah*. Any system, which either subjects human beings to serfdom or gives them undue freedom to overstep the constraints imposed by the Creator Himself through the *Shari'ah*, is in conflict with the dignity and accountability embodied in the concept of *khalifah* and cannot contribute to the well-being of all human beings.

## *ADALAH* (JUSTICE)

Human brotherhood worldwide regardless of faith, which is an integral part of the concepts of *tawhid* and *khalifah* would remain a hollow concept having no substance if it were not accompanied by socio-economic justice. Justice has been held by the jurists to be an absolutely indispensable ingredient of the intent of laws (*maqsad al-Shari'ah*), so far so that it is impossible to conceive of an ideal Muslim society where justice has not been established. Islam is absolutely unambiguous in its objective of eradicating from human society all traces of injustice (*thulm*), which is a comprehensive Islamic term referring to all forms of inequity, injustice, exploitation, oppression and wrongdoing, whereby a person deprives others of their rights or does not fulfil his obligations towards them.

Establishment of justice and eradication of all forms of injustice have been stressed by the Quran as the primary mission of all God's Messengers (Quran, 57:25). There are no fewer than a hundred different expressions in the Quran embodying the notion of justice, either directly in such words as '*adl, qist, mizan*', or in a variety of indirect expressions. In fact the Quran places justice 'nearest to piety' (Quran, 5:8) in terms of its importance in the Islamic faith. Piety is naturally the most important because it serves as a springboard for all rightful action, including justice. The Prophet, peace and blessings of God be on him, was even more emphatic. He equated the absence of justice with 'absolute darkness' and warned: 'Beware of injustice for injustice will lead to absolute darkness on the Day of Judgement.' No wonder Ibn Taymiyyah felt encouraged to assert that: 'God upholds the just state even if it is unbelieving, and that the world can survive with justice and unbelief, but not with injustice and Islam.'

## The Pursuit of Happiness and Good Life

> *O believers! Respond to God and to His Prophet when he calls you towards that which will give you life. (Quran, 8:24)*

It is crucial that there is a model in Muslim countries that embodies the Islamic vision of success (*falah*) and good life (*hayat tayebah*). This model, as articulated by Chapra (1970, 1992, 2008), depends on both moral uplift and socio-economic justice. However, after a colonial era, many Muslim countries are still constrained by debt and poverty due to their adoption of capitalism, socialism and the welfare state. The paradox of wealth is illustrated by the fact that rich countries are not typically happier than poorer ones as argued by Korten (1995).

The paradox of having poverty within wealth in the Western model is attributed to the illusion that the media promotes which conveys the message that happiness is a function of material possessions and accumulation. In Islam, happiness is a reflection of peace of mind (*alnafs al mutma'innah*), which is possible to attain only if an individual's life is in harmony with his inner nature. This happens when both the spiritual and the material urges are adequately satisfied. Since the material and the spiritual are not separate identities, the desired satisfaction takes place only when a spiritual dimension is injected into all material pursuits to give them meaning and purpose.

It is probably not possible to satisfy the needs of all members of society, unless all wasteful and inessential uses of resources are eliminated or minimised and all socio-economic institutions that promote inequities are reformed. This in turn is not possible if individuals take into account their own individual preferences and financial ability. Every individual therefore needs to be made aware of the social priorities in resource use and to be motivated to behave in conformity with these priorities. Humans need to be concerned about the well-being of others while striving for their own well-being. What could be more conducive to the creation of such a discipline than a moral system given by the creator of the Universe Him-self, combined with accountability before Him. Within the framework of such a discipline, material possessions do not command a value for their own sake. They are of value as long as they fulfil the objective of their creation as defined by the value system. Such an attitude creates a voluntary restraint in the use of scarce resources that minimises unnecessary consumption and over-exploitation of resources. Such a moral system makes it possible to satisfy the needs of all by living lightly on earth and by realising that we can attain prosperity without growth. This in turn will result in social cohesion and solidarity where all members of the community feel empowered by the sense of belonging, not their belongings.

In the absence of a moral dimension, material possessions become an end in itself. Satisfaction then does not remain a function of need fulfilment but of much more than that, of vying with others. Conspicuous consumption creates only temporary satisfaction. Without any meaning and purpose of life; fashions and models only exchange one kind of emptiness for another. Everyone is constantly busy acquiring the necessary resources, leaving little time to fulfil obligations towards family and community. The pressures on the individual to expand beyond his or her ability lead to human suffering. The entire machinery of production becomes directly or indirectly directed toward the satisfaction of a maximum amount of wants. When the banking system promotes easy lending, it becomes possible for people to live beyond their means. Claims on resources, therefore multiply and imbalances increase and those unable to keep pace with this struggle fall behind. This will lead to dissatisfaction, social tensions and human alienation.

Realisation of the intent of laws (*maqasid*) requires different priority setting. This includes the realisation that public goods need to be shared in an equitable manner so as to achieve public interest (*maslaha*) through Fairtrade schemes as will be outlined in the following section. This also means that all stakeholders or riparian states sharing a water resource like a river need to formulate a social contract that respects the needs of all. An illustration to the notion of equity and sustainability will be presented in the Box below by looking at the water allocation of the Nile River as summarised from the work of Allan (2000).

---

## CASE STUDY: THE NILE WATER BASIN – WHAT IS AN EQUITABLE WATER DEAL?
### (Adapted from Allan, 2000)

The Nile is an important river in the Middle East although all its waters come from the tropical and equatorial Africa. The ten riparians of the Nile comprise about 29 per cent of the African continent. The tropical and equatorial south of the catchment comprise over 50 per cent of the catchment. The humid segments of the catchment enjoy average annual precipitation of over 1,000 mm per year. The arid half of the basin receives no useful rainfall as potential evaporation ranges from two to three metres depth per year. This makes the Nile a long but low volume water river.

The lower Nile was only significantly controlled by the new works at Aswan in 1906. These works allowed secure access to a minimum of about 30 cubic kilometres per year by 1930s enabling about 80 per cent of Egypt's irrigated area to be double cropped. Works in the Sudan at the Sennar in 1925 on the Blue Nile commanded water sufficient to irrigate the Gezira Scheme just south of Khartoum – initially one million fedans (400,000 hectares) extended in the 1960s to 800,000 hectares. Not until 1970, with the building of the Aswan High Dam, was the utilization of the surface flow of the Nile boosted to an average of about 40 cubic kilometers per year (including the unaccounted re-use in irrigation). The additional water from the new storage at Aswan was sufficient to enable double cropping throughout the six million irrigated feddans (2.5 million hectares) of Egypt by the early 1970s. Two million feddans (800,000 hectares) have been a perpetual land reclamation target since early 1890s.

In terms of the water use of the Nile, the only major user of the Nile waters is Egypt. In 1929, during the British mandate in Egypt, the Nile Basin Agreement allocated 96 per cent of the average flow to Egypt and 4 per cent to Sudan. The Aswan Dam which was constructed in that era was able to store about 168 cubic kilometres of the Nile flow. Later, the Nile Water Agreement in 1959 recognized the entitlement of Sudan to 25 per cent of the flow to Sudan. Hydromet organization, formed in 1960s and founded in 1980s, was a UN inspired agency put in place with the good will of most of the then nine riparians, not Ethiopia, to monitor the Nile Hydrology to enable better basin-wide management and technical discussions. In 1999, Hydromet was reformed to be the Nile Basin Initiative with the aim to enhance cooperation and equitable water allocation. The key question is how can water users agree on a sustainable solution in a new era of democracy in the 21st century?

## Fairtrade as a Model for Justice (*Adl*)

This section presents the case of fair and assesses its relevance to Islamic worldviews. Fair trade is an economic model that emphasises the payment of a 'fair' price to producers that covers production cost and enables production that is socially just and environmentally sound. Fair trade is in line with Islamic values which aim to promote distribution of wealth between rich and poor. As outlined in this chapter, Islam supports notions and principles of public interest, fairness, and equity. Public interest (*maslaha*) means that a person or organisation, therefore, should not undertake an action or instigate a business transaction that will cause greater harm than benefit to the community or environment. The Quran instructs people to be just and fair:

> God loves those who are fair and just. (49:9) Eat not up each other's property by unfair and dishonest means. (4:29)

At the global level, the Fairtrade movement addresses the market imbalances and access of small producers to markets and support them to market their products in a fair price. Also, it promotes people-centred development, sustainable livelihood and sustainable development.

According to Krier (2005) and the Fairtrade Foundation, the number of Fairtrade certified producer organisations worldwide amounts to 632 or 1.5 million farmers and workers, and the number of certified traders is over 800. Fairtrade has directly benefited over 7 million people -farmers, workers, and their families – in 58 developing countries across Asia, Africa and Latin America (Fairtrade Foundation, 2007: 11). Annual Fairtrade sales in Europe reached almost £1.2 billion in 2007 (ibid., Bashir, 2008). Fairtrade sales have increased by almost tenfold in the UK in recent years, from £50.5 million in 2001 to £493 million in 2007 (Fairtrade Foundation).

Besides, Kenya's significant flower export industry also benefits from the economic and social advantages of the Fairtrade system. The Fairtrade Foundation contends that the farm workers are better off with the introduction of certified Fairtrade flower production in Kenya, since the workers now possess the right to join trade unions and reinvest in their communities the 8–12 per cent premium from the export value of the flowers. These cases highlight the extent to which producers and workers in some poor countries benefit from the Fairtrade system (Dolan, 2007).

This section presents the linkages between Islamic values and Fairtrade. Historically, trade and commerce played a key role in the expansion of Islam. The city of Mecca, the birthplace of Islam, was a market and centre for commerce. The early Muslims were not only engaged in trade but they went to distant lands in connection with business. Islam, in fact, reached East and West Africa, as well as South and East Asia through merchants. The Prophet Muhammad (peace be upon him) was himself a successful trader and known for his integrity.

Islam stresses the need for precise and correct weights and measures. Islam condemns the *spirit* of injustice in commercial dealings and of giving too little and asking too much in return. Furthermore, greed is considered a threat to social and economic justice. The Prophet Muhammad (pbuh) in his struggle against the elite of Mecca consistently criticised their greediness and stated '*Two qualities are never coupled in a believer: miserliness and immorality*' (reported by Bukhari). Along similar lines, Islam strongly discourages a monopoly, because it produces 'unlawful' profit and ensures inequality. The Prophet Muhammad (pbuh) therefore forbade monopolies warning '*Whosoever monopolises is a wrongdoer*' (reported by Muslim).Thus, these Islamic principles and guidelines highlight Islam's compatibility with the concepts of fairness and equality.

Fair trade aims to create opportunities for producers and disadvantaged workers in poor countries. Fair trade helps to protect producers and workers in poor countries against the imbalances of the market-oriented policies. Fair trade and justice and interrelated. Social justice includes a fair and equitable distribution of wealth to ensure human dignity for the poor. Striving for social justice involves the struggle against poverty and inequality. The Prophet Muhammad (pbuh) said, '*He who sleeps on a full stomach whilst his neighbour goes hungry is not one of us*', (reported by Bukhari and Muslim). The importance of justice as a human value is emphasised in the following verse:

*Be just, that is closest to Godliness.* (5:8)

Fairtrade is a good example of people-centred development which is in line with Islamic values. This includes the promotion clean energy, organic farming and sound environmental practices that respect human and nature. In this respect, Fairtrade can be viewed as a model that adheres to Islamic values. Muslims believe that Allah has given mankind stewardship over the earth. Stewardship implies taking care to manage, preserve and protect the natural environment for future generations. Furthermore, Islam preaches moderation in consumption, exhorts human to avoid wasteful use of natural resources, and enjoins humankind to maintain the natural balance – principles important in the production of Fairtrade products and to the consumers who purchase them. The Quran states:

*Verily all things have we created in proportion and measure. (54:49)*

The principles of Fairtrade encompass transparent management and commercial relations that aim to promote fairness and respect between trading partners. Islam encourages mutual consent between parties as a necessary condition for a valid business transaction. Islam condemns acts of intermediary intervention that involve exploitation of one's ignorance of market conditions. These principles of mutual consent and of buying and selling at fair market prices in Islam are in harmony with Fairtrade principles.

Fairtrade advocates decent wages and working conditions for workers, as well as long-term trading contracts to provide greater security and a safe and healthy working environment for producers and workers. There are several key principles that guide the treatment of workers. Firstly, there must be clear and proper contracts. Secondly, all agreements whether oral or written must be clear, transparent, just and lawful. And lastly, employees should know their duties and responsibilities and be informed of their rights in terms of holidays and other allowances. It is the duty of both the employers and the employees to fulfil their agreements to the best of their capacities, for the Quran states:

*O you who believe, fulfil your contracts. (5:1)*

The Prophet Muhammad (pbuh) asserted, 'Muslims must abide by their agreements, unless there is an agreement that makes *halal* (permitted) what is *haram* (prohibited) or makes *haram* what is *halal*' (reported by Tirmidhi). The dignity of workers must also be respected. Workers should be treated with dignity and honour and have a humane and safe environment for work. The Prophet Muhammad (pbuh) said:

*Your brothers are your responsibility. Allah has made them under your hands. So whosoever has a brother under his hand, let him give him food as he eats and dress as he dresses. Do not give them work that will overburden them and if you do give them such task then provide them with assistance.*

*(Reported by Bukhari)*

Finally, workers should be given adequate, timely and fair wages. In fact, the Prophet Muhammad (pbuh) considered denying a worker his or her full wage to be an immoral act Exploitation of any person is not allowed in Islam and everyone should receive proper compensation. The Quran says:

> Give just measure and weight, nor withhold from the people the things that are their due. (7:85)

In common with Fairtrade practices, Islam advocates that workers be paid promptly and on time. Indeed the Prophet Muhammad (pbuh) said: '*Give to the worker his wages before his sweat dries*' (reported by Tirmidhi and Ibn Majah). Based on all the above principles, we can also infer that workers have a right to exercise freedom of association and the right to form unions in order to establish and safeguard their rights and gain the bargaining power to receive just compensation.

The ability of workers to exercise these rights is important because Fairtrade aims to work through farmer or producer cooperatives so that the benefits are felt community-wide. The establishment of cooperatives may also enhance the ability of producers to negotiate for fair wages and prices outside the Fairtrade system – 'Fairtrade producers gain value from long- term relationships, direct trade and credit provision, all of which help them in their non-Fairtrade sales negotiations' (Nicholls, 2005).

One of the primary justifications for Fairtrade, therefore, is that it can promote diversification, long-term sustainability and greater returns by encouraging investment in poorer communities. In Islam, the basic principle with regard to trade is that the market should be left free to respond to the forces of supply and demand and natural competition. This means that price controls, tariffs and any other barriers should be removed so that trade can be free and fair. In sum, we see that Islamic worldviews can adopt and adapt modern Fairtrade models as part of cross-fertilisation. The following section is another example of how Islam addresses common pool resources or protected areas (*hima*) as a community-based natural resource management.

## Protected Areas (*Hima*) as a Model for Natural Resource Management

This section reviews one of the Islamic practices in natural resource management called *hima*. Historically, the Middle East and North Africa region had hosted and nurtured a system for communal natural resource management called *hima*, which means protected area. Local knowledge and wisdom promoted and refined appropriate local governance systems as a means to co-manage common-pool resources in a collaborative approach to overcome spillover effects, externalities and free-rider problem. Deep within local Arab culture, the notion of sustainability, resilience and managing bounded instability are key elements for survival in a harsh and scarce natural environment but rich in social and human capital. These natural protected areas, *himas*, were managed by sound local governance that are found on a culture of coexistence, integrity, trust, care and respect for nature and life.

In the Arab peninsula where the natural environment is characterised by aridity, fluctuation and uncertainty, it is crucial to understand the drive for community-based natural resource management which is based on sharing, solidarity and cooperation. *Hima* contributed positively to save and protect the natural resources, range lands and forests in the Middle East region for 5,000 years. Besides, *hima* system provided the enabling environment for managing conflicts over natural resources, rangelands and forests. The deep understanding of the cycles of nature, the seasonal variations and the carrying capacity of the natural environment in an arid and scarce environment, informed social innovation in community-based natural resource management known as *hima*. A new social contract evolved through social learning and adaptive management that is based on respect of human rights and nature, public interest (*maslaha*) and sustainable use of resources.

Historically, many types of *hima* existed to address various social contexts which range from restricted use of grazing to seasonal and sustainable use concepts. Islam contributed and added to the value system and ethical dimension for *hima*. It also instilled a rational imperative and judgement for measuring trade-offs between public and private interest and between human rights and nature conservation. *Hima* can be viewed as civil society and communal approach to manage common pool resources in a collaborative and adaptive manner. *Hima* system provided a framework for sustainable development with good local governance that can inform our existing governance structures in the twenty-first century. This system of local governance added value to the livelihood and well-being for local communities and demonstrated and activated the human role in the construction of the universe (*Imarat al Kawn*) and living lightly on Earth and sufficiency (*zuhd*).

Sardar (2006) commented that one key pitfall of some Western models of development is that they undermine communal existence by promoting urban development, increasing insecurity by displacing traditional agriculture and promoting debt finance. Al-Jayyousi (2008) argued that Islamic values, local knowledge and practices can be viewed as a model for sustainability and good life (*hayat tayebah*) which embodies equity, economic prosperity and environmental sustainability. Besides, public participation (*shura*) and reaching consensus through consultation is key to community decision-making. The notion of social justice and equity (*adl*) for all people in a community regardless of their culture or belief system is the cornerstone in Islamic values.

Islamic law has devised and formalised specific rules for formulating public policies and making trade-offs between public and private interest and in assessing costs or injury (*darar*). The notion of *maslaha* (public interest) may lead to an understanding of sustainability in its broader terms. *Hima* system operationalised a social contract which prohibits ecological degradation (*fasad*) and human and social alienation. This social contract was constantly reformed and adapted by a community of practice (*Ummah*) who set standards for ethical codes of conduct and also to create new knowledge based on the public interest and necessity.

In my synthesis of the key principles of *hima* system, it is evident that Islamic conservations laws and principles are in harmony with the key concepts of ecosystem approach as documented by Ba Kader et al. (1983). These include building consensus and sense of ownership with the stakeholders, dealing with the natural system as one integral unit including socio-economic, ecological and governance, ensuring process for feedback and social learning as evident in local knowledge and culture which is framed and shaped by Islam.

*Hima* as a social institution resulted as a response to a need to promote coexistence between humans and nature. This social innovation, inspired and informed by local culture, was developed through human reasoning, experimentation and innovation (*ijtihad*). *Hima* is a good example of human-centred development model where the human is viewed as a trustee and a witness who is responsible for the 'construction of the world' (*Emmarat Al-kawn*). *Hima* can be sustained and resourced by community-based financing models like *Waqf* (trust funds). This is an innovative way to secure resources like land, energy and water for the poor by enhancing the social responsibility and solidarity. *Waqf* can be harnessed and institutionalised to promote people-centred development that is resourced and managed by civil society (Al-Jayyousi, 2007).

*Hima* contextualised the notion of public goods that are co-managed by local community in accordance to customary laws. In terms of sharing natural resources and the definition of common pool resources, Islam teaches that water, fire (fuel) and grass are public goods. The prophet Muhammad (peace be upon him) declared free access to three types of public goods; that is, water, pasture and fire (Caponera, 1973, 1992). The prophet stated:

> *People are partners in three resources: water, pasture, and fire.*
> *(Ibn Majah after Ibn Abbas, from Zuhaily, 1989)*

In conclusion, in a globalised world, there is a concern that natural resources will be commercialized and local people will suffer alienation from their land and culture. In today's economic model we are witnessing that the institutions of money rule the world. This implies that inevitably the interests of firm and financial institutions will take precedence over the interests of local people. The following outlines some key conditions for the revival of *Hima* which include a focus on knowledge synthesis, community of practice (reflective practitioners), investment in R&D and implementing pilot projects.

In order to revive the *hima* system in the Middle East, it is imperative to embody the key principles, of justice, human rights and ecological sustainability along with adaptive management and community-based natural resource management. Four conditions are to be purposefully met to revive *hima* in the Middle East. These include the ability to assimilate and synthesise knowledge about *hima*; the formation of a community of practice (*ummah*) of reflective practitioners and knowledge navigators who can de-construct and re-construct a new paradigm for *hima* in the twenty-first century; R&D using action learning; and implementing pilot projects based on *hima* concepts. The above four requirements represent the value chain for co-creation of new knowledge about new models of community-based natural resource management inspired from culture.

## References

Abd Al-Kader, Ali. (1959). 'Land, Property and Land Tenure in Islam'. *Islamic Quarterly*, 5: 4–11.

Abouleish, I. (2005). *Sekem: A Sustainable Community in Egyptian Desert*. Floris.

Ali, Abdullah Yusif. (1989). *The Holy Quran: Text, Translation and Commentary*. (New rev. edn.) Amana Corporation, Maryland.

Al-Jayyousi, O.R. (2007). 'Environmental *Waqf* and Sustainable Development' (in Arabic). *Environment and Development Magazine*, 7. Beirut, Lebanon. August.

Al-Jayyousi, O.R. (2008). 'Rural development and Islam', Vol. 41, Issue 3. *Rural 21*, Germany.

Allan, T. (2000). *The Middle East Water Question: Hydropolitics and Global Economy*. London: I.B. Tauris.

Ba Kader, A., Al Sabagh, A., Al Glenid, M. and Izzi Deen, M. (1983). *Islamic Principles for the Conservation of Natural Environment: A Joint Publication by the International Union for the Conservation of Nature (IUCN) and the Meteorological Protection Administration (MEPA) of the Kingdom of Saudi Arabia*. Gland, Switzerland.

Caponera, D.A. (1973).*Water Laws in Muslim Countries*. Food and Agriculture Organisation of the United Nations, Rome: Irrigation and Drainage Paper No 20/1.

Caponera, D.A. (1992). *Principles of Water Law and Administration: National and International*. Rotterdam, Netherlands: Balkema Publishers.

Chapra, M. Umar. (1970). 'The Economic System of Islam: A Discussion of its Goals and Nature', *Islamic Quarterly*, 14: 3–23.

Chapra, M. Umar. (1992). *Islam and the Economic Challenge*. Jordan: The Islamic Foundation and the International Institute of Islamic Thought, International Islamic Publishing House.

Chapra, U. (2008). *Islam and Economic Development*. New Delhi: Adam.

Esposito, John. (1980). *Islam and Development: Religion and Socio-political Change*. Syracuse: Syracuse University Press.

Dolan, C. (2007). Market Affection: Moral Encounters with Kenyan Fairtrade Flowers. *Ethos* 72 (2): 239-261.

Fairtrade Foundation. (2007). *Annual Report 2007*. Available at: www.fairtrade. org.uk/includes/documents/cm_docs/2008/a/annual_review.pdf.(site accessed Dec. 12, 2011).

Faruqui, Naser I., Asit K. Biswas and Murad J. Bino. (2001). *Water Management in Islam*. Tokyo: IDRC/UNU Press.

Forni, Nadia. (2005). *Land Tenure Policies in the Middle East*. Rome: FAO. www. fao.org//docrep/005/Y8999T/y8999t0f.htm.(site accessed Dec. 12, 2011).(site accessed Dec. 12, 2011).

Hammoudeh, M. (2011). *Islamic Values and Management Practices*. Farnham, Surry, UK: Gower Publishing.

Ishaque, Khalid M. (1983). 'The Islamic Approach to Economic Development', in Esposito, John (ed.), *Voices of Resurgent Islam*. New York, Oxford: Oxford University Press.

Iqbal, M. (1934). *Reconstruction of Religious Thought*. Oxford: Oxford University Press.

Izzi Deen, M. (1990). 'Islamic Environmental Ethics, Law and Society', in *Ethics of Environment and Development*, ed. J. Ronald Engel and Joan G. Engel, Tucson: University of Arizona Press, pp. pp. 189–98.

Khalid, Fazlun M. (2002). 'Islam and the Environment: Social and Economic Dimensions of Global Environmental Change', in Timmerman, Peter (ed.), *Encyclopedia of Global Environmental Change*. Chichester: John Wiley, pp. 332–9.

Khan, Muhammad Akram. (1994). *An Introduction to Islamic Economics*. Islamabad, Pakistan: International Institute of Islamic Thought and Institute of Policy Studies.

Korten, D. (2009). *Agenda for New Economy*. San Francisco: Berrett- Koehler.

Korten, D. (1995). *When Corporations Rule the World*. San Francisco: Berrett-Koehler.

Krier, J-M. (2005). *Fairtrade in Europe 2005: Facts and Figures on Fairtrade in 25 European Countries*.www.european-fair-trade-ussocieties.org/efta/Doc/FT-E-2007.pdf; accessed in Dec. 2010.

Lessem, R. and Palsule, S. (1997). *Managing in Four Worlds*. Oxford: Blackwell.

Lessem, R. and Schieffer, A. (2009). *Transformation Management: Towards the Integral Enterprise*. Farnham, Surrey: Gower Publishing.

Nicholls, Alex. (2005). 'Thriving in a Hostile Environment: Fairtrade's Role as a Positive Market Mechanism for Disadvantaged Producers'. Fairtrade Foundation.

Nomani, F. and Rahnema, A. (1994). *Islamic Economics*. London: Zed Books.

Normani, Farhad, and Rahnema, Ali. (1995). *Islamic Economic Systems*. Kuala Lumpur: S. Abdul Majeed & Co.

Rodinson, M. (1973). *Islam and Capitalism*. (trans. Brian Pearce; 1st edn, French, 1966). New York: Pantheon.

Sardar, Z. (1987). *The Future of Muslim Civilisation*. London: Mansell.

Yunus, M. (2008). *Creating a World without Poverty*. NY: Public Affairs.

Zuhaily W. (1989). *Islamic Fiqh and its Evidence*, part 4. (3rd edn; Arabic). Beirut, Lebanon: Dar Al-Fikr.

# 4

# Beauty (*Ihsan*) and Sustainable Development

*The visible world is a trace of the invisible one, and the former follows*
*the latter like a shadow.*

(*Al-Ghazali*, The Niche of Lights)

## Summary

This chapter intends to shed some light on the essence of *ihsan* by exploring the notion of Islamic art and architecture with linkages to sustainability. Also, notions of *ihsan* and naturalistic intelligence will be discussed with reference to metaphors and analogies in Qura'n so as to inform debate on sustainability and Islam. Later, Mecca as a model of a good city and a good life will be discussed as a vision for the future.

## Objectives

1.  Restore the notion of naturalistic intelligence from an Islamic perspective.

2.  Review the principles of Islamic art and the Islamic city as part of constructing sustainability.

3.  Value and nurture the sense of beauty and art in cosmos, nature and human life so as to address ecological degradation.

4.  Highlight the implications of appreciating beauty (*ihsan*) for a transition towards a sustainable civilisation.

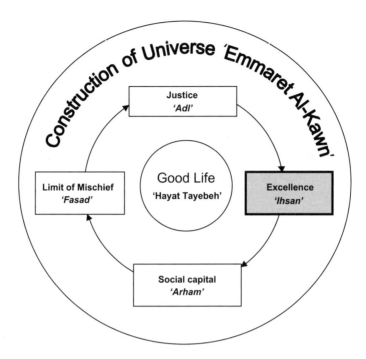

**Figure 4.1      A model for sustainable development based on Islamic worldviews – Excellence (*Ihsan*)**

This chapter intends to shed some light on the notion of *ihsan* from four domains: the individual, organisation, society, the community of life and cosmos. According to Azzam (2006), the art and architecture in Islam are more than just an aesthetic or spatial experience; they represent a symbolic vision of a higher reality. Islamic art is synonymous with scared art. It is an art which transmits a Divine message and transcends time and place. It draws its roots from the spirits and manifests itself in our physical world. Sacred art in general is an expression of human's relationship with God. Its function is to express the primordial Truth, to transform the invisible into visible from through the language of symbolism.

Ali (1996) documented the history of Islamic Art and its key features as summarised below. Art and architecture have always held a central role in the civilisation of Islam; a role which encompasses the wide range of values which make up the civilisation. The art of calligraphy is always considered to be the highest form of visual art in Islam, since it expresses the divine word which is the essence of the Quran. In the Islamic worldview, art cannot be separated from technique or craft or from science. Islamic art transcends the realm of reason to communicate wisdom (*hikmah*) and the universal principles. Technique and beauty were always complimentary parts of artistic creativity and the arts of Islamic world always conveyed the highest principles and values.

To Plato, the good life is one in which a person exhibits perfect virtue and is therefore closer to higher realm of existence. This satisfaction and therefore happiness occur when a person arrives at the mystical understanding of the world. According to Plato, dialogue embedded in love, or what I refer to as intelligent-communicative action, is the medium in which humans will attain the trusted knowledge to attain and realise good life and happiness. This implies a transformation from appreciating one's physical beauty to loving the beauty of mind and beauty in general.

According to Ibn Sina (Avicenna), nature is the venue and setting where everything acquires meaning and God's will is manifested. Therefore, any manifestation of nature tends toward the perfect and the divine. It should be noted that the Islamic worldview, as argued by Foltz et al. (2003), calls to remove the obstacle of human passion from intelligence in order to reach absolute and true faith. Hence, the natural phenomenon induces rational wonder for a marvellous working relationships, processes, systems and mechanisms. When Quran talks about the wonders on the cosmos, human creation, birds, bees and ants it intends to nurture naturalistic intelligence and to enhance learning by analogy from the perfect natural organisation of a self-organising system and a community (*ummah*) that we should mimic so as to attain a sustainable human civilisation.

The symbolism of garden (*Gardens of Eden, ferdaws, rawdah*) in Quran has many references so as to guide the human to good conduct and to help him/her in the journey to the Hereafter. As articulated by Wescoat (1995), the expulsion of Adam and Eve from the garden of the creation was mentioned in short text in Quran so as to signify that Islam in less concerned with paradise lost than with the path towards salvation (*itq*). In sum, the notion of beauty and excellence (*ihsan*) can enlighten and evolve a new sense of self-mastery by appreciating the value and meaning of the unity between inner and outer beauty. Moreover, this self-realisation of beauty will translate to evolve a value-based and ethical organisation that aspires to unify the soft and hard or the majesty (*jalal*) and beauty (*jamal*) for individuals, organisation and societies at large.

The deeper feeling and embodiment of the sense of beauty and excellence (*ihsan*) is likely to transcend national boundaries and will have a universal meaning to deal with the global aesthetic degradation as manifested in physical pollution, human alienation, injustice, species extinction, deforestation, consumerism and unjustified wars for economic gains to control energy and material resources. Reclaiming our human sense of inner and outer beauty (*ihsan*) becomes an imperative to convey a common word (*kalema sawa'*) between all nations on this planet to reconcile the past and history and to co-create a shared reality of unity and togetherness within diversity.

## *Ihsan* and Islamic Art: A Transition to a Sustainable Human Civilisation

The transformation of the inner beauty to the outer world so as to construct a world (*emart al ard*) of beauty and excellence at all domains; that is, the individual, the organisation and society is the cornerstone for a transition to a sustainable human civilisation. The Islamic worldview is about instilling a deeper sense of beauty, order, harmony and system in the human conscience so as to reflect this on the organisation and society. The following section outlines the approach of how this sense of beauty is nurtured as part of the belief and practice in Islam.

### UNITY (*TAWHID*) OF INDIVIDUAL AND COMMUNITY

*Ihsan* as an Arabic term has many meanings like excellence and beauty. This also refers to a higher level of evolving consciousness which is higher than *Islam* (worship of body) and *iman* (worship of heart). The Arabesque art in its repetition of single elements and shapes illustrates the contribution of an individual element to the whole and to the community (*ummah*). *Ihsan* is about the continuous improvement of the individual to the community and the awareness of the Divine in every act which results in evolving of an inner beauty and insight. Hence, through this inner renewable consciousness, human actions are regulated to protect the freedom of the community. True individual value and freedom is found in doing what is good and beautiful for the community (*ummah*). The unveiling of beauty in human, nature and cosmos provides an inspiration for *ihsan* which is doing what is good and beautiful for all the community of life.

### UNITY (*TAWHID*) OF TRADITION AND MODERNITY

Islamic art is manifested in landscape, art, architecture and urban design through integrating pre-existing artistic traditions and adapting them to their own scope and demands as reflected in the Dome of the Rock in Jerusalem – the first monument of Islam (688–92) and the Ummayed Great Mosque in Damascus (706–16). In its creative phases, the art of the Muslim world was the product of a new syntax and of a new semantic order for an older visual structure. The City of Jerusalem in the 21st century can be a model for celebrating ethnic and cultural diversity as it was before during the Islamic rule where all people have a space and a role to play in a city that embraced 'togetherness and unity within diversity'. It was this deep sense of *ihsan* that inspired Omar bin Khattab (the second Muslim Khalifa after Prophet Muhammad) not to make prayers in the church so as to respect the Christian space.

For Muslims, the Islamic art was not a new invention but an assimilative selection, refinement, and recombination of the past and the new and the blending of tradition and modernity. This process, in essence, is a core meaning of the process of excellence and constructed beauty (*ihsan*). This selective assimilation was a defining one in creating early Islamic art since the new Muslims needed an aesthetic mode that could satisfy the spiritual aspirations and link them to the roots of Abrahamic monotheism.

## UNITY OF THE VISIBLE (*THAHER*) AND THE INVISIBLE (*BATIN*)

The key role of the Islamic art is to reinforce the awareness of God and realisation of the Hereafter (*Akherah*) and the fusion of the invisible (*batin*) and the visible (*thaher*). The challenge of a transition to sustainability from an Islamic perspective as well as art is to do what the early Muslim scholars had done, that is to reform and transform old notions, concepts and techniques from all cultures and develop new hybrid models that resonate with local knowledge and culture. If we can restore the state of aesthetic degradation through communicating the notion of *ihsan* to the younger generation, then we are on the right track to achieve a sustainable human civilisation.

## UNITY OF LOCALISM AND GLOBALISM

The global influence of the Islamic civilisation in all directions of the globe from Spain to the Philippines helped spread the aesthetic unity within diversity through Islamic art and architecture. A hundred and fifty years after the coming of Islam, Islamic art had formed its own language and aesthetics. For example, the Great Mosque of Cordoba (785) in Al-Andalus and Ibn Tulun Mosque (879) in Egypt no longer represented phases in a tentative evolution but were, in their own right, unsurpassable masterpieces that set standards for proportions for beauty and harmony. It is interesting to visit the Islamic art museum in Doha, Qatar which was designed by a Chinese artist who wrote that he was inspired by the Ibn Tulun mosque in Egypt.

## UNITY WITHIN DIVERSITY IN CULTURE, SPACE AND TIME

One of the key characteristics of Islamic art, around which almost all views meet, is its unity within diversity. This unity is best expressed in Arabic by the doctrine of *tawhid* which means the Oneness of God or Unity of God. Despite the major differences in style and performance that are found in the countries ranging from Spain and Morocco to India and Indonesia, one can identify an Islamic character of a city or a piece of art. Despite variations in space and time, unity of Islamic art was a unique characteristic that is reflected in Islamic landscape and architecture. This unity can be attributed mainly to the core of Islamic worldviews informed by the Quran and Arabic language which inspires eco-imagination, eco-analogies, eco-metaphors and eco-images informed from cosmos, nature and human being.

## UNITY OF STABILITY AND CHANGE

A critical feature of Islamic art is mobility of ideas and people due to trade and pilgrimage (*Haj*). The mobility of people within and outside the Islamic Empire made artists and artisans spread artistic ideas is space and time. Extensive commercial activities within the empire and travelling to Mecca for pilgrimage (*Haj*) from all over the Muslim world caused the widest artistic interaction and made possible the exchange and introduction of artistic ideas and notions of *ihsan*. The key question in the twenty-first century is how the Islamic cities in general like Mecca and Jerusalem in particular can be the hub for learning and for reclaiming and meaning of both inner and outer beauty.

## UNITY OF ART AND SCIENCE

Another feature of Islamic art is the ability to transform the 'normal and familiar' to 'extraordinary and exciting'. It was evident that Islamic artists were able to transform mundane objects of daily use such as rugs, clothes, lamps, jars and plates into rich and stimulating works of art. For Muslim artistic conscience, an artefact is in itself an object of art whose function is both aesthetic and practical. For a traditional Muslim artist, there are no minor and major arts. No boundary exists that separates fine art from applied art. All artistic production demands the same degree of care, planning, creativity, attention and skill. Separating art from handicraft is a modern Western concept which first was evident during the Renaissance era when art was divorced from spirituality, and only gained ground in the nineteenth century during the Industrial Revolution. In Islam, artist and artisan are one, both are the instruments of God in creating beauty, and none of them is a creator on his own.

In a traditional society, every act whose application requires skill is called art, so that there is an art of agriculture, architecture, smelting, painting and poetry. No distinction exists between a 'fine' and an 'applied' art. When the industrial revolution took place, industrial design was unheard of and the daily lives of the masses in the West were totally devoid of aesthetics. Only in the twentieth century did industry recognise the aesthetic value of the utilitarian objects.

## UNITY OF THE BEAUTY IN THE COMMUNITY OF LIFE AND COSMOS

According to Islam, human is the manifestation of the creation of God (*Allah* in Arabic). Humans have a mandate and a trusteeship (*amanah*) by being the vicegerents of God on earth, trusted to create a harmonious relationship between cosmos, nature and people. All creation reflects the cosmic beauty, magnificence and intelligence (*ihsan*). From an Islamic worldview, Islamic art is one of the means by which humans can nurture and enhance 'aesthetic intelligence' as signs (*ayat*) in all species and cosmos for deeper learning and reflections from nature and cosmos.

From the spiritual and ethical point of view, Islamic art originates essentially from the Quranic Message which aims to translate concepts and notions into shapes. This implies that external message (*thaher*) is complimented by an inner reality (*batin*) that represents the invisible internal essence. The outward form, or *thaher*, underlines the quantitative aspect that is obvious, while the qualitative aspect is the inner beauty or the hidden *batin*. In order to fully realise full meaning of beauty and excellence, one must seek to comprehend both types of knowledge, the visible and the invisible (*batin and thaher*) or the software and hardware of things.

## UNITY OF WORK AND WORSHIP

Of specific value, Islamic art belongs to a culture that is characterised by the role of a community (*ummah*) and shaped the ideal to be liberated from one's self and ego, and where human individuality becomes a means rather than an end. The Islamic worldview is informed by the sayings of the Prophet: *'God has inscribed beauty upon all things'*, *'God desires that if you do something you perfect it'*, *'Work is a form of worship'* and *'God is beautiful and He loves beauty'*. Hence, perfecting one's artistic work becomes a form of worship and a religious obligation easily fulfilled by the artist through adherence to the faith and its convictions. Islamic artists' key role is to search for new ideas and techniques that could further intensify human fascination with the whole life.

It is the combination of reason, intellect, skill and insight that are to be harnessed by the Muslim artists to project the inner self in a form that reflects to the outside reality. Accordingly, all Islamic art is created as a result of the wedding of formal sciences and the crafts. During the golden age of Islam, professionals, artisans and artists followed the Prophet's saying *'God desires if you do something you perfect it'*. This code of conduct ensures quality control, standards, inspiration and continuity. Islamic art is to be viewed as a tool that compliments and supports spiritual life. There is evidence that when there is an eclipse of the spiritual life, this will be reflected negatively on art and urban design. The absence of a spiritual atmosphere breeds professionals who lack reflection and innovation (*ijtihad*).

The relationship of a Muslim with the Quran is an organic and lively one that influences human's visual and intellectual abilities and intelligences. This relationship characterises the identity of Islamic art in terms of harmony, repetition, multiplicity, regularity and variety. Islamic spirituality is related to Islamic art. Through the five daily prayers, reading the Quran and repeating certain prayers as a form of remembrance (*dhikr*), the soul of the Muslim is remoulded into a mosaic of spiritual attitudes that emphasise the grandeur of God.

The Quran says: *'Nothing is greater than the Remembrance of God'* and this can be attained through the meditation and reflection on the creation of human, cosmos and natural environment. Thus, art appears to transform the physical environment into a reflection of the spiritual world. The key mission of the artist is to translate Islamic values into an aesthetic language of patterns and designs that are reflected in urban design and the built environment. Hence, the objective of Islamic art is to enhance naturalistic intelligence and human consciousness of the Creator.

## UNITY OF THE PHYSICAL AND THE SPIRITUAL

Aesthetically, Islamic art and architecture represent the spiritual and physical aspects in the lives of Muslims which revolve around the concept of unity (*tawhid*) as discussed by Al-Faruqi (1998). The geometrical shapes, centre in a circle or axis all convey spiritual and physical meanings with respect to the cosmos and the human life. The central reference of God in the Universe and the spiritual world is followed by the central location of the *Ka'ba* and Mecca city on earth. Thus, the spiritual and temporal life of Muslims is regulated in circles which revolve around an axis and represent the constant revolving movement of the believer's life toward human journey for conscious evolution of God and human destiny. This is also manifested in the pilgrimage and moving around *Ka'ba* (*tawaf*).

The following section discusses a model of the Islamic city, Mecca, as a manifestation of a global forum of a green and good city (*tayebah city*) as a model for human space for healing, renewal and emancipation.

## Mecca as a Model of a Good City (*Tayebah* City)

> *I swear by the city, and you yourself are a resident of this city, by the begetter and all whom he begot: We created human to try him with affliction.*
>
> (Quran: Sura 90:1–The City)

The term Mecca, which was mentioned in Quran in the above verse, has been coined with a preferred destination (*qibla*) and an attraction point not only in Arabic but also in other Western languages. This generic term refers to a focal point for people to attain value and benefits (*manafei*) in a broader sense in all aspect of life from medicine, education, business, art, innovation, science and enlightenment. The key question is how we can view and transform Mecca as a global eco-city for spirituality, enlightenment and transformation. The story of Malcom X and his journey to Mecca was a unique experience of changing his mindset and worldview about the equality between all races. In the twenty-first century, with a world plagued with poverty, financial crisis, HIV, climate change, pollution and scarcity of food, water and energy, branding Mecca as a global forum for transformation, dialogue, peace and celebrating unity within diversity becomes a mission of transformational human leadership. The notion of Green JIZ (*Jihad-Ijtihad-Zuhd*) can be contextualised and manifested in Mecca as a city for a renewed mind, soul which can help realise the notion of good life.

It is illuminating to see that Mecca was a source of enlightenment for a US leader, Malcom X, in the civil rights movement in the sixties of the twentieth century on a volatile issue like race. In the twenty-first century, the Islamic city and Mecca in particular, as a manifestation of Islamic values and worldviews, can play a new role to promote dialogue and understanding on 'global commons' and to inspire new thinking on global pressing challenges like global finance, poverty, HIV-AIDS, multiculturalism, human security, combating terrorism, governance and human prosperity. Mecca can and should be the place for reflection and crafting new solutions for the current financial issues by instituting a global *Waqf* (endowment fund) for Green Earth to ensure that the current economic model consider ecosystem services and the needs of the poor as part of new metrics for human development and progress of societies.

Historically, the built environment and urban centres were informed and inspired by specific concepts and notions. For example, Greece was a city that reflected intellect, morality and ethics, while Rome was about order and beauty, and Jerusalem was about multiculturalism and empowering the weak and the voiceless. In the twenty-first century, how can Mecca be a model that embodies a good life (*hayat tayebah*) in all domains of life from spirituality, human rights, peace and governance, to social equity, human well-being and sustainable livelihood? Simply, how Mecca can be a model and an embodiment for sustainability and good life (*hayat tayebah*). This section is an attempt to view and harness the genuine meaning of Mecca as a venue to host and convene a global humanitarian forum. Besides, it is an attempt to revisit the underlying value and meaning of pilgrimage (*Haj*) which is in essence is an emancipation journey for nurturing self-mastery and new consciousness. It will be illuminating to transform Mecca as a city that unifies all three global fora (economic, social and environmental) and unify a human discourse with a new narrative and a story of a city embodies unity (*tawhid*) of good life.

In this section, I will shed some light on key dimensions of the added value and meaning for having Mecca as a model for an eco-city which seeks to manifest good life (*Hayat Tayebah*) and the purposeful efforts to establish a model for the built environment (*Imran* and *Imaratu Al-ard*) that produces benefits (*manafe'*) beyond space and time. These dimensions include (a) Mecca as a global forum (*qibla*), (b) Mecca with multiple benefits (*manafe'*), (c) Mecca as a green city and (d) Mecca as a model of good life.

## MECCA AS A GLOBAL FORUM

Mecca is blessed by the prayer of Prophet Abraham (peace be upon him) in which he asked that people's hearts long to visit Mecca for both spiritual renewal and transformation. There is an opportunity to brand and harness Mecca as a global city for dialogue by hosting before pilgrimage (*Haj*) time in Jeddah a global forum to address humanity's pressing challenges from governance, democracy, human rights, finance, human health, women rights, learning and innovation. The essence of pilgrimage (*Haj*), besides the spiritual dimension, is to share the wisdom and best practices and to address the current risks, threats and challenges worldwide. The same can be said about Jerusalem, as a city which Prophet Muhammad (pbuh) led all prophets in a payer at Al-Aqsa mosque in Jerusalem, which shows, from an Islamic worldview, that Islam is not a new religion but a continuum for all monotheistic religions.

## MECCA WITH MULTIPLE BENEFITS

The notion of benefits (*manafe'*), as stated in the context of Prophet Abraham prayer (peace be upon him), is a generic term that encompasses human well-being, livelihood, socio-economic development and human-centred development. Benefits also encompass human dignity and the nurturing of human mind, soul and well-being. Also, living the experience of Mecca should be a transformational experience and learning from the history and personal journey of prophet Muhammad (peace be upon him) as he inspired a community (*ummah*) to shoulder a human responsibility and to embody a global vision and mandate so as to spread mercy (*rahmah*) to humanity.

## MECCA AS A GOOD AND GREEN CITY

Realising the global challenges from climate change, pollution, over-consumption, biodiversity loss and poverty, Mecca can be the stage to demonstrate how a transition to a low-carbon economy and also it can contribute to new ideas for green economy like protected area (*hima*) and trust funds (*waqf*). Mecca and the Middle East and North Africa are rich in solar energy and if this renewable energy is well-harnessed in the built environment, auto-industry and ICT it can be a model for achieving prosperity without being addicted to fossil oil.

## MECCA AS A MODEL OF GOOD LIFE (*HAYAT TAYEBAH*)

Harmony, balance, governance, human dignity and reconciliation between human and nature are key ingredients for good life. The rich historical experience of pilgrimage is a story of social cohesion and human empathy; all of which are the cornerstones for a good life and a good city. Living for few days in Mecca encompasses good practices, good food (prophet food), unity of appearance in white clothes and unity in remembrance of God (*thiker*). In essence, it is about Green struggle (*jihad*), innovation (*ijtihad*) and living lightly on earth (*zuhd*).

> *There were tens of thousands of pilgrims from all over the world. They were of all colors, from blue-eyed blonds to black-skinned Africans. But we were all participating in the same ritual displaying a spirit of unity and brotherhood that my experience in America had led me to believe never could exist between the white and the non-white.*
>
> *America needs to understand Islam because this is the religion that erases from its society the race problem.*
> *Malik Shahbaz (Malcom X speech after Haj to Mecca).*

The following section will discuss how Quran promotes the notion of naturalistic intelligence as a means for deep learning, reflection and transformation.

## Naturalistic Intelligence: Inspiration from Signs (*Ayat*) in Quran

The following illustrates a set of examples which sheds some light on the magnificence, order, harmony and beauty that was revealed in Quran as documented by Yahya Harun (2002) and summarised below.

Ever since the Quran was revealed, it has possessed an easily understandable language and tone, accessible to all people and in all times. Allah tells us of this style in the Quran:

> *We have made the Quran easy to remember.*
>
> *(Quran, 54:22)*

The perfection of the literary language of the Quran, the incomparable features of its style and the superior wisdom contained within it are some of the definitive proofs that it represents the word of the Creator. In addition, the Quran contains within its words many miracles which prove it to be Allah's word. One of these attributes is the remarkable number of scientific truths which are contained in the Book of Islam. In this book which was revealed over 14 centuries ago to the Prophet Muhammad (pbuh), there are innumerable examples of information that humanity have only been able to uncover by the technology of the twentieth and twenty-first centuries. The following is a set of examples which illustrate the notion of *ihsan* and its linkage to sustainability:

## *ISHAN* AS ORDER AND EQUILIBRIUM

The billions of stars and galaxies in the universe move in perfect equilibrium in the paths set out for them. Stars, planets and satellites rotate not only around their own axes but also together with the systems of which they are an integral part. Sometimes, galaxies containing 200–300 billion stars move across each other's paths. Yet amazingly, no collisions take place that might damage the great order in the universe. This miracle is something over which all of us should reflect.

In the universe, the concept of speed assumes giant dimensions when compared to earthly measurements. Stars, planets, galaxies and conglomerations of galaxies – whose numerical properties can only be conceived by mathematicians – weigh billions or trillions of tons, and move through space at extraordinary speeds.

For example, the Earth rotates at 1,670 km/h (1,038 mph). If we consider that the fastest-moving bullet today possesses an average speed of 1,800 km/h, we can see how fast the Earth is moving, despite its enormous size and mass. If we were able to construct a vehicle capable of moving at that speed, it would be able to circumnavigate the Earth in 22 minutes. These figures apply only to the Earth. Those for the Solar System are even more fascinating. The speed of that system is such as to exceed the bounds of reason: The larger the systems in the universe, the greater their speed. The Solar System's speed of orbit around the centre of the galaxy is 720,000 km/h. The Milky Way, with its 200 billion or so stars, moves through space at 950,000 km/h.

There is no doubt that there is a very high risk of collisions in such a complicated and fast-moving system. Yet nothing of the sort actually happens and we continue with our lives in complete safety. That is because everything in the universe functions according to the flawless equilibrium set out by Allah. It is for this reason that, as stated in the verse, there is no 'discrepancy' in the system.

> *He Who created the seven heavens in layers. You will not find any flaw in the creation of the All-Merciful. Look again-do you see any gaps? Then look again and again. Your sight will return to you dazzled and exhausted!*
>
> (Quran, 67:3–4)

Materialist philosophy emerged with the claim that all the systems in nature and the universe were like machines that functioned on their own, that the flawless order and balance within them were the work of chance. The scientific discoveries of the twentieth century that followed swiftly, one after the other, in the fields of astrophysics and biology have proved that life and the universe were created. Discoveries have revealed that there is a great design and fine-tuning in the material world and this has categorically demonstrated the groundless nature of the claims of materialism.

Considering the conditions necessary for life, we see that only the Earth meets these particular conditions. For an environment suitable for life, there are innumerable conditions taking place simultaneously and unceasingly all around us. There are some hundred billion galaxies, each with-on average a hundred-billion stars. In all the galaxies, there are perhaps as many planets as stars. In the face of such overpowering numbers, one can better comprehend the significance of the formation of such an exceptional environment on the Earth.

From the force of the Big Bang explosion to the physical values of atoms, from the levels of the four basic forces to the chemical processes in the stars, from the type of light emitted by the Sun to the level of viscosity of water, from the distance of the Moon to the Earth to the level of gases in the atmosphere, from the Earth's distance from the Sun to its angle of tilt to its orbit, and from the speed at which the Earth revolves around its own axis to the functions of the oceans and mountains on the Earth: every single detail is ideally suited to our lives. Today, the world of science describes these features by means of the concepts of the 'Anthropic Principle' and 'Fine-Tuning'. These concepts summarise the way that the universe is not an aimless, uncontrolled, chance collection of matter but that it has a purpose directed towards human life and has been designed with the greatest precision.

Attention is drawn in the above verses to the measure and harmony in Allah's creation. The word 'taqdeer', meaning 'to design, measure, create by measuring', is employed in Quranic verses such as Surat al-Furqan. The word 'tibaaq', meaning 'in harmony', is used in Surat al-Mulk and Surah Nuh. Furthermore, Allah also reveals in Surat al-Mulk with the word 'tafaawut', meaning 'disagreement, violation, non-conformity, disorder, opposite', that those who seek disharmony will fail to find it.

The term 'fine-tuning', which began to be used towards the end of the twentieth century, represents this truth revealed in the verses. Over the last quarter-century or so, a great many scientists, intellectuals and writers have shown that the universe is not a collection of coincidences. On the contrary, it has an extraordinary design and order ideally suited to human life in its every detail as documented by Yahya Harun (2002 a, b).

The existence of carbon, the basis of all life, depends on the temperature remaining within specific limits. Carbon is an essential substance for organic molecules such as amino acid, nucleic acid and protein: these constitute the basis of life. For that reason, life can only be carbon-based. Given this, the existing temperature needs to be no lower than –20 degrees and no higher than 120 degrees Celsius (248° F). These are just the temperature limits on Earth.

These are just a few of the exceedingly sensitive balances which are essential for life on Earth to have emerged and to survive. Yet even these are sufficient to definitively reveal that the Earth and the universe could not have come into being as the result of a number of consecutive coincidences. The concepts of 'fine-tuning' and the 'anthropic principle' that began to be employed in the twentieth century are further evidence of Allah's creation. The harmony and proportion therein were described with magnificent accuracy 14 centuries ago in the Quran.

Today, the relativity of time is a proven scientific fact. This was revealed by Einstein's theory of relativity during the early part of the twentieth century. Until then, it was not known that time was relative, nor that it could change according to the circumstances. Yet, the renowned scientist Albert Einstein proved this fact by discovering the theory of relativity. He showed that time is dependent on mass and velocity. However, the Quran had already included information about time's being relative. Some verses about the subject read:

> *A day with your Lord is equivalent to a thousand years in the way you count.*
>
> (*Quran, 22:47*)

> *He directs the whole affair from heaven to Earth. Then it will again ascend to Him on a day whose length is a thousand years by the way you measure.*
>
> (*Quran, 32:5*)

## *IHSAN* IN THE DUALITY IN CREATION

> *Glory be to Him Who created all the pairs: from what the earth produces and from themselves and from things unknown to them.*
>
> (*Quran, 36:36*)

While 'male and female' is equivalent to the concept of 'pair', 'things unknown to them', as expressed in the Quran, bears a broader meaning. Indeed, we encounter one of the meanings pointed to in the verse in the present day. The British physicist Paul Dirac, who discovered that matter was created in pairs, won the Nobel Prize for Physics in 1933. This finding, known as 'parity', revealed the duality known as matter and anti-matter. Anti-matter bears the opposite characteristics to matter. For instance, contrary to matter, anti-matter electrons are positive and protons negative. Science proved that every particle has its antiparticle of opposite charge. Another example of duality in creation is plants. Botanists only discovered that there is a gender distinction in plants about a hundred years ago.

The Arabic word 'zawjayn', translated as 'two types', comes from 'zawj', meaning 'one of a pair'. As we know, fruits are the final product produced by ripening plants. The stage before fruit is the flower. Flowers also have male and female organs. When pollen is carried to the flower and fertilisation takes place, they begin to bear fruit. The fruit gradually ripens and starts to release seeds. The fact that fruits have gender-specific features is another piece of scientific information indicated in the Quran.

## *IHSAN* IN HUMAN CREATION

> *From what thing did He create him? From a drop of sperm He created*
> *him and proportioned him. Then He eases the way for him.*
> (Quran, 80:18–20)

When the father's sperm cell fertilises the mother's egg, the parents' genes combine to determine all of the baby's physical characteristics. Each one of these thousands of genes has a specific function. It is the genes which determine the colour of the eyes and hair, height, facial features, skeletal shape and the countless details in the internal organs, brain, nerves and muscles. In addition to all the physical characteristics, thousands of different processes taking place in the cells and body-and indeed the control of the whole system-are recorded in the genes. For example, whether a person's blood pressure is generally high, low or normal depends on the information in his or her genes.

The first cell which forms when the sperm and the egg are joined also forms the first copy of the DNA molecule which will carry the code in every cell of the person's body, right up until death. DNA is a molecule of considerable size. It is carefully protected within the nucleus of the cell and this molecule is an information bank of the human body as it contains the genes we mentioned above. The first cell, the fertilised egg, then divides and multiplies in the light of the programme recorded in the DNA. The tissues and organs begin to form: This is the beginning of a human being. The coordination of this complex structuring is brought about by the DNA molecule. This is a molecule consisting of atoms such as carbon, phosphorus, nitrogen, hydrogen and oxygen.

The information capacity recorded in DNA is of a size which astonishes scientists. There is enough information in a single human DNA molecule to fill a million encyclopaedia pages or 1,000 volumes. To put it another way, the nucleus of a cell contains information, equivalent to that in a one-million-page encyclopaedia. It serves to control all the functions of the human body. To make a comparison, the 23-volume *Encyclopaedia Britannica*, one of the largest encyclopaedias in the world, contains a total of 25,000 pages. Yet a single molecule in the nucleus of a cell, and which is so much smaller than that cell, contains a store of information 40 times larger than the world's largest encyclopaedias. That means that what we have here is a 1,000-volume encyclopaedia, the like of which exists nowhere else on Earth. This is a miracle of design and creation within our very own bodies, for which evolutionists and materialists have no answer.

Bearing in mind that the structure of DNA was unravelled by Francis Crick in 1953, it is truly amazing that the Quran pointed to the concept of 'genetic planning' in an age when, as we have mentioned previously, mankind's knowledge was very limited. Geneticists were unable to discuss until the end of the nineteenth century and these remarkable facts act again as proofs that the Quran is the word of Allah as documented by Harun (2002b).

> The notion of *Ihsan* is illustrated in Olive tree in Quran. Research in recent years has revealed that the olive represents an important source of good health. In addition to the olive itself, olive oil is also an important source of nutrition. Attention is drawn to the oil of the olive tree in these terms in the Quran:
>
> > *Allah is the light of the heavens and the Earth. The metaphor of His light is that of a niche in which is a lamp, the lamp inside a glass, the glass like a brilliant star, lit from a blessed tree, an olive, neither of the east nor of the west, its oil all but giving off light even if no fire touches it. Light upon light. Allah guides to His light whoever He wills and Allah makes metaphors for humanity and Allah has knowledge of all things.*
> >
> > *(Quran, 24:35)*

## *IHSAN* IN SPECIES AND HABITATS

> *There is no creature crawling on the Earth or flying creature, flying on its wings, who are not communities just like yourselves.*
>
> *(Quran, 6:38)*

As a result of modern-day animal and bird ecology study, we know that all animals and birds live in the form of separate societies. Lengthy and wide-ranging studies have shown that there is a rather systematic social order among animals. Honey bees, for example, whose social life amazes scientists, build their nests in colonies in tree hollows or other covered areas. A bee colony consists of a queen, a few hundred males and 10–80,000 workers. There is only one queen in every colony and her fundamental task is that of laying eggs. In addition, she secretes important substances which maintain the unity of the colony and allow the system within the hive to function. The males' only function is to fertilise the queen. All other functions, such as, building honey combs in the hive, gathering food, creating royal jelly, regulating the temperature of the hive, cleanliness and defence are carried out by the workers. There is order in every phase of life in the hive. All duties, from caring for the larvae to provision of the general needs of the hive, are performed without fail.

Despite having the greatest numbers in the world, ants also exhibit an order which can serve as an example to human beings in many areas: technology, collective labour, military strategy, an advanced communications network, a hierarchical order, discipline and flawless town planning. Ants live in societies known as colonies and in such order amongst themselves that one could even say that they have a civilisation similar to that of human beings.

As ants produce and store their food, they also watch over their young, defend the colony and wage war against their enemies. There are even colonies which engage in 'sewing', 'agriculture' and 'animal rearing'. These animals have a very powerful communications network amongst themselves. Their social organisation and expertise are far superior to any other living thing. Communal animals with ordered lives also operate together in the face of danger. For instance, when birds of prey such as hawks or owls enter the area, smaller birds surround these birds en masse. They then produce a special sound to draw other birds to the area. The aggressive behaviour displayed by small birds en masse generally drives birds of prey away.

A flock of birds flying together protects all its members in the same way. For instance, a flock of starlings flying together leave a wide distance between one another. When they see a hawk, however, they close the distance between them. They thus make it harder for the hawk to dive in amidst the flock. Even if the hawk does so, it will be acting to its own detriment. Its wings will be damaged and it will be unable to hunt. Mammals also act in consort when there is an attack on the group. For example, zebras take their young into the middle of the herd when they flee from enemies. Dolphins also swim in groups and fight off their greatest enemy, sharks, as a group.

## *IHSAN* AND BIOMIMICRY

> *There is instruction for you in cattle. From the contents of their bellies, from between the dung and blood. We give you pure milk to drink, easy for drinkers to swallow.*
>
> *(Quran, 16:66)*

Before scientists and research and development experts embark on new projects, they usually look for models in living things and imitate their systems and designs. In other words, they see and study the designs created in nature by Allah and, inspired by these, go on to develop their own new technologies. This approach has given birth to biometrics, a new branch of science that seeks to imitate living things. In recent times, this branch of science has come to be widely applied in the world of technology. The use of the word 'ibrah,' (to learn from, advice, importance, important thing or model) in the above verses is most wise in this regard.

Biomimetics refers to all of the substances, equipment, mechanisms and systems that people produce in order to imitate the systems present in nature. The scientific community currently feels a great need for the use of such equipment, particularly in the fields of nanotechnology, robot technology, artificial intelligence, medicine and the military. Biomimicry was first put forward by Janine M. Benyus, a writer and scientific observer from Montana. This concept was later analysed by many other people and began to find applications.

The theme of 'biomimicry' is that we have much to learn from the natural world, as model, measure and mentor. What these researchers have in common is a reverence for natural designs, and the inspiration to use them to solve human problems. David Oakey, product strategist for Interface Inc., a company that uses nature to increasing product quality and productivity, says that nature is his mentor for business and design, a model for the way of life. Nature's system has worked for millions of years. And thus biomimicry is a way of learning from nature.

Scientists who began to favour this rapidly spreading idea accelerated their studies by using nature's incomparable and flawless designs as models. These designs represent models for technological research, for they provide the maximum productivity for the least amount of materials and energy, and are self-maintaining, environmentally friendly, silent, aesthetically attractive, resistant and long-lasting. The *High Country News* described biomimetics as 'a scientific movement' that uses natural systems to create technologies that are more reliable and sustainable. Janine M. Benyus (1998), who believed that models in nature should be imitated, gave the following examples in her book, *Biomimicry: Innovation Inspired by Nature:*

- Hummingbirds cross the Gulf of Mexico on less than 3 grams (one tenth of an ounce) of fuel

- Dragonflies outmanoeuvre our best helicopters

- Heating and air-conditioning systems in termite mounds are superior in terms of equipment and energy consumption to those made by human beings

- A bat's high-frequency transmitter is more efficient and sensitive than our own radar systems,

- Light-emitting algae combine various chemicals to illuminate their bodies

- Arctic fish and frogs freeze solid and then spring to life, having protected their organs from ice damage

- Chameleons and cuttlefish change the pattern of their skin to blend instantly with their surroundings

- Bees, turtles and birds navigate without maps

- Whales and penguins dive without scuba gear

These astonishing mechanisms and designs in nature, of which we have cited only a few, have the potential to enrich technology in a wide range of fields. This potential is becoming ever more obvious as our accumulated knowledge and technological means increase. All animals possess many features that amaze human beings. Some have the ideal hydrodynamic shape that allows them to move through water, and others employ senses that appear very foreign to us. Most of these are features that researchers have encountered for the first time, or, rather, that they have only recently discovered. On occasion, it is necessary to bring together prominent scientists from such fields as computer technology, mechanical engineering, electronics, mathematics, physics, chemistry and biology in order to imitate just one feature of a living thing.

Scientists are amazed when confronted with the incomparable structures and systems they are discovering with every passing day, and use that amazement to inspire themselves to produce new technologies for humanity's benefit. Realising that the existing perfect systems and extraordinary techniques applied in nature are far superior to their own knowledge and intellect, they became aware of these matchless solutions to existing problems and are now resorting to the designs in nature to resolve problems that have eluded them for years. As a result, they will perhaps achieve success in a very short time. Moreover, by imitating nature, scientists are making very important gains with regard to time and labour and also to the targeted use of material resources.

Today we see the developing technology gradually discovering the miracles of creation and using the extraordinary designs in living things, as in the case of biomimetics, in the service of humanity. Benyus has stated that 'Doing it nature's way' has the potential to change the way we grow food, make materials, harness energy, heal ourselves, store information and conduct business. A number of articles were published with titles that include: i) 'Science is Imitating Nature, Life's Lessons in Design'; ii) Biomimicry: Secrets Hiding in Plain Sight; iii) Biomimicry: Innovation Inspired by Nature; Biomimicry: Genius That Surrounds Us; iv) Biomimetics: Creating Materials from Nature's Blueprints, and Engineers; v) Ask Nature for Design Advice.

In the nineteenth century, nature was imitated only in aesthetic terms. Artists and architects of that time were influenced by nature and used examples of the structures' external appearances in their works. Yet the realisation of nature's extraordinary designs and that these could be used to benefit human beings only began in the twentieth century with the study of natural mechanisms at the molecular level.

The Quran indicates, when recounting Prophet Sulayman's (pbuh) life, that ants have a communication system:

> *Then, when they reached the Valley of the Ants, an ant said: 'Ants! Enter your dwellings, so that Sulayman and his troops do not crush you unwittingly.'*
>
> *(Quran, 27:18)*

Scientific research into ants has revealed that these tiny animals have very organised social lives and that, as a requirement of that organisation, they also have a very complex communication network. For example, *National Geographic* reports that an ant carries in her head multiple sensory organs to pick up chemical and visual signals vital to colonies that may contain a million or more workers, all of which are female. The brain contains half a million nerve cells; eyes are compound; antennae act as nose and fingertips. Projections below the mouth sense taste; hairs respond to touch.

Even if we are not aware of it, ants use a variety of methods to communicate, thanks to their very sensitive sensory organs. They use these organs at all times, from finding prey to following one another, and from building their nests to waging war. With 500,000 nerve cells squeezed into their 2–3 mm bodies, they possess a communications system that astonishes human beings. The reactions in their communications have been divided into several specific categories: alarm, recruitment, grooming, exchange of oral and anal liquid, group effect, recognition, caste determination. Ants, which establish an ordered society by means of these reactions, live a life based on the mutual exchange of information. To bring about this exchange, they sometimes exhibit more flawless communication in areas that human beings often cannot resolve through speech, such as coming together, sharing, cleaning and defence.

Ants mainly communicate on the chemical level. These semiochemicals, known as pheromones, are chemical compounds that are perceived by smell and secreted by internal glands. In addition, they play the most important role in organising ant societies. When an ant secretes a pheromone, the other ants receive it by means of smell or taste and duly respond. Research into ant pheromones has revealed that all signals are emitted according to the needs of the colony. Moreover, the intensity of the pheromone emitted also varies according to the urgency of the situation at hand.

As we have seen, ants require a profound knowledge of chemistry to do what they do. The fact that the Quran emphasised this fact 1,400 years ago, a time when there was no such knowledge about ants, is another one of its scientific miracles and the *ihsan* in the creation.

> *Allah splits the seed and kernel. He brings forth the living from the dead, and produces the dead out of the living. That is Allah, so how are you misguided?*
>
> *(Quran, 6:95)*

In the above verse, our attention is drawn to a food cycle of which people at the time of the Quran's revelation could have known nothing. When a living thing dies, micro-organisms quickly cause it to decompose. The dead body is thus divided up into organic molecules that mix with the soil and form the basic source of food for plants, animals, and, ultimately, humanity. Were it not for this nutritional cycle, life would not be possible.

Bacteria are responsible for meeting all living things' mineral and food needs. Plants and some animals, which remain almost dead (hibernation) throughout the winter, revive in the summer and meet all of their mineral and food requirements through the activities of bacteria during the winter. Throughout the winter, bacteria separate organic wastes (that is, dead plants and animals) and turn them into minerals. Thus, when living things reawaken in spring, they find food ready and waiting for them. Thanks to bacteria, a 'spring cleaning' has been carried out in their environment and the necessary amount of food has been prepared for nature as it returns to life in the spring.

As we have seen, dead creatures play a vital role in the emergence of new ones. This transition, indicated in the Quran as *'He brings forth the living from the dead, and produces the dead out of the living'*, is carried out in the most perfect manner that is full of *ihsan*.

In summary, we see from this journey of *ihsan* how the essence of beauty and excellence is manifested in human well-being, nature and cosmos which is a source of reclaiming the inner and outer beauty to ensure a sustainable human civilisation that celebrates the notion of a good living for a good life where all communities of life live in a world that is based on systems, order, innovation and beauty.

## References

Al-Faruqi, Ismail. (1998). Islam and Other Faiths. Ataullah Siddiqui (ed.), Leicester: The Islamic Foundation, in association with the International Institute of Islamic Thought, Herndon, VA.

Ali, Wijdan. (1996). *What is Islamic Art?* Mafraq, Jordan: Al- al Bayt University.

Azzam, Khaled. (2006). The Principles and Philosophy of Islamic Art. www. mullasadra.org (website accessed: Dec. 2010).

Ball, Philip. (2001). 'Life's Lessons in Design'. *Nature*, 409: 413–16.

Benyus, Janine M. (1998). *Biomimicry: Innovation Inspired by Nature*. New York: William Morrow and Company, Inc.

Bess, Philips. (2003). The City and the Good Life. The Christian Century. The Christian Century Foundation. www.christiancentury.org (website accessed Dec.1st 2010).

Capra, F. (1997). *The Web of Life: A Scientific Understanding of Living Systems*. Port Moody: Anchor.

Capra, F. (2002). *The Hidden Connection: A Science for Sustainable Living*. NY: Doubleday.

Davies, Paul. (1984). *Superforce: The Search for a Grand Unified Theory of Nature*, Simon Schuster Printing

Denton, Michael. (1998). *Nature's Destiny: How the Laws of Biology Reveal Purpose in the Universe*. New York: The Free Press, 12-13.

Foltz, Richard et al. (2003). *Islam and Ecology*. Cambridge, MA: Center for the Study of World Religions, Harvard Divinity School.

Harun, Yahya. (2002a). *The Creation of the Universe*. Ontario, Canada: Al-Attique Publishers.

Harun, Yahya. (2002b). *The Miracle of Creation in DNA*. New Delhi: Goodword Books.

Hawking, Stephen. (1988). *A Brief History of Time*. London: Bantam Press, 121–5.

Hölldobler, Bert and Wilson, Edward O. (1990). *The Ants*. Cambridge, Massachussetts: Harvard University Press.

Husaini, Waqar. (1999). *The Quran for Astronomy and Earth Exploration from Space*. (3rd edn.) New Delhi: Goodword Press.

La'li, Mahdi. (2003). *Comprehensive Exploration of the Scientific Miracles in Holy Quran*. Canada: Trafford Publishing, 35–8.

Moore, Keith. (1982). *The Developing Human*. (3rd ed.) Philadelphia: W.B. Saunders Company.

Moore, Keith et al. (1992). *Human Development as Described in the Quran and Sunnah*. Makkah: Commission on Scientific Signs of the Quran and Sunnah.

Sagan, Carl. (1983). *Cosmos*. Avenel, NJ: Wings Books, 5–7.

Wescoat, James L. (1995). 'From the Gardens of the Quran to the Gardens of Lahore', *Landscape Research*, 20: 19–29.

# 5

# Social Capital in Islam (*Arham*)

## Summary

This chapter addresses the third component of the sustainability model which is the social capital. The social order in Islam is intricately linked to human existence as it represents the arena where humans find the possibilities of self-realisation and growth. The Islamic social order can be viewed at three levels: the community (*ummah*), the family and the individual. In this chapter, a focus will be on the community since this domain captures the essence of collective action and choice. This valued-based community is called a 'median community' (*ummah wassat*) to be commissioned to provide the common ground and common word for all people.

The social capital (*arham*) encompasses the human and social dimension from an Islamic perspective. The social system, community social contract and social norms will be addressed as part of holistic Islamic worldview. Trust fund (*waqf*) will be presented as a case study to explain the social cohesion and societal responsibility.

## Objectives

1.  Introduce the meaning and value of social system and social capital in Islam.

2.  Explore the social theory in Islam as part of systems theory.

3.  Present a case study of trust fund (*Waqf*) as a model for social cohesion.

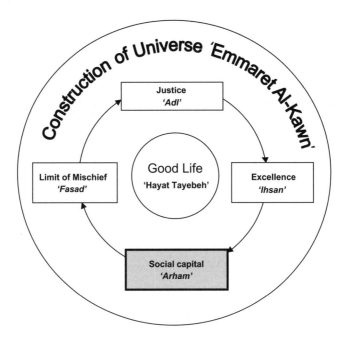

Figure 5.1     A model for sustainable development based on Islamic
               worldviews – Social capital (*Arham*)

## Background: Social Theory in Islam

In March 2011, I was on a mission to Senegal, Dakar in which I had the chance
to visit Goree Island which witnessed the slave trade for about 300 years during
the twelfth to fifteenth centuries between the triangle that connected Europe,
Africa and the United States. The vivid experience of human civilisation that
was driven by materialistic gain and exploitation of the humans in Africa left
me with many scars and compelled me to rethink the basic underpinning of the
capitalist thinking which is driven by growth, power and money.

On the same mission, I had the chance to visit a fishing village in Dakar where
about 13,000 local people live entirely on fishing with their own social housing
connected with about one-metre-wide alleys in a fascinating organic mosaic
that connects people and bricks. It was heartening to see a woman who just had
caught two big fish with a big smile on her face that she secured her family's
meal for the day. However, local people in this village were complaining that
huge international ships from all over the world come along the Atlantic Ocean
to fish in millions of tonnes and compete with the local people in their local
livelihood. There was no means for those people to enforce laws or prevent

these ships from taking away their daily food. These simple stories convey a message of the extent and level of equity and justice in a globalised world with free trade agreements.

These cases set the scene for this chapter in which I attempt to address the social theory in Islam. Ul Haq (1996) and Chapra (1970, 1992, 2008) documented the socio-economic paradigm in the Islamic worldview. This chapter is based on their work. I intend to frame the key ingredients of the social theory in Islam within a systems approach, since all Islamic sub-systems, including spiritual, cultural, economic, political, social and educational, are viewed as one continuum. I used the Arabic term *arham* which is the plural of womb since all humanity share the same origin. The following is a synthesis of the key components in the social theory in Islam

## UNITY OF NORMATIVE AND PRESCRIPTIVE

Islam takes a unique view of human's social existence since it views all humans are linked to the same origin, Adam and Eve, and hence we all have kinship and we are all from the same family tree regardless on colour, ethnicity or religion. It is a system that is all encompassing and all inclusive. It addresses the human's multidimensional needs and points to their satisfaction through the operation of the natural laws and society. It prescribes normative individual behaviour and gives ordinances, laws and principles for society, economy and politics. It outlines the foundations of a good society as manifested in the city of Medina when the Prophet Muhammad initiated the first model society. Besides, Islam points to the need of organised community and defines the 'cement and glue' for building community action, societal responsibility and local governance.

Moreover, Islamic worldview has a critical look and insights on the human history and the rise and fall of early civilisations. It urges to utilise and harness analytical and logical reasoning to explain the cause and effect of human activity on sustainability.

## UNITY OF INDIVIDUAL AND COLLECTIVE ACTION

The creation in the Islamic worldview was created for a purpose and hence humans are responsible and accountable. This was evident in Quran '*a human has not been created in vain*' (Quran, 23:115). Humans, as trustees and witnesses, are created for a mission that is to serve and be guided by the code and laws of God. On the individual level, it means that a human has to worship the one

God, behave in an ethical manner and realise his/her higher tendencies. On the collective level, his/her task is to establish an ethical social order to attain good life (*hayat tayebah*). Human's life is one unceasing moral struggle and challenge. It is this task that the Quran refers to as the trust (*amanah*), that is, the use of reason and intellect to ensure balance and order 'natural state' on earth.

The role of a human as a trustee can only be fulfilled when human's actions follow a true understanding of the Faith that are rooted in the oneness and transcendence of God (*tawhid*) and the conviction that all normative values and laws come from God. Human's success or failure in the eyes of God is dependent on his purposeful intent to add value to life and to do good. The Quran states:

> Indeed, We have conferred dignity (or honour) on the children of Adam, and borne them over land and sea, and provided them with sustenance out of the good things of life, and favoured them far above most of Our creation: (but) one Day We shall summon all human beings (and judge them) according to the conscious disposition which governed their deeds (in life). (17:70–1)

## UNITY OF SOCIAL ORDER AND HUMAN EXISTENCE

The social order in Islam is intricately linked to human existence as it represents the arena where he/she finds the possibilities of self-realisation, growth and service to God and humankind. As such, the social order in Islam has to be based on divine guidance, ordered and designed on Islamic permanent values and ethics. What the Quran wants to prevent is '*corruption on earth* (*fasad*)', that is, the state of general lawlessness in society-moral, political or social as outlined in a set of verses in Quran (Quran, 2:11, 27, 205; 7:56, 85; 8:64; 11:16; 12:73; 13:25; 16:88; 26:152; 28:77). This can happen when humans 'fall into decadent ways'. The Quran repeatedly points out the end of previous civilisations as lessons for humankind. The function of Prophets was to set models of ethical and social order that balances the human and spiritual needs. In sum, the key goal of the Quran is to establish social orders which are moral, just and egalitarian.

## Islamic Social Order

The Islamic social order can be viewed at three levels: the community (*Ummah*), the family and the individual. In this section, a focus will be on the community since this domain captures the essence of collective action and choice.

## COMMUNITY (*UMMAH*) OF GOOD ACTION AND REFLECTION

Islam considers the social order as natural and necessary because it is in this theatre that the human can realise his/her potential. The social order is where the value-based policies, decisions and choices are formed as inspired from Islamic values. The Quran states:

> *Those (are Muslims) who, when We give them power on earth, establish prayers (salah), pay charity (zakah), command good and prohibit evil. (22:40)*

In this context, prayers (*salah*) symbolise the overall normative and the philosophy of economic justice and support for the weak. The role of community (*ummah*) in commanding good and prohibiting evil highlights the collective intent for good work in all domains of life including social, political, economic and cultural. This also defines and prescribes the desired and normative function of the community as a collective force of good. The Muslim society is meant not only to comprise of individuals detached from societal concerns, rather the community to be described as the best community (*khair ummah*) is mandated to reform and transform the society to ensure social cohesion, security, welfare and prosperity.

Fulfilling this mission of doing good and forbidding evil implies that this community becomes the ideal and best community (*khair ummah*). The Quran points this out:

> *You are indeed the best community (ummah) that has ever been brought for (the good) of mankind: (because) you enjoin the doing of what is right and forbid the doing of what is wrong, and you believe in God. (3:110)*

This criteria for becoming the best community (*khair ummah*) was stated in a number of context in Quran (Quran, 2:177, 9:71, 22:41) to demonstrate that the task of the Muslim community is to establish an ethical social order on earth where human and social security are promoted and injustice is abolished. Besides, this valued-based community is being labelled in Quran as a 'median community' (*ummah wassat*) to be commissioned to seek and provide the common ground and common word for all people. Of vital significance, the characteristic of being (*ummah wassat*) convey a clear message of the Islamic community as a balanced, fair and far from extremism as the mathematical meaning of 'median' refer to in pure mathematics.

## A MEDIAN COMMUNITY (UMMAH WASSAT) AS A WITNESS

The mission and function of the 'median community' are clearly defined in Quran:

> *Thus We have appointed you as a median community (ummatan wasat an) that you may be witnesses to mankind and the Messenger be a witness over you.*
>
> *(Quran, 2:143, 22:78)*

It should be mentioned here that the term witness (*shahed*) also implies the meaning of a role model and an example. Hence, the Muslim community should be a model nation like the Prophet was an example model for Muslims. Historically, the role of Islam represented the intermediate/middle nation compared to previous religions and nations. In the twenty-first century, using the same analogy, there is a crucial role for the current Muslim communities in all parts of the globe in US, Europe, China, India, Brazil, Malaysia, Turkey, Iran, Indonesia, Australia, Philippines and Southeast Asia to be the median (*ummah wassat*) and the witness (*shahed*) so as to balance out extremes on the globe in all domains of life including spiritualism versus materialism; totalitarianism versus social anarchy; command economy versus market economy. In other words, the Quran assigns the Muslims the task of being the community of the golden mean so as to promote good and balance and to smooth out social, political, economic and religious extremes on earth.

## UMMAH AS A UNIVERSAL COMMUNITY OF SHARED DESTINY

*Ummah* is a unique Islamic concept which describes a community of faith and universal community of voluntary association or membership. In this association, a member's race, nationality and ethnicity are purely functional categories while faith is the organic bond. Thus, loyalty to the community overrides loyalties to one's family, kinship, race, nation and linguistic group. The Quran states:

> *O People! We have created (all of) you out of a male and female, and We have made you into different nations and tribes so that you might come to know one other; (otherwise) the noblest of you in the sight of God is the one most possessed of God consciousness (taqwa).*
>
> *(Quran, 49:13)*

This indicates that humanity as one large human family with no one possessing inherent superiority over another. It also implies that equality in human dignity is common to all. It is this equality which is the essence of all human rights and which is and confirmed by the Islamic worldview. The distinction between humans is based on their goodness, virtue and moral acts, that is, consciousness (*taqwa*).

These teachings were reflected in the Farewell Pilgrimage address of the Prophet Muhammad (pbuh) in which he stated that nobody has superiority over another except through piety and good action as the Prophet said: '*We are all children of Adam and Adam was of dust*'.

The oneness of the *Ummah* is declared to be moral and it is not to be limited by geographic, political, linguistic, ethnic, cultural or national considerations. This means that the Islamic view of the concept of *Ummah* is a transnational, trans-racial and a universal community of believers, joined together by Islamic belief, teachings and values. It also means that the *Ummah* whose membership is constituted by free will and conscious choice, should not allow discrimination based on race, colour, ethnicity, religion between its members. Simultaneously, the solidarity and concerns of each part of the *Ummah* should be reflected in the whole Ummah, that is, the suffering, adversity and hardship of its members should be of equal value and concern to the whole as well as the prosperity, resourcefulness and affluence of its members should benefit those less privileged.

Quran does not envision the Islamic *Ummah* to be one in religious identity alone but it envisions the *Ummah* to transcend to a functioning community of experts and professionals with a formal entity and identity. The ideal form of *Ummah* is one that is a corporate, organised and civic body that addresses the global commons of humanity including governance, poverty, climate change, education, health and energy. This community of practice (which I call *Ummah*) will be charged to identify and solve human sufferings worldwide.

## *UMMAH* AS AN INSTITUTION

The migration of the Prophet (pbuh) and the early Makkan Muslims to Madinah was motivated, among other factors, by the necessity of living a secure social and communal life. In Makkah, while the Muslims were able to practice the personal aspects of faith like worship they were not able to lead an organised collective life. Lack of power and authority and constant threats and persecution contributed to the vulnerability of the early Muslim community. However, since Islam was meant to serve and guide all aspects of human life, then a social and economic order was necessary. It is also instructive that the migration was followed by the instituting of the state of Brotherhood (*mu'akhat*) between the migrants from Mecca and the people in Madinah. Besides, the *Ummah* was formed as an institution as manifested in the establishment of the mosque, the school and the business marketplace in Madinah.

## Islamic Values and Ethics

The Islamic worldview provides a set of values, guidelines and principles on which the social order is to be based. The following is a brief description of these values.

### EQUALITY OF PEOPLE

Islam as a universal way of life asserts that people originate from one source; hence, they are inherently equal. This means that all people, regardless of religion, are equal in essential human rights. This also means that people should be treated equally under the law regardless of position, gender or status in society. This implies giving equal weight to the happiness or hardship of people as well as treating people equitably.

The principle of equality implies that non-Muslims living under Islamic rule have all the religious freedoms, economic rights and social privileges as Muslims have. Non-Muslim communities, therefore, can function as autonomous units with their own religious structure, laws and practices. The autonomous status was given by the Prophet Muhammad (pbuh) to the Jewish community when he established the constitution of the Islamic state of Medina. Similarly, he granted autonomy to the Christian community when they came under the domain of Islam. The principles of religious tolerance, justice and peaceful coexistence toward all members of the Islamic society were equally followed and applied by the successors of the Prophet. Hence, the Islamic social order accepts multiculturalism where now in the twenty-first century we see hesitation and resentment for the accepting Muslim communities in the West.

## MUTUAL COOPERATION FOR PRIVATE AND PUBLIC GOOD

Islam views the community (*ummah*) as a body of people mutually cooperating, helping and protecting each other in all aspects of life. This principle is embodied in various verses with the words 'commanding good, prohibiting evil, establishing prayers and paying *zakah*', in the directives to establish justice and equality, and in numerous verses relating to human transactions. The establishment and maintenance of the ethical social order itself is dependent upon societal cooperation and collective action. The Quran states:

> *The believers, men and women, are friends and protectors of one another; They all enjoin good and forbid evil, establish prayers, pay zakah, and obey God and His Messenger- these are the ones upon whom God is going to have His mercy. Verily, God is Almighty, Wise!*
> (Quran, 9:71)

The theme of mutual cooperation is the cornerstone in the ethical code in the Muslim community.

## SOCIAL COMMITMENT AND ACTION

Farook (2007) highlighted the notion of corporate social responsibility in Islamic financial institutions. Islam regards belief and action as inseparable since action is a reflection and an outcome of the belief. This is reflected even in the worship aspects of faith like prayers, fasting, paying *zakah* and performing the pilgrimage (*haj*). Moreover, whereas a small part of the rules and laws of Islam have to do with rituals, like worship, the larger part of the rules, laws and public policies deal with the social order and trade-offs .

Social responsibility is not confined to corporate sector but includes the individuals and policy makers. This implies that believers are to have corresponding evidence through both personal acts of worship and economic welfare to reflect social concern and responsibility. It is this social solidarity that helps ensure the sustainable development of the community. The Quran states:

> *Let there be of you a community (ummah) who call (people) to virtue, enjoin good and prohibit evil – these shall be the successful ones.*

> (Quran, 3:103)

The key message in this context is the necessity for having positive collective action for the preservation and welfare of society. Unless community members strive to address the moral, economic and socio-political issues and cooperate in society building activities, there will be chance for social development, good life and happiness. Asad (1980) points that the improvement is a nation's moral structure is bound, in the long run, to lead to greater material well-being and political power, however, moral decay results in social, economic and political decay. Hence, it is the duty of every thinking Muslim to subject his social environment to continuous criticism for the common good.

It should be borne in mind that in the Islamic terminology, oppression (*thulm*), evil and wrongdoing (*munkar*) and their opposites are justice (*adl*), right and good (*ma'ruf*) encompass all actions that relate to morality and good life. Therefore, the Muslim *Ummah* is responsible for what goes on in society and has to exert every effort to reform and resolve all socio-economic problems. The Quran affirms this point repeatedly when it refers to the histories of the past civilisations. The key lesson is that a civilisation is doomed to collapse if it abandons social justice and ecological sustainability principles, like the early Yemeni civilisation called Saba.

The social laws in Islam (*sunnat Allah*) have continuously operated in human history upon previous civilisations when they deviated from the guidance of God. Therefore, unless conscious, concerned and collective efforts are made to tackle problems of governance, poverty, pollution, waste, unemployment and climate change, the human civilisation is at risk.

## SOCIAL SOLIDARITY

The Quran views the Islamic social order to be based on unity of faith, oneness of purpose and social cohesiveness. It states: '*The believers are indeed brethren to one another*' (49:10). It is a religious and moral community (*ummah*) and a free association of individuals who come together for the purpose of actualising the whole realm of values of Islam.

Moreover, the Islamic social order is not limited to the Muslim community (*Ummah*). Other expert communities of practice (*Ummah*) in specialised domains of knowledge like scientific, legal and other professions can be part of construction of knowledge. Therefore, the social ethics of mutual cooperation, empathy, compassion, assistance, justice, mercy, virtue and good human relationships equally apply to relations between all members of a society being Muslims or non-Muslims.

The Islamic values respect and celebrate cultural diversity as documented by Al-Jayyousi (2001, 2009). This implies that there is a social contract that all members of a community have to adhere to that is based on justice, mercy and solidarity. This is guided by the instructions in Quran which calls for cooperation through virtue (*al-birr*) and justice (*al- qist*).

It is important to note the attitude and policy of the Prophet towards non-Muslims (who are called *people of covenant*). He upheld their rights, and declared:

> *Those who commit an act of aggression against a member of the non-Muslims, who usurp his rights, who make any demand upon him which is beyond his capacity to fulfil, or who forcibly obtain anything from him against his wishes, I will be his (that is, the oppressed's) advocate on the Day of Judgement.*

Prophet Muhammad (pbuh) further said: '*He who harms a non-Muslim harms me, and he who harms me, harms God.*' These and other statements of the prophet coupled with the above quoted verse from Quran clearly establish the state's duty to guarantee safety and security of the non-Muslim communities. This concern was reflected in the actions of the early caliphs, the teachings of the Muslim jurists (*fuqaha'*), as well as in the general policy of the Muslim community.

Given this perspective, the Islamic social order envisions a pluralistic society living harmoniously with each other, mutually cooperating on the basis of commonly perceived interests and working together to build and sustain an ethical society motivated to achieve the ideals of social solidarity, egalitarianism and social justice for all.

## ALTRUISM AND SELF-SACRIFICE

Altruism, the doctrine that the general welfare of society is the proper goal of an individual's actions, is one of the central social teachings or ethics of Islam. Islam does not assume humans to be totally selfless. On the contrary, it argues that humans be concerned for their personal welfare. It simultaneously suggests that this welfare is determined both by personal acts of worship as well as by acts of social welfare. The Quran views altruistic behaviour as a means for personal growth, as an instrument of promoting societal wealth and as a manifestation of the individual's God consciousness.

Therefore, altruism is a source of human happiness and success (*falah*) in the worldly life and success in the Hereafter (*akhera*). In economic terms, the Islamic concept of altruism is very much like a move toward optimality which means that it makes at least someone better off without making anyone worse off. Hence, the Quran continuously appeals to a human's heart and mind to urge everyone to engage in the promotion of public welfare. The highest form of altruism and self-sacrifice is self-exertion for God's social causes and for the establishment and maintenance of an ethical social order. The prophet described human's struggle for self-mastery against his own desires, passions and weaknesses as the greatest struggle (*jihad*). He also strongly emphasised the need for a Muslim to reform and to raise once voice against wrongdoing, particularly when the wrongdoer is the established authority: '*The highest kind of jihad is to speak the truth in the face of the authority (sultan) that deviates from the right path.*' The youth voices in many countries in the Middle East including Tunisia and Egypt in early 2011 were a vivid form of *jihad* that transformed the political landscape in many counties in Middle East and North Africa.

## Family System in Islam

I recall one of the German water experts in a meeting in Cairo in 2006 in a discussion near Tahrir Square saying that when she visited the Ummayed mosque in Damascus, Syria and she wore the Islamic costume (*abaya*) that covers all body to enter the mosque she commented: 'Wearing the "*abaya*" was a liberating experience.' My response to her was that before Islam, women used to dress semi-naked; Islam came with the civilising power and made social codes that have modest dress for women so as to value mind, human dignity and inner values of the human. We are challenged by the global media which makes the 'unknown familiar and the familiar (natural state or *fitra*) unknown'.

The economic order is part of the larger moral-social order to ensure the creation of conditions whereby the possibilities of prosperity, happiness and well-being for the community. All facets of the Islamic systems are meant to provide an opportunity for people to evolve new consciousness so as to do good and hence to actualise the divine will. It is within this perspective that the concepts of *jihad* and *ijtihad*, as forms of collective social struggle, should be understood.

One of the basic needs of a human is the sense of belonging which is realised at the family and the community at large (*ummah*) at national, regional and universal arenas. Family is the core unit in the social system in Islam, hence, it becomes the anchoring point whose strength becomes the strength of society. In short, family is a positive permanent value of Islam as well as a necessary institution of its social order. Islam views men and women as equal but with some role differentiation. In general, it views them as partners complimenting each other and helping each other in family responsibilities. The Quran states:

> *The believers, men and women, are protectors of one another: They enjoin what is just and forbid what is evil, and establish prayer and pay zakah and obey God and His apostle. On them will God bestow his grace.*
>
> (Quran, 9:71)

The Quran assigns men and women equal status in terms of religious and ethical rights, duties and responsibilities. It clearly recognises the women's rights to participate in public affairs as well as her role in social defence. Also, it needs to be pointed out that there is nothing in the Quran against women earning or being economically self-sufficient. Islam only exempts women from the responsibility of supporting a family. It recognises the full economic personality of a woman; it envisions her as owning a property and lays on her the duty to pay *zakah*. Moreover, Islam does not place limits on the activities of Muslim men and women can do except for the few prohibited categories.

A serious appraisal of the doctrines of Islam suggests that they provide an appropriate moral ethical framework for all members of society to participate in collective life and to be productive in a variety of ways. Islam attaches equal value to efforts of men and women, regardless of the field of activity. It adopts a median way, a balanced approach, to the division of labour. Men carry the larger responsibilities of family and consequently of society. Women, on the other hand, have the basic freedom to work and earn without the livelihood earning responsibility. Similarly, they have the freedom to participate in public life, yet no more is demanded of them in the social sphere than what they may be able to bear. In sum, using the metaphor from ecology, while we witness the role of women in the west as displayed in the media, music, fashion industry and Hollywood film industry of being about 'exploitation', the Islamic worldview sees her role in the domain of 'cultivation' by focusing on her role in the family, education and all the productive and ethical sectors.

## Islamic Social Spending

I recall one of the American professors at the University of Illinois in Chicago who teaches a graduate course in public policy analysis commenting that the Quran is the best reference in public policy. This can be evident when we examine the following policy issues.

In the Islamic worldview and values if one wants his money to multiply and be blessed then one has to give charity (*zakah*). The literary meaning of the action of *zakah* is to purify. While the Western terminology of tax refers to a financial burden on the individual, the Islamic term *zakah* has a spiritual meaning of purification, value creation and self-mastery. In essence, the value of an individual is measured by the value added to the community and life (*emart al kawn*).

In terms of setting criteria for equity, justice and trade-offs, The Quran defines one of the goals of the state to be distributive justice. The general principle is that '*No person shall be burdened beyond his capacity*' (Quran, 2:233) and '*Allah does not burden any person with more than he is well able to bare*' (Quran, 2:286). Although the first verse is specifically in the context of economic burden or expenditure while the second is more in the spiritual context, the essence is the same: that God desires no one to be taxed beyond what is reasonable and bearable.

The implications for fiscal policy in *zakah* system are summarised below:

1.  Given that a certain minimum level of income is required for living expenses or meeting basic needs, that level of income should be exempt from taxation.

2.  Taxation on the total income should begin after the income reaches the minimum basic need level.

3.  Taxes should be proportional or progressive, but not regressive.

The following are a set of principles for a taxation structure and social spending in Islam to ensure balanced and human-centred development.

## AVOIDANCE OF THE CONCENTRATION OF WEALTH

The Quran lays down the principle that '*wealth should not circulate only among the rich*' (Quran, 59:7). This verse, revealed in the context of the utilisation of state income asserts that such income, besides being meant for avoiding unnecessary state expenditures, is also meant to uplift the weaker section of society. Hence, money should not become a benefit for those who already are well off. In other words, state expenditure policy should be designed to avoid the concentration of wealth, among the well-to-do section of society, while ensuring the dispersion among the less well-to-do. This principle is consistent with other measures of Islam like the law of inheritance and the rules of *zakah* which help ensure a wide dispersion of wealth and welfare expenditures respectively.

## THE UNDERPRIVILEGED AS BENEFICIARIES OF GOVERNMENT EXPENDITURES

While specifying the use of *zakah* funds for numerous needy categories of people and general welfare purposes, Islamic law emphasises that government resources and its income should also target the weaker sections of society. In other words, the Quran seems to be saying that government expenditures should be largely meant to satisfy the basic necessary needs and/or targeted toward raising living standards and income potentials of the underprivileged members of society. This principle, therefore, constitutes an important element in the fiscal priorities in Islam. This social spending can be done privately as philanthropy and/or through public institutions and the government. In a sense, the Quran is encouraging the people to contribute generously for social development and helping the needy in society.

## SOCIAL RESPONSIBILITIES TO BE SHARED BY EVERYONE ACCORDING TO ABILITY

The Quran clearly establishes the principle of sharing of the collective burden by everyone. However, it also takes into account people's abilities to do so. It points out that everyone may not have the financial means to share the burden. In such cases, the contribution of labour and intellect suffices and is considered valuable and worthy. The Quran, in other words, seems to argue that every person has the potential to return to society at least some portion of what society gives him. This he/she can do either in the form of taxes and voluntary contributions and/or in the form of social service. That is why in the eyes of God, a Muslim who strives and exerts himself through his wealth and his capabilities to satisfy public wants is higher in rank than someone who makes no effort.

## COLLECTIVE RESPONSIBILITY

The principle of collective responsibility implies the essence of the principle of compensation which forms part of the basis of the Islamic legal system. The implications of the principle of collective responsibility are firstly that financial burdens should be spread and shared widely and equitably, and secondly that those who are incapable of paying taxes should be given opportunities to be socially productive as well as helped to become economically productive and, therefore, taxpaying members of society. In other words, the state should not be looked upon as a source of charity, but rather the recipient of public support both obligatory and voluntary, financially and with in-kind support.

The following section will outline the types of social spending both voluntary (*sadaqat*) and compulsory (*zakat*).

## Types of Social Spending

The following are brief descriptions of the social charity in Islam, namely charity (*sadaqat*) taxes (*zakat*) and trust funds (*waqf*).

### AL-SADAQAT

The term used by the Quran to denote all social expenditure or spending is *sadaqat*. It comes from the root *sadaqa* which means to speak the truth and to be sincere. *Sadaqat*, therefore, are the free-will offerings given for the sake of God by a Muslim out of love, compassion and concern for others, as well as what he/she is morally or legally obliged to give without expecting any worldly return. In other words, *sadaqat (plural of sadaqa)* are charitable deeds and also the obligatory tax of *zakah*, which literally means 'the purifying dues'. Hence, while *zakah* is a form of *sadaqa)*, the latter also includes *non-zakah* voluntary, charitable and social spending (*infaq*). *Sadaqah*, therefore, implies self-purification from a false sense of security, and from greed and vanity.

*Sadaqah* is an act of sharing one's resources with relatives or next of kin, as well as other members of the human community, including those of other faiths. It is important, however, that this be done without asking or expecting and return whatsoever. Then only does such sharing become a *sadaqa*. Islam is encouraging the Muslims to invest in society by taking care of and satisfying social needs, and is placing such acts with the greatest value in the hierarchy of values of Islam. This is the Islamic methodology of emphasising altruism which, if practised, can place substantial resources in the local community or government for promoting sustainable development programmes.

The role of *sadaqat* or social and charitable expenditures in general, should not be viewed as legitimising the existence of poor and needy people in society. On the contrary, Islam views the presence of poverty as the greatest social and economic problem and is equivalent to disbelief (*kufr*). *Sadaqat* play a critical role in Islamic society in promoting social safety nets and social cohesion. Even where basic needs may have been met and poverty removed, they continue to play an important role in sustainable development through providing funds for charitable endowments, trusts and foundations for educational and general welfare purposes.

In this sense, the Quran, through *sadaqat*, has provided perpetual private resources for meeting public wants and promoting sustainable development and prosperity. On the other hand, it has provided the members of a society a means for self-development through altruism, as well as a mechanism to participate and contribute toward the quality education, innovation, health, peace and prosperity of society.

## ZAKAH

*Zakah* is the compulsory levy on the income and wealth of Muslims. It literally means 'to clean' and 'to purify' and it signifies integrity and compassion for the community. It is a tax which is meant to purify the property of a person from selfishness and make it permissible (*halal*) for one's personal use and benefit. According to the rules delineated by Islamic law, *zakah* is levied at 2½ per cent of total net worth after the worth reaches a minimum level (*nisab*) on most physical and financial assets.

Similarly, *zakah* is levied at 5 per cent for agriculture produce from artificially irrigated land and at 10 per cent for naturally irrigated land after the produce reaches a minimum level (*nisab*). The proceeds of the *zakah* tax are to be spent for social welfare purposes in a broad sense, as specified by the Quran:

> The zakah is (meant) only for the poor and the needy, those who collect the tax, those whose hearts are to be won over, for the freeing of human beings from bondage, for the relief of those overwhelmed by debts, for the cause of God (all priority social needs), and for the wayfarer an ordinance from God-and God is All-Knowing, Wis.'
>
> (Quran, 9:60)

What is most significant and critical about *zakah* is its association with prayers (*salat*). They have been mentioned together in 25 out of 29 Quranic verses. This is to illustrate the significance and linkage of both pillars of Islam. In fact, the Quran points out that the prayers (*salat*) of a Muslim is meaningless if it does not help motivate him to satisfy the wants of the poor and needy (Quran, 107:1–7). *Zakah* is not only a moral obligation toward God and society, a basic element of worship and faith, it is also a legal right of society. In this sense, *zakah* is not strictly a tax, as this word is commonly understood (that is, something given in exchange for certain services received), but rather an obligatory contribution for socio-economic and human development.

Since *zakah* is levied on the wealth of all members of society except the poor, the tax base is fairly wide, giving the entire population the sense of participation in social uplifting. Realising that *zakah* is largely collected and spent at the local level implies the value of the concept of people-centred development where local resources benefit local people. Hence, the Islamic development model is pro decentralized and small-scale local development. *Zakah* is an important public policy domain that should be formalised and enforced to provide security for all. The Quran views *zakah* as the opposite of usury (*riba*). While *riba* was meant to bring the capital lender a multifold increase through an exploitive practice, *zakah* brings the investor a several fold increase in a beneficial way. The two are opposites also in terms of distributive effects; whereas *riba* transfers wealth away from society to the rich, *zakah* redistributes wealth from the have-groups to the have-not groups.

In sum, the *zakah* levy embodies several implications for the economy. Firstly, it encourages and stimulates investment and it discourages hoarding of capital. Secondly, the exclusion of the means of production from *zakah* taxation provides an incentive for investment in plant and equipment. Likewise, exemption of housing from *zakah* taxation encourages home ownership and in investment in construction. All these lead to a high level of capital utilisation, which in turn, promote employment, output and income in the economy. By taxing money savings, *zakah* motivates the channelling of funds to investment and this contributes to sustainable development and prosperity without pursuing growth for the sake of growth.

Thirdly, *zakah* finances consumption expenditures of the poorest groups in society. In this way it directly contributes to increased consumption expenditures and hence effective aggregate demand goes up significantly. This leads to increased employment, output, income and consequently economic growth. If the supply of basic goods is managed effectively, then the economy moves toward higher output levels without inflation. The market size also increases as well as the absorption capacity of the economy for goods and services.

Fourthly, *zakah* expenditures for public goods and services increase beneficiaries' overall health, education and productivity levels. While this raises the income levels of the target beneficiaries, it also increases the growth potential of the economy. Finally, *zakah* is an economic stabilising influence. This means that when the economy is operating much below its full-employment potential, *zakah* expenditures increase aggregate demand, thereby reducing the output gap. Also, when the economy approaches or reaches full employment, *zakah* expenditures are reduced in proportion. Besides, *zakah* surpluses, when they occur, can be saved for harder times, used for infrastructural, ecosystem restoration, education, R&D and sustainable development.

Finally, *zakah* is multi-dimensional in content. It is both a value as well as an institution and beneficial for the giver as well as the recipient. It has a moral and socio-economic dimension. Therefore, *zakah* is very representative of Islam's socio-moral teachings, and that is probably why the Quran urges its establishment as a human and global institution. If we imagine the proposal of having a global *Zakah* Fund from the 1.4 billion Muslims, this global fund will resolve the wealth and power asymmetry between the North and the South. Therefore, the larger institutional reform at the social political and economic levels ('doing what is right') is a necessary condition for the institution of *zakah*. However, *zakah* has not played a significant role in the collective life of the *Ummah* in recent centuries due to the lack of the needed social innovation (*ijtihad*) and lack of framing an Islamic Dream for reform, renewal and enlightenment. However, since early 2011, we have been witnessing a wave of youth activism asking for good governance, democracy and reform and in the Middle East and

North Africa. Seeking inspiration from local knowledge and culture is crucial to blend it with the Western techniques.

## Trust fund (*Waqf*) for sustainable development

One of the institutions that are mentioned in the Islamic culture is endowments (*awqaf*). This term is used both in the sense of a public benefit or income producing institution, as in the case of the lands of *Khalibar* whose income was equality distributed among members of the community in Madina. Such an institution was established at the behest of the Prophet Muhammad (pbuh) when he said to Umar: '*Give those trees as a whole in waqf so that those might not be sold but their fruits can be spent and given in charity*.' Consequently, 'Umar gave those trees in charity (or established the charitable endowment).' Other instances of the founding of public *waqf* through private support are also reported from the Prophet's period, especially for satisfying basic needs like drinking water and food security. Hence, public welfare endowments can be a useful and beneficial instrument in satisfying different societal needs in the twenty-first century.

Al-Jayyousi (2007) argued that given the level of human dependence on ecosystem functions and services, environmental degradation has enormous socio-economic consequences for human livelihood and well-being. Land degradation and desertification continue to be the most significant environmental issues in the Middle East and North Africa. Well within a human lifetime, landscapes that have thrived for thousands of years are changing as the environment deteriorates. The region depends on groundwater and desalination plants to meet its water requirements. Today, five of the seven countries of the Arabian Peninsula have already exhausted their renewable water resources and are now exploiting non-renewable resources. The use of desalinisation plants has improved access to clean drinking water, but has created other environmental problems, such as disposal of brine, that threaten marine ecosystems and could seriously damage the region's fisheries.

A deficit in food production is growing and is aggravated by the scarcity of both land and water resources that are already over-exploited. Water security will become one of the major constraints to further development and will thus have major socio-economic impacts in the region over the next 30 years. Thus, balancing ecological and human needs must be seen as a priority. Much of the developing world has been used for many hundreds of years for livestock grazing, but it is only in recent years with the improvements in veterinary services and the introduction of subsidies that livestock numbers have increased beyond the carrying capacity of the land, as the more sustainable lifestyles have given way to the wealthier and more consumptive practices of today. Habitat destruction, hunting, deforestation and urban expansion have contributed to the extinction or near extinction of native species of the region. Threats to species are exacerbated by the harsh and unpredictable conditions in arid and semi-arid lands which are predominant ecological features of the region.

Funds available for addressing environmental and conservation issues in the region are not growing in proportion to the growth in the scale and importance of the issues and major increases in investment are crucial. Long-term and stable sources of financing must be applied to address these challenges. There are a number of organisations and development funds in the region including the Arab Fund for Economic and Social Development, the Abu Dhabi Fund for Development, the Islamic Development Bank, the Kuwait Fund for Arab Economic Development, the OPEC Fund for International Development, the Saudi Fund for Development and the Cooperation Council for the Arab States of the Gulf. However, the primary focus of these funds is the financing of economic and social infrastructure, both physical and institutional such as roads, dams, power grids, airports, hospitals and schools. Investments in sustainability and environmental actions are rare. The following is a proposal to initiate a *waqf* for sustainable development.

There is a growing need for not-for-profit fund specialising in conservation and environment. The new *waqf* fund would both complement existing conventional development funds of the region and provide a more flexible and innovative financing mechanisms. The purpose of the Waqf Fund is to ensure an appropriate level of sustainable financing for environmental conservation activities in the developing world. Thus, the Fund will have the following two broad goals:

- To mobilise significant funds for environmental aspects of sustainable development in the developing world from the public and private sectors, foundations and committed individuals.

- To apply those funds to a carefully developed and selected array of human-centred development projects and programmes to be implemented through relevant partner organisations in the world.

The Waqf Fund can promote partnerships among all relevant players (government, banking sector, donors, civil society and the private sector) within and between countries of the world. The Waqf Fund can support activities that address environmental and conservation issues that are considered to be priorities by the specialised experts and institutions. Determining these priorities will require a strategic analysis and planning exercise that engages institutions in all the key sectors in the needy countries of the world.

## CULTURE AND SUSTAINABLE DEVELOPMENT: VALUE CREATION

*Waqf*, in Arabic language, means hold, confinement or prohibition. The word *waqf* is used in Islam in the meaning of holding certain property and preserving it for the confined benefit of certain philanthropy and prohibiting any use or disposition of it outside that specific objective. This definition accords perpetuity to *waqf*, that is, it applies to non-perishable property whose benefit can be extracted without consuming the property itself. *Waqf* can be related to land, buildings, water, species, agriculture, plants and cash.

In the history of Islam, the first religious *waqf* is the mosque of Quba' in Madina, a city 400 kilometres north of Makkah, which was built upon the arrival of the Prophet Mohammad in 622. It stands now on the same lot with a new and enlarged structure. Six months later, Quba' was followed by the mosque of the Prophet in the centre of Madinah. Mosques and real estate confined for providing revenues to spend on mosques' maintenance and running expenses are in the category of religious *waqf*.

Philanthropic *waqf* is the second kind of *waqf*. It aims at supporting the poor segment of the society and all activities which are of interest to people at large such as libraries, scientific research, education, health services, care of animals and environment, lending to small businessmen, parks, roads, bridges, dams and so on. Philanthropic *waqf* began by the Prophet Muhammad (pbuh). A man called Mukhairiq made his will that his seven orchards in Madinah be given after his death to Muhammad. In year four of the migration from Mecca to Madina (*hijrah*) calendar, the man died and the Prophet took hold of the orchards and made them a charitable *waqf* for the benefit of the poor and needy. This practice was followed by the companion of the prophet and his second successor Umar, who asked the prophet what to do with a palm orchard he got in the northern Arabian peninsula city of Khaibar and the Prophet (pbuh) said *'If you like, you may hold the property as waqf and give its fruits as charity.'*

A third kind of *waqf* started shortly after the death of the prophet during the reign of Umar (635–45), the second successor. When Umar decided to document in writing his *waqf* in Khaibar, he invited some of the companions of the prophet to attest this document. Jaber, another companion, says that when the news broke out every real estate owner made a certain *waqf*. Some of those put a condition that the fruits and revenues of their *waqf* to be first given to their own children and descendants and only the surplus, if any, should be given to the poor. This kind of is called family *waqf*.

## LEGAL CONDITIONS OF *WAQF*

*Waqf* creation requires certain conditions, the most important among them including:

1.    The property must be a real estate or a thing which has some meaning of perpetuity. Muslim societies has *waqf* land, buildings, camels, cows, sheep, books, jewellery, swords and other weapons, agricultural tools, and so on.

2.    The property should be given on a permanent basis. Some jurists approve temporary *waqf* only in the case of family *waqf*.

3.    The *waqf* founder should be legally fit and apt to take such an action, that is, a child, an insane or a person who does not own the property cannot make *waqf*.

4.    The purpose of the *waqf* must, in the ultimate analysis, be an act of charity from both points of view of Shari'ah and of the founder.

5.    Beneficiaries, person(s) or purpose(s), must be alive and legitimate.

## MANAGEMENT OF *WAQF*

In principle, the *waqf* founder determines the type of management of his\her *waqf*. The *waqf* manager is usually called *mutawalli* and his/her responsibility is to administer the *waqf* property to the best interest of the beneficiaries. The first duty of *mutawalli* is to preserve the property and to maximise the revenues of the beneficiaries. The *waqf* document usually mentions how the *mutawalli* is compensated. The judicial system, that is, courts, is the authority of reference with regard to all matters and disputes related to waqf. In the early part of the eighth century, a judge in Egypt established a special register and office to record and supervise *awqaf (plural of waqf)* in his area. This culminated in the establishment of a *waqf* office for registration and control which was linked to the supreme judge who used to be called the 'judge of judges'. In the twenty-first century, the corporate sector had developed codes for audit, good governance and transparency measures that should be all used to activate and govern the *waqf* for sustainable development.

## SOCIO-POLITICAL ROLE OF *WAQF*

The permanent nature of *waqf* resulted in the accumulation of *waqf* properties all over the Muslim lands and the variety of its objectives provides support for widespread religious and philanthropic activities. The size of *waqf* and its objectives play important role in the socio-political life of societies and communities. Information extracted from the registers of *awqaf* (plural of waqf) in Istanbul, Jerusalem, Cairo and other cities indicates that lands of *awqaf* cover considerable proportion of total cultivated area. For instance, in the years 1812 and 1813 a survey of land in Egypt showed that *waqf* represents 600,000 feddan (=0.95 acre) out of a total of 2.5 million feddan (Ramadan, p. 128); in Algeria the number of deeds of *awqaf* of the grand mosque in the capital Algiers was 543 in the year 1841 (Ajfan, p. 326); in Turkey about one third of land was *awqaf* (Armagan, p. 339); and finally in Palestine the number of *waqf* deeds recorded up to middle of the sixteenth century is 233 containing 890 properties in comparison with 92 deeds of private ownership containing 108 properties.

*Waqf* financing of education usually covers libraries, books, salaries of teachers and stipends to students. Financing was not restricted to religious studies especially at the stage of the rise of Islam. In addition to freedom of education this approach of financing helped creating a learned class not derived from the rich and ruling classes. There is also *waqf* on animals whose example is the *waqf* on cats and the *waqf* on unwanted riding animals both in Damascus. There are *awqaf* for helping people go to Mecca for pilgrimage and for helping girls getting married, and for many other philanthropic purposes.

## Conclusion

Islam views human as having a purposive existence which is to create an ethical social order on earth that is just and humanitarian. Islam's social philosophy is a based on the perspective of human intent, the satisfaction of needs and wants and the enjoyment of things, as well as on the primacy of individual and collective responsibility, all within the guidelines given by Islamic values. Islam argues that all people are part of one large human family hence they are equal and should be treated as such. The diversity of mankind is itself a divinely created phenomenon for the purposes of identification and social learning.

Islam constitutes the principle of a median community (*ummah wassat*) as a platform of commonality based on faith, values and ethics. It envisions the social order embodying several *ummahs* living in peace and harmony. It suggests mutual cooperation for private and public good through social commitment, social solidarity and altruism. It diffuses collective responsibilities among all citizens. Therefore, it becomes the task of all members of society to contribute toward the establishment and maintenance of the ethical social order and trust funds (*waqf*) so as to maximise socio-economic welfare as well as the opportunities for self-development and personal growth for the largest possible number of people.

## References

Al-Jayyousi, Odeh (2001). Islamic Water Management and Dublin Statement, in Faruqui N., Biswas and Bino, M, (ed.), *Water Management in Islam*, Tokyo: UNU Press, pp. 33-8.

Al-Jayyousi, Odeh (2008). The State of Ecosystem and Progress of Societies. Proceeding of the International Conference on Statistics, Knowledge, and Policy: Measuring and Fostering Progress of Societies, Istanbul, Turkey.

Al-Jayyousi, Odeh (2009). 'Islamic Values and Rural Sustainable Development', *Rural 21 Journal*, Vol. 41, Issue 3.

Armagan, Servet (1989). A Glance at the State of Awqaf in Turkey, Islamic Research and Training Institute of the Islamic Development Bank, Jeddah, pp. 335-344.

Asad, Muhammad. (1980). *State and Government in Islam*. Gibraltar: Dar al-Andalus.

Capra, F. (1997). *The Web of Life: A Scientific Understanding of Living Systems*. Port Moody: Anchor.

Capra, F. (2002). *The Hidden Connection: A Science for Sustainable Living*. NY: Doubleday.

Chapra, M. Umar. (1970). 'The Economic System of Islam: A Discussion of its Goals and Nature', *Islamic Quarterly*, 14: 3–23.

Chapra, M. Umar. (1992). *Islam and the Economic Challenge*. Jordan: The Islamic Foundation and the International Institute of Islamic Thought, International Islamic Publishing House.

Chapra, U. (2008). *Islam and Economic Development*. New Delhi: Adam.

Farook, Sayd. (2007). 'Corporate Social Responsibility of Islamic Financial Institutions', *Islamic Economic Studies*, 15, no. 1.

Korten, D. (2009). *Agenda for New Economy*. San Francisco: Berrett- Koehler.

Ramadan, M. (19830. The Role of Awqaf in Al-Azahar. Proceeding of the Symposium of Awqaf Institution in the Arab and Islamic World. Institute of the Arab Research and Studies, Baghdad, pp. 93-112.

Sen, A. (1999). *Development as Freedom*. NY: Anchor.

Soros, G. (1999). *The Crisis of Global Financial Capitalism*. NY: Little, Brown.

Soros, G. (2000). *Open Society*. NY: Little, Brown.

Ul Haq, Irfan. (1996). 'Economic Doctrines of Islam. The International Institute of Islamic Thought'. Academic Dissertation No. 3., Washington, DC.

Yunus, M. (2008). *Creating a World Without Poverty*. NY: Public Affairs.

# 6

# Pollution, Corruption (*Fasad*) and Climate Change: Islamic Perspectives

## Summary

This chapter intends to discuss the concept of pollution and corruption (*fasad*) from an Islamic perspective. The unity of universe, humanity and destiny dictates the need of a transformational global leadership to address the potential threats of climate change. The global debate on climate change needs to be informed by Islamic discourse of trusteeship (*amanah*). Islamic worldviews on economic development and finance can be of value to inform current global debate with respect to key policy issues like finance, equity and global governance. Besides, a Green *Jihad-Ijtihad-Zuhd* (*JIZ*) model will be presented as an Islamic perspective on climate change.

## Objectives

1.  Introduce the Islamic views with respect to climate change as a global threat.

2.  Highlight the role of transformational leadership to address the climate change debate.

3.  Develop a holistic approach (Green JIZ model) for dealing with climate change and the need for a transition to a low carbon economy.

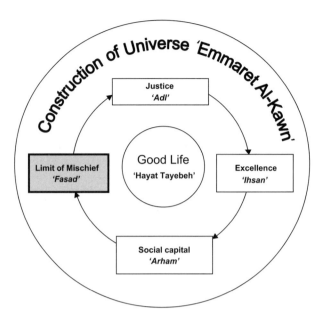

**Figure 6.1     A model for sustainable development based on Islamic worldviews – Limit of mischief (*Fasad*)**

## Introduction

The Islamic mind can be characterised by three types when confronted with the climate change issue. These types include the fatalistic mind (*qadari*) that believes humans are doomed and have no choice, the suspicious mind who believes in conspiracy theory, and the rational and pragmatic mind. I argue that the first two types or forms of thinking are risky for humanity and will get us nowhere. I believe that through science and reason humans can be responsive and can play a responsible role in the global debate and action on climate change. Any society which does not base its policies on rigorous science will not be able to recognise, comprehend and respond to future risks and will be doomed to collapse.

There is scientific evidence that climatic changes have been occurring since the existence of humans on this planet. Also, there is evidence that climate change has reached a point of irreversible system disruption. It was argued by Houghton (2004) that planetary factors have a significant influence over the earth's temperature due to gradual shifts in the earth's relationship with the sun. Besides, volcanic activity and solar radiation influenced global climate. However, human activity, industrialisation, urbanisation and deforestation had contributed to rising concentration of greenhouse gases in the earth's atmosphere. It was estimated that about 70 per cent of anthropogenic $CO_2$ comes from the use of fossil fuels like oil, coal and gas. Historically, according to Met Office (2005) the pre-industrial carbon dioxide concentration was 280 ppm (parts per million) and has increased by about 35 per cent to reach about 380 ppm. This in turn is likely to cause a tipping point as earth temperature will approach 2 degrees C above pre-industrial levels.

IPCC (2007) projections to the end of the century under a high emissions scenario predict a 0.9 m rise in mean sea level, which is likely to displace 15 million in Bangladesh. The debate on climate change is linked to concept of environmental justice and spillover effects where states that have limited role in pollution may suffer larger consequences of climate change risks in terms of crop yields and rainfall fluctuations. North–South variations in food distribution are likely to cause risks to at least 60 million more people in Africa. Moreover, more extreme rainfall and flooding would be increasingly common. There is a cost for inaction and there is a need for urgent action to mitigate and limit the adverse effects of climate change.

In the next 30 years, biodiversity declines are likely to accelerate and ecosystems will be increasingly less able to provide the services people need in terms of air, water, food, medicine and energy. Global economic and ecological systems will be more vulnerable and hence climatic disruptions are likely to occur. To minimise potential risks and threats, we need a global immune system to build resilience and we need a much enhanced capacity to deal with risks, uncertainty and indeterminacy. We know problems such as climate change exist, but they are complex, and the interactions of future environmental changes are unpredictable. The global environmental governance systems are sub-optimal at dealing with uncertainty and indeterminacy. The IPCC, through its attempts to identify areas of consensus, failed to consider the North–South perceptions and policy options, development paradigms and energy options. This chapter will attempt to develop a framework or a model to address the climate change issue from an Islamic perspective.

## Climate Change: Islamic Perspectives

In 1987, the United Nation Commissions of Environment and Development concluded that, unless sustainable development becomes a global initiative, human civilisation and survival could be jeopardised in the future. In the twenty-first century, it will be insightful to re-examine the role of sustainable development in developing human civilisation. The gradual introduction of measures to promote sustainable development strongly reinforces the quest of sustainable society and the development of human civilisation. Hence, it will be crucial to reflect and learn why civilisations rise and fall based on cultural views, like Islam, so as to have the civic intelligence and the collective memory to avoid collapse. The following is a description of how Islam views the climate change issue.

Islamic texts view humans as unique in creation. All of creation is considered to be in submission to God's will, whereas human beings have the unique attribute of being able to stand aside and choose to deviate away from what God is said to have prescribed for them. This power to disobey, coupled with the fact that humans exist within the rest of creation, means that human beings are being trusted to behave responsibly. This responsibility is one that is regarded as being so overwhelming and the Human took this trusteeship (*amanah*).

In the Quran this concept of trusteeship or guardianship is called *khalifah* (*trustee*). Llewellyn (2003) is of the opinion that considers *khilafah* (*trusteeship*) to be not a privilege, but a trust and responsibility. Khalid (2002) and Chishti (2003) assert that the environment crisis is a failure of the trusteeship, viewing the natural world as a barometer whose reading indicates how well a society has fulfilled its responsibility given to it by *Allah*. A change in worldviews, mindset, life styles and development models are necessary if humans are to meet their test of guardianship.

The notion of oneness of God (*tawhid*) is fundamental to Islam. The centrality of it to the faith is evident simply by the fact that the first part of the very first pillar of Islam makes the statement that 'there is no God, but God'. These two themes, one God and the reference to nature as 'signs' or *ayat*, are perhaps more directly related than may first appear. The concept of one God, or *tawhid* in Arabic, is also symbolic of the unity of creation, in Islam, is said to originate from one source, and that source is God (Khalid, 2002).

Ultimately the path to God-consciousness is thus a path along which one lives one's life in a state of increasing awareness of this oneness, understanding better ones place in the wider creation and fulfilling ones role as *khalifa* or guardian of the earth, with greater ease. Islam as a worldview contributes to new discourse in explaining the root causes and possible remedies of climate change. There is a need for a macro-shift in harnessing local knowledge, innovation, ethics and new development models to address both poverty and conservation. The following is an outline of key Islamic notions on climate change. The Islamic views on climate change cover three domains which include: Green activism (*jihad*), Green innovation (*ijtihad*) and Green life style (*zuhd*). I will refer to this as a *Green JIZ* model which represents an Islamic response to climate change as depicted in Figure 6.2 below.

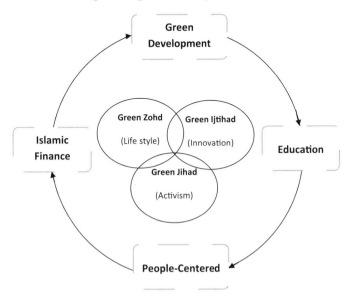

**Figure 6.2**    **A model for addressing the climate challenge from an Islamic perspective**

## GREEN JIHAD

The basic meaning of Jihad is a struggle against imbalances, injustice or mischiefs that disturb the 'natural state' (*fitra*). Muslim community should manifest the optimal and balanced way of life as a median community (*ummah wasat*). The key role of *ummah* is to ensure justice, beauty and balance in universe through exercising stewardship and being a *khalifah* (trustee). Civil society activism in the Muslim world should support and nurture a green way of life is in line with Islamic worldview. This activism is one form of *jihad* to ensure balance and harmony between humans and nature. Transforming the positive energy of youth in the Muslim world towards a *Green Jihad* which supports all principles of equity (*adl*), beauty (*ihasn*), saving our social and human capital (*arham*) and saving our natural capital to support progress and prosperity (*emartu al ard*). Llewellyn (2003) comments on the Quranic view that each species is a community (*ummah*) and it is part of the community of life (*ummam*) and each life-form warrants special respect. He adds that each creature glorifies its Creator, even if we do not understand its glorification or the symphony of life. The Quran says: '*There is not a thing but celebrates His praise, but you understand not how they declare His glory'* (Quran, 17:44)'.

Green *Jihad* is about appreciating and preserving the balance and beauty in the universe. As outlined in the framework of sustainability, *ihsan* means beauty and excellence. Besides, *ihsan* refers to a higher stage of belief above *Islam* and *iman* which is awareness and consciousness of God.

As articulated by Majeed (2003), *ihsan* is the inner beauty which necessarily emanates outward, transforming every human activity into an art and every art into the remembrance of God. The concept of beauty is intimate to God and *ihsan* can be manifested through humans in the form of beautiful geometry, gardens, calligraphy and arches. Hence, art and beauty (*ihsan*) can be viewed as feedback loop for reflection and meditation. In essence, the inner beauty of the heart is manifested and reflected in outer the beauty to evolve new consciousness.

Green *Jihad* is also about being in line with the natural state (*fitra*). Khalid (2002) describes *fitra* as 'the pure state, a state of intrinsic goodness'. Chishti (2003) points out that Islam describes itself as the religion of the natural state (*fitra*). This refers to pure state of intrinsic goodness which already exists within humans. The notion of natural state (*fitra*) is one in which a human being is in constant recognition of his/her own place in the wider creation and hence humans are primed to respond in a caring way to their environment and with more of the inner light of *ihsan*.

In the twentieth century, we witnessed the birth of three movements, that is, human rights, local people and the environment. Social and environmental movements joined forces on human-environmental justice issues with a strong emphasis on issues of mining, extraction and pollution. They tend to position themselves in opposition to oil industry, corporate power, donor agencies and public policies. Green *Jihad* is about the unity of all these movements (human, social, environmental) to address the inequities between the 'have' and 'have nots'. This form of Green *Jihad* was vividly manifested in the rainbow youth revolution in Tunisia and Egypt in early 2011. People in the Middle East were calling for the adoption of core values for equity and justice which underpin the sustainability of any human society and civilisation.

As argued by Adams (2008), there are areas of common interest between environmental and justice movements, for example the conversion of mangroves to shrimp aquaculture. This brings environmental degradation and loss of biodiversity, and often involves the privatisation of communal fishing grounds where both the poor and biodiversity lose out.

In essence, green *Jihad* is a purposeful positive force to ensure equilibrium and 'natural state' and to protect the community of life and to ensure good and justice. Nasr (2003) draws attention to the implications of species extinction from this spiritual standpoint when he states that all creatures in the natural world sing the praise of God. When we cause threat or extinction of any species, we are in reality silencing a whole class of God's worshippers, or what I call disturbing or interrupting the symphony of life. Quran informs us that when humans abuse power, this results in the degradation of both the natural and social capitals. If Muslims are part of the global civil society activism, this will enhance the role of Muslims as change agents for global peace, democracy and freedom.

The essence of Islam is being in a state of harmony and 'natural state' (*fitra*) and in respecting balance (*mizan*) and proportion (*mikdar*) in the systems of the universe. All these notions embedded in the Islamic value system can provide an ethical dimension for Muslims on the climate change issue. Translating this into the technical terms of measuring the concentration of climate in parts per million (ppm). The climate debate is about the increase in the concentration or proportion of greenhouse gases which can be measured in ppm. Due to human development model and consumption patterns, we are seeing an increase in carbon dioxide concentrations of more than 420 ppm as compared to pre-industrial levels of 280 ppm.

Hence, addressing climate change from an Islamic perspective is about assuming the human role as a trustee and steward (*khalifah*) and the role of the median community (*ummah wasat*) to enjoin good and forbid evil and ensure harmony, balance, and right proportion (*fitra*). This balance has been disturbed due to human choices which result in overconsumption, over-exploitation and overuse of resources. The ethical dimension of Islam is about linking theory and practice through evolving new consciousness and spiritual development. Embodying Islam in turn will lead to environmental activism to save the integrity of planet through protecting life on earth and to respect of rights of other species and the protection of the diversity of all communities of life.

## GREEN INNOVATION (*IJTIHAD*)

The Quran consists of many signs and guidelines to inspire the human mind and imagination to learn from the systems in the cosmos and nature. Islam defines rules and principles that provide a reference frame for policy makers and jurists to devise sound trade-offs and decisions to ensure balance between public and private interest and between people and nature. The process for devising law from the Quran and the Sunna is called *ijtihad* which is a process of interpretation and extrapolation to solve current issues in light of the understanding of the text in various contexts. However, the application of core Islamic principles in real world problems would depend on the adaptation and the selective assimilation of Islamic laws which require a sound understanding of current issues, including science, politics and social sciences as stated by Kamali (1991) and Ramadan (2001).

Islamic thought was challenged by the notion of 'closing of *ijtihad*' by the religious scholars of the third Islamic century, as well as to ignore innovations from the end of the eighteenth century. Kamali (1991) explains this closure to be part of the reason why a gap has developed between Islamic law and the changing conditions of society. The thinking and conceptual thinking to apply Islamic laws and principles to contemporary issues including global climatic change would require the process of *ijtihad*, as pointed out by Llewellyn (2003). I believe that promoting a culture of *ijtihad* requires a reform in the following domains:

a)  interdisciplinary learning and unity (*tawhid*) of social and physical sciences;

b)  interpretation and extrapolation of the balance between public and private interest in light of the intent of Islamic law (*maqasid*);

c)  understanding the physical and social laws (*sunan*) and their interdependence.

The term *maslaha* (public interest) is an instrument of *ijtihad* (innovation). One aspect of *maslaha* is to consider the policy that will better off the community at large away from private or self-interest. Five fundamental public intents (*maqasid*) have been defined by Islamic Jurists, which provide a framework and value system to derive legal rulings. These include five domains in the following order of priority: the protection of *din* (religion), *nafs* (life), *nasl* (progeny), *aql* (intellect) and *mal* (wealth).

Trade-offs among these five domains can be resolved based on the potential impact, benefit and priority. For example, public interest has priority over private or group interest. These principles and guidelines frame a code of conduct and inform the debate over climate change. The lack of global eco-ethics and principles is the root cause of complacency over action on climate change as was evident in climate summits in Copenhagen in 2009 and Cancun in 2010.

The lack of global leadership in the US and the industrial world including China and India in the climate change debates was evident in the political positions in the climate summits in 2009 and 2010. The US rationale for not ratifying the Kyoto Protocol was justified on the basis of not harming the US economy which illustrates the illusion or the blind spot in the market economy which gives priority of wealth (*al mal*) above life (*al nafs*). Realising the Islamic law term of necessities (*darurat*) informs public policy on setting priorities as in light of the intent of laws (*maqasid*) where human security and life has a priority over money. One critique to the current economic Western model is that it does not tell us the ecological truth since it promotes economic growth at the expense of human and natural capital.

Islamic rulings based on the five necessities, as outlined in *maqasid*, address both the needs of present and future generations. Hence, the well-being and security of future generations is of fundamental value in Islam. Climate change potential risks and threats can affect the human security and life on earth and, hence it is imperative to embody new ethics, rules and public policy that enhance innovation (*ijtihad*) and leadership to save people and nature.

## GREEN LIFE STYLE (*ZUHD*)

Islamic teachings emphasise the concept of living lightly on earth (*zuhd*), conservation and limit of waste and extravagance (*israf*). Also, Islam encourages humans to reflect on the bounties of God, and according to Armstrong (2001) they should look at the signs of His goodness and power that were evident wherever they looked in the natural world. This reflection on the marvels of the natural world would elicit innovation and nurture naturalistic intelligence.

The Quranic verses revealed in Mecca addressed the oneness of God and also discouraged Meccans from greed, injustice and material accumulation.

The early Islamic teachings made a clear connection between nature and the Creator. This correlation is clear by the use of word *ayat* which means signs. The term signs (*ayat*) refer to both signs in Quran and nature. Nasr (1998) explains that Islam views nature as having sacred qualities and that Muslims viewed in every creature a message and a sign to be read from the cosmic Quran. He further explains that to remember God's quality of encompassing all things, (in Arabic, *Muhit*), is to maintain awareness of the sacredness of nature into which God's presence permeates.

As articulated by Nasr (2003), our need for nature is not only to feed and shelter our physical bodies, but also and above all to nurture our souls. Nature has value to humankind and this benefit transcends the obvious physical and encompasses a spiritual nurturing, thus satisfying a deeper need. These linkages between the signs of cosmos and Quran strengthen one's connection to the Creator, and provides an antidote to the effects of living in a culture fixated on production, profit and the growth of the economy that have a causal effect on fuelling climate change.

Green life style and local development implies conservation as a way of life and supports small-scale development models as applied in Egypt by Abouleish (2005). Islam supports conservation of resources including water, food and energy regardless of its apparent abundance. The current economic model is addicted on fossil oil which is the root cause of climate change challenge. To produce any commodity, we need natural resources and energy. Energy is essential for manufacturing, processing raw materials and for shipping final products across the globe. It is the use of energy during these processes that is most pertinent to a discussion on climate change. The different types of fossil energy (coal, oil and gas) or renewable energy (wind, solar, hydrogen and hydropower or nuclear or bio-fuels) determine the future of climate and the health of the planet which is based on our policy options, development objectives and social choices.

Within Islamic worldview, small-scale and people-centred development is encouraged to minimise ecological footprints which are too high due to global trade. This means that production should be more according to need not for maximisation of profit and creating demands for luxury goods. In Islam, there is a religious constraint for Muslims to conserve and respect the carrying capacity of the earth. Hence, Islamic values encourage policies that reduce the dependence on fossil fuel use regardless if climate change risks exist or not or if there is scarcity of resources. From this perspective, climate change could be seen as one possible symptom of a deviation away from the principle of conservation (*zuhd*). The key message is that even if the threats of climate change do not exist, it is imperative for Muslims to embody and follow Islamic principles as act as a median community (*ummah wasat*) to save the planet and human well-being as part of the global commons.

The three components Green *Jihad, Ijtihad and Zuhd* and the Islamic approach to address climate change through a development that is *local-centred and green along with having quality education and Islamic finance models*. The model, called Green JIZ, represents a holistic response to climate change from an Islamic perspective. Specifically, Green *Jihad* is about harnessing the civil society activism to save nature and people's right in a free, safe and healthy living. Green *Ijtihad* is about unlocking the potential of human innovation to improve human well-being. Moreover, Green *Zuhd* is about living lightly on earth and to avoid over-consumption, overuse and over-exploitation of resources. However, media and advertising play key roles in shifting human needs to wants. Islam urges all humans not to be obsessed by the culture of consumerism and to gain greater mastery in their life styles. Muslims, as a median community among all nations (as *ummah wasat*), should take responsibility and transcend the consumer culture and to develop models of renewable energy, clean production, fair trade and localised production which in turn will lead to less carbon emissions and minimise risks and potential disasters of climate change.

According to Armstrong (2001) the Quran does not consider natural disasters to happen at random but there are results of human activities as indicated in the following verse:

> *Mischief (fasad) has appeared on land and sea because of the deeds that the hands of men have earned, that (God) may give them a taste of some of their deeds: in order that they may turn back (from evil).*
>
> (Quran, 30:41)

'Mischief' or 'corruption or natural disasters' in the above verse means *fasad* in the original Arabic. This broad meaning of *fasad* implies a cause–effect relationship which is linked to human purposeful acts in terms of all human activities. In our current times, the notion of *fasad* can include besides economic and political corruption, environmental impacts such as sea level rise, increased flooding, droughts and hurricanes which are associated with anthropogenic climatic change. The economic cost for corruption is immense.

According to the World Bank (2009), more than US$1 trillion is paid in bribes every year. Corruption is considered among the obstacles to sustainable development since it distorts the rule of law and good governance practices. Also, corruption in all its forms can impact the environment at many scales and domains as it can be seen in pressure from corporate sector to reform laws and regulations to their interests by the commodification of natural resources and burden the poor to cover the additional cost of corruption. Besides, corruption harm the economic, social and ecological balance in a society and it is viewed as an opportunity cost from money lost away from responsible development and sustainability.

Justice, ethics and morality are key pillars in Islamic worldview to attain peace and harmony for people and nature. Islam refers to corruption as an ethical and social problem attributed to human behaviour. Islamic looks at climate change issue in a holistic manner which includes justice, equity, honesty and decency. It is about the adoption of a transformative way of finance, human development and education so as to embody the notion of *Green JIZ*. For example, the climate change risks are linked to global energy demand to sustain the existing market economy which can be the motive for wars and monopolies. During 1990s, the US policy was able to deviate and distract the public opinion from the risk of climate change and focus on war on terrorism as articulated by Al Gore (2007). The Iraq war in 2003 and the issue of Weapon of Mass Destruction (WMD) are good examples of poor global governance and corruption at many domains from reasons and motives of war to issues related to oil firms and human dignity. The economic rationality in this debate was so pervasive that it did not consider the human, ecological and social impact of such a war that is so costly. For example, the total cost for veterans' health care and disability in Iraq war was in the range of $422 to $717 billion according to Stiglitz and Bilmes (2008).

In essence, the lack of human stewardship in the Islamic world resulted in a state of pollution, risk and mischief (*fasad* in Arabic). The leadership at all levels has a lot to do to transform and address the issue of climate change by addressing the root causes not the symptoms of the issue. In the dominant economic model, media, the culture of consumerism and the life style are harming both human and nature. The underlying economic theory which defines the pursuit of happiness and economic growth needs to be re-thought and examined. The underlying rationale of the banking system and the compound interest rate are based on over-exploitation of natural resources by adopting the notion of *discounting the future* while undermining the intergenerational equity.

In an attempt to devise a causal relationship between human activities and pollution (*fasad*) and its relevance to climate change, the following depicts the following cause–effects relationships:

### Case A: Harmony

Oneness of God (*tawhid*) ➔ Harmony (*fitra*) ➔ Justice (*adl*) ➔ Trusteeship ➔  Conservation (*zuhd*)

### Case B: Imbalance

Over-consumption ➔ overuse of fossil energy ➔ increase in $CO_2$ emissions ➔ climate change (*fasad*)

### Case C: Restoration

Feedback learning loops ➔ Green *jihad*è Green *ijtihad* ➔ Green life style (*zuhd*) ➔ restoration of *fitra*

Case A represents the ideal state where a society adheres to the ethos of Islam and embodies the role of a trustee and steward and thus the construction of earth (*emartu al ard*) is balanced and causes no risk to future generations. While case B represents the overuse and over-exploitation of resources which results in $CO_2$ emissions and climate imbalances which is a state far from natural state (*fitra*). The third state, Case C, is a sought vision in which a society strives to reform and transform to restore a natural state (*fitra*) through Green *Jihad, Ijtihad and Zuhd* which I refer to as *Green JIZ* model as depicted in Figure 6.2.

In the following section, I will discuss the carbon crisis and Islam using metaphors and explaining their impacts on the global political discourse.

## The Carbon Cycle, Climate Change and Islam: New Metaphors

The US experience in climate change demonstrates that their approach to reform environmental laws was based on science which framed and defined the problem as an environmental one without linkages to political, socio-economic development and human security. Besides, they argue that there is a tendency from the environmental community to focus on the policies without giving much thought to the politics that made the policies possible. Environmentalism is viewed as just another special interest. This is evident in the justification, reasoning and definition of what is considered as an environmental issue. Environmentalism is today more about protecting 'the environment' than advancing a new sustainability thinking and worldview about human and nature.

On the other hand, Europe is leading a transition towards a low-carbon economy. Denmark is investing in renewable energy and Britain has agreed to cut carbon emissions by 60 per cent over 50 years, Holland by 80 per cent in 40 years, and Germany by 50 per cent in 50 years. Besides, China is investing in solar energy and in eco-friendly cars.

The protest industry claims that action on global warming will cost billions of dollars and millions of jobs as argued by Al Gore (2007). They repeat this claim through advertisements, lobbying, public relations and alliance-building among businesses and labour unions. The debate can be framed in the context that reducing greenhouse gases will not be detrimental to labour. On the contrary, it can be argued that conservation will enhance innovations and create new jobs in the green economy. The following section will attempt to draw some analogies and metaphors between the climate change and Islam.

## THE CONSTRUCTED OR IMAGINED RISK OF CLIMATE CHANGE AND ISLAM

Carbon and Islam needs to be re-thought in terms of risks, threats and challenges. Both of them paradoxically offer two sides of the coin, that is, $CO_2$ and Islam can be seen as a potential risk when they are not understood in a balanced manner and in line with the natural laws (*fitra*). Global challenges from both carbon and Islam cannot be addressed unless there are framed and conceptualised in a systemic manner as part of natural systems in ecology and humanity. In an attempt to draw parallel metaphors and analogies between Carbon and Islam, it is imperative to understand the carbon cycle and the Islamic cycle (as a system) of thought so as to de-construct the stereotypes and misconceptions of both cycles of life and energy.

Carbon is an abundant element that is necessary for life on Earth. The carbon cycle is about the exchange of carbon between all of the earth's components – the atmosphere, oceans and rivers, rocks and sediments and living things. The processes of photosynthesis and respiration are the basis of carbon cycle. In photosynthesis, plants use energy from the sun and carbon dioxide ($CO_2$) from the atmosphere to create carbohydrates (sugars) and oxygen ($O_2$). As shown in the following equation:

*Photosynthesis (Sun + $CO_2$ = ➔ energy (sugar) + $O_2$ ...*      *(1)*

Carbohydrates are then stored (or sequestered) in their biomass (living parts, such as leaves, stems and roots) as plants live and grow. Stored carbohydrates can be used as energy. To use the energy, carbohydrates need to be broken down in respiration and $CO_2$ is released back into the atmosphere. The rate at which $CO_2$ is produced is variable. For example, decomposition – where fungi and micro-organisms breakdown carbohydrates to gather energy – is a slow but significant way the carbon is returned to the atmosphere.

The carbon cycle involves the *flux,* or flow, of carbon between different earth systems. An object or process that absorbs and stores carbon is called a *sink,* while one that releases carbon faster than it is absorbed is termed a *source.* For example, a healthy plant is a carbon sink because it is taking in $CO_2$ from the air and storing it in new leaves and roots and a larger stem. However, a plant can become a source of carbon in the amount of $CO_2$ going out exceeds the amount taken in. This might happen if a plant is eaten and an animal utilises its carbon for energy or if $CO_2$ is sent back into the atmosphere through decomposition or fire.

Humans have a large impact on the worldwide carbon cycle. Fossil fuels, including coal, oil and natural gas all contain large amounts of carbon that was formed during the decomposition of plants and animals over millions of years. Burning fossil fuels releases large amounts of $CO_2$ and other greenhouse gases into the atmosphere faster than natural processes. Changes in land use, especially deforestation, also contribute to elevated levels of atmospheric $CO_2$. Although plants absorb some of the additional $CO_2$, most of the greenhouse gases remain in the atmosphere and contribute to climate change.

Islam, as the carbon cycle, can be seen as an ecological system which metaphorically consists of photosynthesis which is having renewable energy from revelation and innovation as shown in the following equation:

*Knowledge-synthesis (revelation + innovation = ➔ activism + good life ...*   *(2)*

In trying to draw an analogy between the above equations (1 and 2), we can see that in equation 2, there is a process of 'knowledge synthesis' which is a combination of selective assimilation as a result of 'revelation and innovation' as inputs to the equation. This yields a positive energy and good life under the condition we apply sound innovation '*ijtihad*'. Hence, one can argue that the lack of proper knowledge mining and wisdom is a symptom of the stagnation of the Islamic communities worldwide. This stagnation means lack of innovation and hence this will result in negative energy (terrorism and extremism). Paradoxically, the mercy for humanity, Islam will not be seen as a remedy to human problems but rather a potential risk. The same can be said about equation (1), when excess carbon dioxide is not absorbed by natural systems due to human consumption or abuse behaviour, climate change will be taking place because of lack of balance.

The imbalance takes place when we have a source where the amount of $CO_2$ sunk is less than that released which can be viewed as the lack of innovation (*ijtihad*) and dialogue between cultures. In essence, the stagnation in the world of notions, ideas and dialogue with the 'other', enhances the imagined clash of civilisations and the so-called phenomenon of Islamophobia. These misconceptions are the human-made 'fires' that destroy the wealth of our forests which are in reality (like Islam) our pharmacy, playground, class room and source of inspiration.

The rise and fall of Islam and nations can inform how cycles of life follow the natural and social laws (*sunnan*) are not being understood and acted upon by people. The following section will address this concept of a learning civilisation.

## The Way Forward: Learning for Ecology and History

Diamond (2005) lists several reasons for the collapse of societies which are mainly related to environment damage. He noted that the Anasazi people of the south-western United States witnessed the collapse of their society because of environmental damage and climate change, just as the fall of the Maya civilisation of Mesoamerica. Many past societies collapsed due to the failure to solve problems similar to those we face today like problems of deforestation, water management, topsoil loss and climate change as documented by Diamond (2005). In every case, however, people contributed to their own downfall by over-exploiting their environment for short-term gains while ignoring the long-term consequences.

The notion of the rise and fall of nations was articulated by Ibn Khaldoun in his theory of the cycles of civilisations. He argued that when societies lose their moral fibre and the cultural elite exploit the masses, then societies fall and civilisations die. Ancient civilisations, such as that of Mesopotamia and Egypt, were established because of the technological improvements in agriculture, allowing people to live in the same place for longer periods of time. However, limited land availability and increasing population led to intensify food production. However, the lack of rain during the growing season caused droughts and crop failure. Thus, water storage and irrigation were necessary but the rapid evaporation of moisture from the soil, caused by high temperature and high water tables led to the concentration of salts on the soil surface. Indeed, this is a classic example of an unsustainable agricultural system. The ancient agricultural civilisation chose short-term food production practices that caused environmental degradation of the natural capital. The same pattern of short-sighted treatment of the environment continues in most other cradles of civilisation like India and China. In China, massive deforestation added to catastrophic erosion of the soils. Silt accumulated from the erosion clogged Chinese rivers, causing frequent flooding of the river valleys, resulting in massive destruction and loss of life.

Hence, we argue that the necessity of sustainable development is actually a human need and a priority. Sustainable development is a programme to combat unbalanced development patterns rooted in the mismanagement of resources and absence of ethics. Sustainable development requires a reconsideration of the link between humankind and nature. It is also about adopting a holistic approach that is rooted in culture and ecology, like Islam, for addressing the root causes of human problems. In short, to ensure survival, humans must live in harmony with nature and this notion is especially important in the era of globalisation, in which more serious problems including environmental destruction, reduction of biological and cultural diversity, poverty unemployment and significant gap between the 'haves' and the 'have-nots', are deepening.

At the core of the current ecological crisis, as argued by Nasr (1998), lies the destruction of the sacred and spiritual vision of nature at the hands of the modern world and in the name of growth and development. In sum, the solution for the global ecological crisis is to turn to the intellectual and spiritual resources of the world's religious traditions for guidance.

## Conclusions

The Islamic worldview presents an interactive and integrated outlook to sustainability and human civilisation. The intent of law (*maqasid*) sets a framework for public policy analysis and for devising trade-offs between the public and private interests. Islam represents the natural state (*fitra*) or the intrinsic state of goodness. The natural state (*fitra*) implies a full harmony with nature, people and the built environment. The role of the human as a trustee and a witness (*khalifa*) gives him/her a responsibility to be a change agent who embodies all forms of reform and enlightenment. Islam also provides new perspectives for explaining and addressing the root causes for the current environmental crisis of environment as manifested in climate change, poverty and human security. For example, the Islamic perspective on climate change is that the root cause of this global issue is the absence or lack of human stewardship and ethics.

This chapter presented a model to address the climate change issue from an Islamic perspective. The model consists of three components Green *Jihad, Ijtihad and Zuhd* and four strategies to address climate change through a transformative development that is *local-centred and green along with having a quality education and Islamic finance models*. This model, called Green JIZ, represents a holistic response to climate change from an Islamic perspective. Green *Jihad* is about harnessing the civil society activism to save nature and people's right in a free, safe and healthy living. Green *Ijtihad* is about unlocking the potential of human innovation to improve human well-being. Green *Zuhd* is about living lightly on earth and to avoid over-consumption, overuse and over-exploitation of resources. Muslims, as a median community among all nations (*as ummah wasat* ), should take responsibility and transcend the consumer culture and to develop models of renewable energy, clean production, fair trade and localised production which in turn will lead to less carbon emissions and minimise risks and potential disasters of climate change.

In essence, the stagnation in the world of notions, ideas and dialogue with the 'other', enhances the imagined clash of civilisations and the so-called phenomenon of Islamophopia. These misconceptions are the human-made fires that destroy the wealth of our forests which are in reality our pharmacy, playground, class room and source of inspiration.

## References

Abouleish, I. (2005). *Sekem: A Sustainable Community in Egyptian Desert*. Floris. University of Michigan.

Adams, W.M. and Jeanrenaud, S.J. (2009). *Transition to Sustainability*. World Conservation Union.

Al-Jayyousi, O.R. (2001). 'Islamic water management and the Dublin Statement', in Faruqui, N., Biswas, A. and Bino, M. (eds), *Water Management in Islam*, Tokyo: United Nations University Press, pp. 33–8.

Al-Jayyousi, Odeh. (2008). The State of Ecosystems and Progress of Societies. Proceeding of International Conference: Statistics, Knowledge and Policy. Measuring and fostering the progress of societies. OECD. Istanbul, Turkey.

Al-Jayyousi, Odeh. (2009). 'Islamic Values and Rural Sustainable Development'. *Rural 21 Journal*. Volume 41, Issue 3.

Armstrong, K. (2001). *Muhammad: A Biography of the Prophet*. London: The Orion Publishing Group.

Chishti, S. (2003). 'Fitra: An Islamic Model for Humans and the Environment', in Foltz, R., Denny, F., Baharuddin, A. (eds), *Islam and Ecology: A Bestowed Trust*. Cambridge, MA: Harvard University Press, pp. 67–82.

Diamond, Jared. (2005). *Collapse: How Societies Choose to Fail and Survive*. New York: Penguin Books.

Gore, Al. (2007). *The Assault on Reason*. London: Bloomsbury Publishing.

Houghton, J. (2004). *Global Warming: The Complete Briefing*. Cambridge University Press.

Hawken, P., Lovins, A. and Lovins, L. (1999). *Natural Capitalism*. CO, USA: Rocky Mountains Institute.

Hussain, Muzaammal. (2007). *Islam and Climate Change: Perspectives and Engagements*. UK. www.lineonweb.org.uk/Resources/reading/htm. Accessed in Dec. 10, 2010.

International Panel on Climate Change (IPCC) 2007. Special Report on IPCC-Renewable Energy Sources and Climate Change Mitigation-Working Group 4.e

Izzi Dien, M. (2000). *The Environmental Dimensions of Islam*. Cambridge: The Lutterworth Press.

Kamali, M. (1991). *Principles of Islamic Jurisprudence*. Cambridge: The Islamic Texts Society.

Khalid, F. (1998). 'Islam, Ecology and the World Order', in Haleem, H. (ed.), *Islam and the Environment*. London: Ta-Ha Publishers, pp. 16–31.

Khalid, F. (2002). 'Islam and the Environment', in Timmerman, P. (ed.), *Encyclopedia of Global Environmental Change*. Chichester: John Wiley & Sons, pp. 332–9.

Llewellyn, O. (2003). 'The Basis for a Discipline of Islamic Environmental Law', in Foltz, R., Denny, F., Baharuddin, A. (eds), *Islam and Ecology: A Bestowed Trust*. Cambridge, MA: Harvard University Press, pp. 185–247.

Majeed, A. (2003), 'Islam in Malaysia's Planning and Development' in Foltz, R., Denny, F. Baharuddin, A. (ed.) *Islam and Ecology. A Bestowed Trust*, Cambridge, MA: Harvard University Press, pp. 463-465.

Nasr, S. (1998). 'Sacred Science and the Environment Crisis: An Islamic Perspective', in Haleem, H. (ed.), *Islam and the Environment*. London: Ta-Ha Publishers, pp. 118–37.

Nasr, S. (2003). 'Islam, the Contemporary Islamic World, and the Environmental Crisis', in Foltz, R., Denny, F., Baharuddin, A. (eds), *Islam and Ecology: A Bestowed Trust*. Cambridge, MA: Harvard University Press, pp. 185–247.

Ramadan, T. (2001). *Islam, the West and the Challenge of Modernity*. Leicester: The Islamic Foundation.

Stiglitz, Joseph and Linda Bilmes. (2008). *The Three Trillion Dollar War*. New York: W.W. Norton and Company.

WCSD. (1987). *Report of the World Commission on Environment and Development*. Oxford University Press.

World Bank (2009). Six Questions on the Cost of Corruption with World Bank Institute Global Governance Director. http://web.worldbank.org/website/external/news. Accessed on 20th October 2009.

# 7

# Education for Sustainable Development

## Summary

This chapter is intended to critique and assess the current educational system which is devoid from cosmology and suffers from a lack of an ecological insight. The philosophy of Western education was influenced by the mechanistic Newtonian model which looks at nature as an opportunity for exploitation not as a source for inspiration and innovation. This paradigm of education led us to a state of 'nature-deficit disorder' and contributed to the current global challenges including consumerism, poverty and climate change. Transformative education that is informed and guided by Islamic worldviews and the unity (*tawhid*) of mind and soul, natural and social sciences and Today (*dunia*) and Hereafter will be proposed in this chapter. This transformative education will be the hope for a sustainable human civilisation.

## Objectives

1. Critique the modern educational system and assess its negative impacts on the natural environment.

2. Outline the foundations of education for sustainability from an Islamic perspective.

3. Define the role and value of education in Islam as part of construction of earth (*emart al ard*).

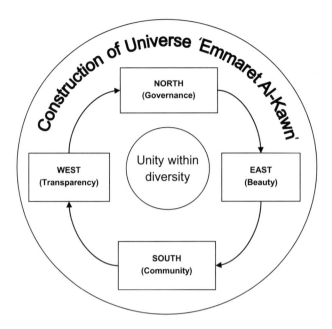

**Figure 7.1      Sustainable development based on four Islamic worldviews**

## Background: Framing the Educational Crisis

During my graduate studies at the University of Illinois at Chicago in the early 1990s, I moved to a new dorm during summer semester. I was stunned to see a big photo, about two metres in length and one metre in height, that covered the wall of my room near my bed which depicted the man landing on the moon and the Earth looking like a small tiny ball floating in space. Whenever I go to sleep I imagine myself immersed in Chicago near the Sears Tower in the moving tiny ball. This fascination of the dynamics, order and beauty of the universe and the communities of life is absent in our educational system. This needs to change if we are to live in peace with all that is around us.

The future of humanity depends to a large extent on the human capacity to evolve and reinvent seamless connections between culture, economy and ecology. Figure 7.1 shows how the Middle East can be the centre where 'unity within diversity' can be attained within the four dimensions of the globe (North, South, East and West) as articulated by Lessem and Palsule (1997, 2009). The Middle East, witness of the birth of early civilisations, is a candidate venue for the fusion of ideas from all corners of the globe, where the good governance from the North, the beauty of the East, the community of the South, and the transparency of the West, all meet in the centre. The prevailing schools of thought in education had constructed boundaries and barriers between and among disciplines (natural science, humanities and physical sciences). This in turn impeded and prevented the human to develop holistic understanding and a worldview of the systems that underpin sustainable development in its cultural, spiritual, ecological, social and economic components. Simply, what is critical is to enable and re-source the human to see unity within diversity.

It is imperative to rethink our educational systems that neglected the beauty and majesty of the powers around us in nature and the cosmos which are essential to nurture our inner world. The extinction of species around us may extend to humankind unless we change our worldviews and redefine and abandon the human goal to conquer nature rather than being in harmony with nature and the community of earth and life, as proposed by O'Sullivan (1999) in his work on transformative learning.

The modern human looks at the natural phenomenon as an external event or as a commodity, while in the past the early man used to communicate and respond to events from nature. Hence, a transformative learning is needed to co-create a holistic view for cosmos, nature and humankind. This is the key role for a 'university' as a domain for the confluence and fusion of ideas, thoughts and insight. The university as a space to celebrate the beauty and majesty of the universe and nature which was lost in our educational mission due to the fact that our development model is informed by economics but not reformed by ecology and culture. Looking at the Earth as our mentor for religion, philosophy, science and economics is a key to evolve a new consciousness towards new modes of learning since the essence of our ecological crisis stems from the philosophical views as argued by Griffin (1995).

The 21st century market economy has exploited, polluted and overused our natural resources and created the illusion which stipulates that the pursuit of growth is infinite and science can provide the needed resources in a finite world. The interdependence between nations and individuals is a measure of the progress of society. Any progress for one or few nations at the expense of others is a recipe for destruction.

The key goal for our educational system should be to make our planet liveable for the all communities of life (*ummam*). It is argued by Wackernagel and Rees (1996) that globalisation and modernism had made us lose our ecological insight and our feelings with the natural world which is essential for our existence. Hence, we need a transformative education and learning systems that embed the story of cosmos and humans and that enhances our eco-cosmic intelligence. This holistic education will transcend the market-based notions of learning to a wider domain and space that is imaginary, immense and infinite which is in line with the Islamic worldview that nurtures the notion of eco-cosmic intelligence.

It is undeniable that the loss of eco-cosmos learning has been addressed in Muslim worldviews with an orientation different from that of Western philosophy. Today, attempts are being made to understand the basic epistemological issues in terms of Islamic orientation. In order to understand and contextualise new 'hidden connections' between culture, economy and ecology, we need to revisit and rethink the philosophy and knowledge in Islam that underpins sustainable development.

With this view, an attempt is made in this chapter to delineate the different connotations of the term knowledge ('ilm) and its relevance to development. It is hoped that this brief attempt will serve as a step for future groundwork for the construction of a framework for an Islamic theory of knowledge and then enable us to lay out the foundations for reinventing and framing sustainable development from an Islamic perspective.

In the Islamic theory of knowledge, the term used for knowledge in Arabic is 'ilm, has a much wider connotation than its synonyms in English and other Western languages. 'Knowledge' falls short of expressing all the aspects of 'ilm. Knowledge in the Western world means processed information while 'ilm is an all-embracing term covering theory, action and education. This notion is critical when we attempt to frame and redefine the notion of development economics and the wider notion of sustainability which covers norms and values (human capital) besides economy (financial capital) and ecology (natural capital).

According to the Islamic perspective, the attainment of knowledge is obligatory at both the individual and societal levels. In fact there is no concept that has been operative as a determinant of the human civilisation in all its aspects to the same extent as knowledge ('ilm). The value of knowledge is deeply rooted in the Islamic culture. This is evident by the fact that the Islamic revelation, Quran, started with the word read (iqra') and there are many references to scholarship, imagination and inspirations of the human to understand the cycles of natural systems that govern the universe (water cycle, seasons) as well as the social laws and transformations that govern the rise and fall of civilisations.

*'Ilm* is of three types: information (as opposed to ignorance), natural laws and knowledge by conjecture. The first and second types of knowledge are considered useful and their acquisition is made obligatory. As for the third type, which refers to what is known through conjecture, or is accompanied with doubt, we shall take that into consideration later, since conjecture or doubt are sometimes essential for knowledge as a means, but not as an end. Besides, various Quranic verses emphasising the importance of knowledge, there are hundreds of Prophetic traditions that encourage Muslims to acquire all types of knowledge from any corner of the world. During periods of stagnation and decline, Muslims confined themselves to imitation which was the main reason attributed to the destruction of philosophy and sciences in the Muslim world.

In the Islamic world, knowledge (*ma'rifah*) is differentiated from knowledge in the sense of acquisition of information through a logical process. 'Ilm is referred to in Quran (revealed by God to prophet Mohammad) as 'light' (*nur*). It is important to note that there is much emphasis on the exercise of the intellect in the Quran and the traditions, particularly in the matter of innovation (*ijtihad*) *and* analogical deduction (*qiyas*). Besides, intuition and judgement are regarded as a higher stage of mental reasoning or inquiry.

Exercise of the intellect (*'aql*) is of significance in the entire Islamic literature which played an important role in the development of all kinds of knowledge. In the twentieth century, the Indian Muslim thinker Iqbal, in his work *Reconstruction of Religious Thought in Islam*, pointed out that innovation (*ijtihad*) was a dynamic principle in the body of Islam. He argued that principles of scientific induction were emphasised by the Quran, which highlights the importance of observation and experimentation in arriving at certain conclusions. It may also be pointed out that Muslim scholars (*fuqaha* and *mufassirun*) made use of the method of linguistic analysis in interpreting the Quran and the Sunnah of the Prophet.

A distinction was made between wisdom (*hikmah*) and knowledge in the pre-Islamic philosophy developed under the influence of Greek thought. In Islam there is no such distinction. Besides, a distinction is made between *khabar* (information) and *nazar* (analytic thought). This applies to most of the Muslim philosophers who sought to attain the ultimate knowledge which could embrace all things. In the Western philosophical tradition, there is a distinction between the knowledge of the Divine Being and knowledge pertaining to the physical world. But in Islam there is no such distinction. *Ma'rifah* is ultimate knowledge and it springs from the knowledge of the self, ('One who realises one's own self realises his Lord'). This process also includes the knowledge of the phenomenal world. Therefore, wisdom and knowledge which are regarded as two different things in the non-Muslim world are one and the same in the Islamic perspective. This ensures that there is room for doubt and scepticism in Islam before reaching certainty in faith (*iman*). The Sufis have described *iman* as consisting of three stages: *'ilm al-yaqin* (certain knowledge), *'ayn al-yaqin* (knowledge by sight) and *haqq al-yaqin* (knowledge by the unity of subject and object).

In Islam knowledge (*'ilm*) is not confined to the acquisition of knowledge only, but also embraces socio-political and moral aspects. Knowledge is not mere information; it requires the believers to act upon their beliefs and commit themselves to the goals which Islam aims at attaining. In brief, the theory of knowledge in the Islamic perspective is not just a theory of epistemology. It combines knowledge, insight and social action as its ingredients. The all-round development of various branches of knowledge pertaining to physical and social phenomena, as well as the process of logical argumentation for justification of Islamic doctrine and deduction of Islamic laws (*ahkam*) with reference to Quranic injunctions and the Prophetic tradition, is indebted to Islam's notion of knowledge (*'ilm*). Scientific knowledge, comprising natural and physical sciences, was sought and developed by Muslim scientists and mathematicians vigorously from the beginning of the last decades of the first century of *Hijrah*. The scientific endeavour found its flowering period with the establishment of the House of Wisdom (*Bayt al-Hikmah*) in the reign of al-Ma'mun.

After the decline of philosophical and scientific inquiry in the Muslim east, philosophy and sciences flourished in the Muslim west due to endeavours of the thinkers of Arab origin like Ibn Rushd, Ibn Tufayl, Ibn Bajah, and Ibn Khaldoun, the father of sociology and philosophy of history. Ibn Khaldoun's philosophy of history and society is the flowering of early work by Muslim thinkers in the spheres of ethics and political science. The credit for giving serious attention to socio-political philosophy goes to al-Farabi, who wrote books on these issues under the titles of the utopian city (*Madinat al-fadilah*).

In brief, it may be justifiably claimed that the Islamic theory of knowledge was responsible for blossoming of a culture of free inquiry and rational scientific thinking that also encompassed the spheres of both theory and practice. The challenge today in the twenty-first century is how to mine, explore and refine this richness of culture and evolve a new version and a model for sustainable development that inspires and resources the human.

In many parts of the world cultural values such as living lightly on earth (*zuhd*) are intrinsic to sustainable development. These norms are rooted in the relationship between people and their environment. In some parts of the world, like the Middle East and Africa, culture permeates all aspects of life. Education for sustainable development should consider and incorporate culture in the learning and interpretation of the cosmos and the community of life, since culture comprises of all the complex and distinctive spiritual, material, intellectual and emotional features that characterise society. However, the cultural challenge is to identify and reclaim indigenous worldviews, perspectives and local knowledge when adopting the notion of education for sustainable development.

## Evolution of Education in Islam

In order to address the notion of education for sustainable development from an Islamic perspective, we need to have a historical overview of education in Islam and then we need to ground education in a conceptual and operational manner as a key element in transformation, reform and enlightenment of societies. It is illuminating to remember that the first word revealed in 610 CE to the Prophet Muhammad (pbuh) was *Iqraa'* ('Recite' or 'Read'). The full verse (96:1) commands '*Read in the name of your Lord Who has created* (all things).' The act of reading, reflection, learning and action in Islam thus took an early emphasis within Islamic worldview. A distinction between learners and non-learners is articulated in Quran: '*Are those who know and those who do not know to be reckoned the same?' asks the* Quran (39:9). The pursuit of knowledge ('*ilm*) is regarded as a religious obligation like prayers.

Besides, the pursuit and purposeful intent to manage knowledge is urged in Islam as the Prophet exhorts, '*The pursuit of knowledge is incumbent on every Muslim, male or female*', a statement that has made the acquisition of knowledge is mandatory for the Muslim individual, irrespective of gender. '*The scholars are the heirs of the prophets*' is another important *hadith* that highlights the role, status of and value of learning and its dissemination in the shaping of communal life and as a basic, integral part of an individual's religious growth.

The earliest venue of education was the mosque, the place of formal worship in Islam as documented by Afsaruddin (2005). During the Prophet Muhammad's time, his mosque in Medina served both as the locus of private and public worship and for informal instruction of the believers in the religious law and related matters. The mosque continued to play these multiple roles throughout the first three centuries of Islam (seventh to the ninth centuries of the Christian or the Common Era). By the tenth century, a new feature, the hostel (*khan*) was increasingly being established next to 'teaching mosques' in Iraq and the eastern provinces of the Islamic world which allowed students and teachers from far-flung areas to reside near these places of instruction. The emergence of the mosque-*khan* complex at this time is a consequence of the lengthier and more intensive period of study required to qualify as a religious scholar.

In the tenth and eleventh centuries of the Common Era, another important institution developed and proliferated known as the *madrasa*, literally meaning in Arabic 'a place of study'. One of the Fatimid's enduring intellectual legacies was the establishment of the oldest continuing university in the world-the al-Azhar mosque-madrasa complex in Cairo – in 972 CE. Perhaps the most prominent name associated with the spread of *madrasas* particularly in Iraq was Nizam al-Mulk (d. 1092), the Saljuq minister. His name is associated with the famous Nizamiyya acadamy in Baghdad, which had the presence of famous scholars like Abu Hamid as-Ghazali (d. 1111).

Henceforth, the *madrasa* became the principal venue and vehicle for the transmission of religious education in the major urban centres of the Islamic world, such as Baghdad, Cairo, Damascus and Jerusalem. It was the institution of higher learning comparable to a modern college of which it was its precursor. In addition to mosques, mosque-*khans* and *madrasas*, other institutions developed over time which played important, supplementary roles in the dissemination of learning. One of the most significant institutions of this type was the burgeoning libraries from the ninth century on. The larger mosques often had libraries attached to them containing books on religious topics. Other semi-public libraries would additionally have books on logic, philosophy, music, astronomy, geometry, medicine, astronomy and chemistry. The first academy in the Islamic world, known in Arabic as *Bayt Al-Hikmah* (lit. 'House of Wisdom'), was built by the 'Abbasid caliph al-Ma'mun (813–33), which had a library and an astronomical observatory attached to it.

According to Afsaruddin (2005), the *madrasa* was typically funded by a trust fund (*waqf*), a charitable foundation, a form of institutional organisation that was borrowed by the West from the Islamic world towards the end of the eleventh century. *Waqf* rendered a person's property safe from confiscation by the state by freezing it as a public asset but which could be passed on to the founder's descendants. In relation to the Quran and *Hadith*, learning by heart (*talqin*) was the principal method of acquiring knowledge and a retentive memory was, therefore, greatly prized.

The saying '*learning is a city, one of its gates is memory and the other is understanding*' captures the approach to learning. In the study of law, the scholastic method of disputation (*munathara*) prevailed, a pedagogical method that originated quite early in the Islamic milieu. As early as the middle of the eight century during the Abbasid period, strong interest began developing in the learning of the ancient world, particularly its Greek sources, but also to a lesser extent in its Persian and Indian ones as well. The intellectual awakening that this interest spawned has rendered this age especially illustrious in the annals of Islamic and world history. Due to the political and territorial expansion of Islam beyond the original Arabian Peninsula, Muslims became the heirs of the older and more cultured people whom they conquered or encountered.

At the time of the Arab conquest of the Fertile Crescent, the intellectual legacy of Greece was unquestionably the most precious treasure at hand. Under the two Abbasid caliphs al-Mahdi and his son Harun-al-Rashid in particular, the Muslim army won decisive victories over the Byzantine enemy forces. One of the most important acheivments of al-Ma'mun's rule in his establishment of the previously mentioned *Bayt al-Hikmah* (*the House of Wisdom*) in 830. The House of Wisdom was a combination library, an academy and a translation bureau. One historian has described the *Bayt al-Hikmah* as the most important educational institution since the foundation of the Alexandrian Museum in the first half of the third century BC. Under al Ma'mun, the *Bayt al-Hikmah* became the centre of translation activity. This era of avid translation would last through the early tenth century.

Greek, Persian, Indian and Syriac learning was selectively synthesised with Islamic scholarship and values which enriched the religious sciences and fostered the cultivation of the natural sciences, philosophy and mathematics. Education served its best purpose when it fostered honest, intellectual inquiry based on critical study of texts and dialectal engagements with one's peers. Scholarly disagreement was welcomed and, as we saw, even publicly staged, in legal and intellectual circles. A statement attributed to the Prophet (pbuh) states, '*There is mercy in the differences of my community*'. This *hadith* embodies a deep awareness that the hermeneutics of reading scripture, or any other text, yields a multiplicity of equally valid readings at any given time or place.

Holistic educational system which promotes spiritual enrichment and critical thinking for men and women, Muslim and non-Muslim, appears to be very closely derived from highly compatible with the classical philosophy of Islamic education which prevailed in the early pre-modern era. Studying God's creation is thus a natural consequence of an individual's faith, leading to deeper knowledge of matters of the mind and the spirit.

## Framing and Concept Development in Islamic Education

In Islam the original source from which every principle of Islamic thought is derived or derivable is the Holy Book, Al-Quran, which was revealed to the Prophet Muhammad piecemeal over a period of 23 years of the Prophet's life. In Islam the doctrine of the infallible word of God, Al-Quran is an article of faith.

Al-Quran recognises revelation as the source of knowledge which is, in the Islamic worldview, a higher guide of reason, but at the same time it acknowledges that the truth of the principles established by revelation is confirmed by reason and denounces those who do not use their reasoning faculties. But human reason in the Islamic view is likely to deviate where there is no revelation as represented in the Quran, and the Prophetic Sunnah.

There emerges from the Quran, taken as a whole, a consistent body of doctrines and of practical obligations. These have remained in all ages the core and inspiration of the Muslim's religious life. Judgements, ideas, derivations (*Ijtihad*, that is, opinions on legal matters), theory-making and concept-formation, as well as educating and being educated in the Islamic way, should be consistent with the Quran precepts and their indications as indicated by Ramzi (1994). Sunnah of the Prophet is the second source from which the teachings of Islam as well as its concepts and theories are drawn. Sunnah literally means a way or a rule or any saying conveyed to the Prophet either through hearing or through revelation.

In its original sense, Sunnah indicates the doings and *Al-Hadith* (the sayings) of the Prophet. In the terminology of Islam, Sunnah and *Hadith* are used interchangeably to convey any saying of the Prophet, or any action or practice of him, as well as his silent approval of an action or practice done by another Muslim in his presence. Scholars in *Hadith* devised strict rules for the critique of the originality of *Hadith*. According to the restrictions of *Hadith*

Critique, only the genuine and the good Ahadith can be regarded as sources of the Islamic conceptualisation, that is, concept formation and development.

Thus, Quran and Sunnah established restrictions and limitations within which concept formation and *Ijtihad* have to be practised. *Ijtihad* is the third source through which Islamic thought is drawn with respect to matters which have not been conclusively decided upon therein. The word *Ijtihad* means exerting oneself, and a *Mujtahid* is the one who exerts himself to form an opinion in legal matters, or 'one who claims the right to reinterpret tradition'. *Ijtihad* or claim that only the early Jurists had the right to be Mujtahidun. *Al-Ijtihad* is correlated with Al-Fiqh which is the technical term for the Science of the Islamic Law. *Al-Ijtihad* is technically applicable to any jurist exerting the faculties of his/her mind to the utmost for the purpose of forming an opinion in the light of Islamic principles.

With respect to schools of Al-Fiqh, there should have been according to the Islamic view because they ought to have been regarded as ways of understanding what *Shari'ah* shows in accordance with the power of evidence (*Ad-Dalil*), instead of being acknowledged as schools or rites. Faith consists of knowledge and belief. Faith, in Islam, is a firm belief arising out of knowledge and conviction. The Islamic life, as well as the Islamic educational system, is open to human achievements and international experience in every related field and in every aspect of life, provided that the respective experience or achievement is consistent with and applicable within the Islamic doctrines. Consequently, according to Ramzi (1994), Islamic faith includes certain rulings that control theory making and concept formation.

The Arabic verb '*Rabba*' means took care of the infant, reared him, taught and guided him from his birth until his adulthood. The verb '*Yurabbi*' is the present tense of *Rabba*. One of the meanings of the verb '*Rabba*' in Al-Quran is 'took care of the child and raised him until he became an adult and able to undertake his responsibilities'. At-Tarbiah in Islam stresses also the permanence and continuation of the process of education. Both parents and teachers give education and receive education all through their lives.

The Prophet Muhammad is the embodiment of the Islamic doctrines revealed in Al-Quran. He is the perfect incarnation of the Islamic personality, the perfect slave of God, the perfect Prophet and Messenger, and the perfect Islamic educationalist. According to the Islamic Faith, the infallibility of the Prophet and his being guided by God through revelation, are basic concepts that underline Islamic concept formation, Islamic education and Islamic learning.

The basic concepts are believed to control and guide concept formation as well as the actions of Muslims and Muslim society in their movement towards becoming Islamic. Through practice, sayings, approvals and disapprovals (the prophetic Sunnah), the Prophet Mohammad established the Islamic ordinance that comprehended life, state, society and the Islamic nation. He also established the fundamental concepts that guide Muslim scholars and educationalists in holding on to Islamic lines of thought.

His lifetime is considered the main part of the reference period for Islamic life, law, education, and conceptualism. That part began from AD 610 until AD 632 – the period of revelation. His Sunnah is believed to be the actual interpretation of Al-Quran, and the essential reference for Fuqaha', jurists and educationalists for all ages after AD 632. Under the dynamic leadership of the Prophet, the final good for Mankind was not merely indicated but was translated into practice and a system and organisation for the realisation of the ideal were established.

The centre of the Prophet's preoccupation was on educating and presenting a role model of transformational leadership for the first Muslim community. The Prophet Mohammad (pbuh) was the messenger of Islam who was sent by God to all humankind as a continuation to previous religions. Being a Muslim, by default, implies the belief is all past prophets. Muslims believe that The Message of Islam is complete, comprehensive and final and was not based on a social, or tribal, or national or racial motives. Allah teaches us in Al-Quran:

> Today I have perfected your religion for you, and I have completed My
> blessing upon you, and I have approved Islam for your religion.

Thus, Muhammad (pbuh), in the Islamic view, is the perfect educator and the perfect educationalist and the unique Islamic personality with respect to education and every aspect of life. His life and his Sunnah are the conclusive and practical application of Al-Quran in particular and Islam as a message. Every one of the prophet's companions (Sahabah) is an example of the Islamic personality that has been educated and brought up through the guidance and companionship of the Prophet. Those people exemplify the product of the Islamic way of life within which the Islamic education process took place and was brought into reality.

Consensus (*Al-Ijmaa'*) of the Companions is regarded as infallible and is eligible to be a source for theorisation in education, in Al-Ijtihad, in jurisprudence (Al-Qadaa'), and in juridical deductions. Through their consensus, Al-Quran has been assembled, and As-Sunnah has been passed on to the following generations. The noteworthy fact is that they practised educating the younger generations and bestowed upon them what they had known and practised in the lifetime of the Prophet without any hint whatsoever to attract followers or to establish schools. Al-Quran enjoins Muslim generations to refer to the guidance of their consensus.

Furthermore, according to Ramzi (1994), through scrutinising the lives of the generation of the Prophet's Companions, one can easily see that Islamic education aimed at maintaining and elevating the unity of the Islamic nation, and at extending and deepening knowledge in all aspects related to Islamic life. During this period of stagnation many events took place in the Muslim world such as closing the gate of *Al-Ijtihad*, in spite of the fact that *Al-Ijtihad* leads the process of concept formation and judgement in Muslim society, and activates the potentialities of Islamic understanding among people. The door of *Al-Ijtihad* was shut once and for all, and that no scholar, however eminent, could henceforth qualify as a Mujtahid (an authoritative interpreter of law). Yet that destructive issue did not prevent some few scholars from claiming the right of Mujtahidun, but the fact remains that a gap of concept formation had been originated and had been existing to a degree which was described to be a state of 'fossilisation'.

Ibn Taymiyyah (1262–1327) applied his capacity to lead Islamic thought along the same lines with an anti-neutral political stand, followed by Al-Fuqaha' and Ulama' of his time, and by the graduates of Al-Azhar Islamic College. He tried to maintain the understanding of Muslims and their concept forming to revive the relation between Islamic faith, life and education.

As modern Arab philosophers discuss the relation between philosophy and religion, the role of philosophy is being tackled again with stress being placed on the relation between *Al-Aql* (reason) and *An-Naql* (Al-Quran and revelation). The view was described as a crisis of reason and religion is the same crisis that started most of the political conflicts which are expressed in the modern liberal Arab literature such as secularisation (the separation of religion from the state). It may be concluded that Muslim philosophers had followed the Greek lines of metaphysics in their long and tedious pursuit for wisdom and did not fully integrate their views with the Islamic context. Secularism for instance, claims that religion had to give way to new forms of associations and social relations and that secularisation is the instrument to transformation of the (nation state) in ideology, law, education and bureaucracy.

The conceptual crisis has been noted by contemporary Western scholars, Arab and Muslim thinkers as what was referred to as 'conflicting and confusing influences'. In Gibb's view, Western ideas have been contributing to conceptual gap in the Muslim world. The fragmentation of Islamic unity since 1850 was the result of the stagnation of governance structures. I believe that nowadays the same root causes of stagnation still exist which compelled the youth in the Arab world to seek freedom and reform in the age of virtual and social media.

The longing and pursuit of reform and freedom in the Middle East started in the early nineteenth century and education was viewed as key element for change and emancipation. Many thinkers including Muhammad Iqbal (1876–1938), Jamalud Din Al-Afghani (1838–1873), Muhammad Abduh (1845–1905), Muhammad Rashid Rida (1865–1935), Ahmad Amin (1886–1954), Taha Hussain (1889–1973), and Abbas M. Aqqad (1889–1964), Adip Ishaq (1856–1885), Kheirud Din At-Tunsi (1825–1889), Rifaah At-Tahtawi represent an individual line of thought regarding the reformation of the Arabic and Islamic world. Their views do no resemble the Islamic concept formation and did not lead towards a new model of Islamic education. Those thinkers tried to reform their societies by means of individual experience, which was influenced the Western model.

Modern Arab and Muslim educationalists, headed by Jamalud Din al-Afghani, tried to revive Arab nationalism and the rise of Islam. Al-Afghani advocated the concept of a 'Muslim League' in which the Muslim states might bond together. This was acknowledged by Muslim educationalists to be the first stroke against the application of the Islamic concept of unity. Abdul-Hassan An-Nadwi suggested a theoretical education programme that comprehended the Muslim nation and the Muslim states. He tried to restore the former status of the Muslims. His programme included the cultivating faith in the hearts of Muslims and originating religious feelings. The fact remains that these parties failed to re-establish the Islamic thinking of the *Ummah*, mainly because a number of them concentrated on the religious and spiritual.

Another look from a different angle may assist us to see that since 1850 Muslim thought can be said, according to Ramzi (1994), to have forked into three schools:

- The Reformist School, which was represented by Muhammed Abduh and Malik Ibn Nabi.

- The Historic School, which was represented by Taha Hussain, Abbas Al-Aqqad and Ahmad Amin.

- The Educational School, which was represented by An-Nabhani and Al-Banna.

Ibn Nabi tried to justify the situation stressing the role of conceptions in organising individual activities. To him, concepts are the basic motives of the individual activities which build the basis of the communal activities. He also called for the general principle from which concept formation emanates. This formation of concepts to Ibn Nabi harnesses reason which in turn shall harness the rational imperatives in a community.

Muslim educationalists, nowadays, who view Islam as a way of life and a system that comprehends all aspects of life observe the Islamic Ummah (nation) to have been losing its Islamic concepts, because, as they express it, the present day generation has not received any Islamic conception or any productive way of thinking from their ancestors. The Islamic nation is supposed to have been living a crisis of thought which causes confusion and obscurity in the vision of Muslims. All through the Arab and Muslim worlds educationalists urge a conceptual reformation as a prerequisite for any other reformation. The majority of present day Muslim educationalists and thinkers are so complacent and satisfied with their ideas and experience that they more or less avoid discussions on the possibility of integrating the educational system with Islamic life and Islamic faith.

Others see that the modern Arab educationist has a great Islamic tradition in education to look up for inspiration and that Islamic education is at present a mere shadow of its past. The product of education in the Arab world is seen as deformed and regressive. There are different and inconsistent systems of education which are caught between conflicting pressures, such as respect for tradition and the necessity for change. The challenge is to find the right and balanced harmony between traditional conceptions to address contemporary issues and challenges.

The Islamic educational theory is not a set of hypotheses proved to be valid through observations and experimentation, nor is it a set of principles stated by humans; instead it is a set of educational concepts that inform and frame the educational system. In essence, religion is not viewed as a societal phenomenon but rather it is the foundation of education. Scholars argued that the main factor behind the backwardness and regressive situation of the Muslim community is the absence of both the educational system and a well-defined philosophy with a clear organisation of concepts.

Another part of the responsibility lies with the effects caused by the theory of the evolution of species and the theory of natural selection through struggle for survival. These two theories were suggested to explain the varieties of plant and animal species, human beings included, and to justify the extinction of certain species and forms of life. They are infused in the sciences and educational fields and in school curricula. These theories, combined with the evidence of evolution suggested by anthropologists and biologists as well as Darwin, did not approach the concept of creation or deal with the concept of its creator. At the same time they did not contradict, if understood soundly, the Islamic principles of Creation.

Ramzi (1994) argues that the theory of evolution which states that that Man had lived about one million years before he began to develop a kind of life that distinguished him from other animals, which is supposed to have begun 20,000 years ago, is not so contradictory with the Islamic concept. According to the Islamic view, the varieties of species and the combinations of the chromosomes, as well as the natural selection in the worlds of animal and plants are manifestations of God's glory and supreme power. God had created the species and instilled in them potential tendencies and capabilities to evolve according to the possibilities of internal as well as external variables. Plants, animals, things, seas, mountains, plants and the whole universe are subservient to man, and are indicators and signs for the God creation. These worlds and forms of life are reservoirs of miraculous treasures for learning and inspiration.

With respect to man, Islam speaks of him as the offspring of Adam and Eve, through which his honourable species originated and populated the earth. According to Quran, changes in environments and in social and physiological relations could not cause the existence of a new human species.

## Reflections and Conclusions

The notion of education for sustainability or education for sustainable development is viewed in different perspectives. While some argue that introducing this concept is of value since it will be used to address issues that are under-represented by conventional environmental education, others show some concerns about the globalising nature of the 'education for sustainability' agenda and stress the need to nurture alternative perspectives.

If environmental thought and ethics are evolving processes, then one task of higher education is to engage students in this process. Moreover, if environmental thinking is to continue evolving, and if students are to be participants in an environmental discourse unimagined today, then we must resist temptations to exclude emerging ideas (like Islamic perspectives) in favour of sustainability. Sustainability is challenged by the fact that both the knowledge base and the value base of sustainability are variable and questionable. However, sustainability debate can bring together different groups of society searching for a common language to discuss environmental issues. It is argued that where different ways of looking at the world meet, dissonance is created and learning is likely to take place.

Moreover, this dialogue allows the socio-scientific dispute character of emerging knowledge and values to surface. Participation in such a debate is an opportunity to learn about a highly controversial topic at the crossroads of science, economy, technology and society. Critical thought depends on transcendental elements in ordinary language, the words and ideas that reveal assumptions and worldviews, and the tools to mediate differences between contesting value systems. Paradoxically, there is a counteractive effect in the power of universal discourse (like sustainability) in reducing the meaning to a minimum. This reduction is likely to result in devaluation of language and linguistic dysfunction.

Educational institutions have a unique freedom to nurture, inspire, develop new ideas and to contribute in the creation of new knowledge. Universities have a unique role in developing the multiple intelligences of the students so that to enable them to critique, construct and act with a high degree of reflection, autonomy and self-determination. Education should develop students' competencies which will enable them to cope with uncertainty, conflicting values and reality construction. The key factor to cause decay in any society or institution is when it stifles creativity, homogenises thinking, narrows choices and limits autonomous thinking and degrees of self-determination.

Education is viewed as a means to evolve self-actualised members of society, looking for meaning, developing their own potential and jointly creating solutions. In this view, a sustainable society cannot be created without the full and democratic involvement of all members of society. We can envision a very transparent society, who actively and critically participate in problem-solving and decision-making, and value and respect alternative ways of thinking, valuing and doing. This society may not be sustainable from an ecological point of view as represented by the eco-totalitarian society but the people might be happier and ultimately capable of better responding to emerging issues.

It seems appropriate to seek some standards for integrating sustainability in education in ways that do not standardise realities. The following are some lessons learned from an initiative for incorporating sustainability in education as documented by Van den Bor et al. (2000) and summarised below. These include:

- Sustainability as a 'socially constructed reality' and a phenomenon to be studied.

- Sustainability as contextual and hence its meaning is dependent on the situation in which it is used.

- Sustainability as a normative, ethical and moral.

- Sustainability as an innovation and a catalyst for change.

Teaching sustainability requires the transformation of conventional mental models. This implies that teachers should consider themselves as learners. Also, teaching sustainability includes a debate on values and ethics. The inclusion of aspects of sustainability in education is very much culturally defined.

Sustainability demands transformations and critical reflections on one's teaching. It also requires the empowerment of learners by enabling them to work on the resolution of real issues that they themselves have identified. It requires appreciation and respect of differences. The transformation in the educational orientation is outlined below:

- from consumptive learning to discovery learning;

- from teacher-centred to learner-centred;

- from content oriented learning to self-regulative learning;

- from institutional staff-based learning to learning with and from outsiders;

- from emphasising only cognitive objectives to also emphasising affective and skill-related objectives.

In an attempt to incorporate sustainability in education, it opens a whole new world of learning and researching. Having this view, sustainability represents an ideal entry into philosophy and ethics. Hence, the contextualisation of Islamic principles in education for sustainable development is of special significance to evolve local solutions inspired from culture.

Islamic worldview sees humans as part of nature rather than separate from it. On an epistemological level it holds knowledge as subjective and maintains that valid knowledge can be both rational and non-rational. This is a different conception of knowledge from that of the dominant in the Western worldview, which separates fact from value and has led to a kind of 'conceptual alienation'. This is attributed to the fact that the Western model is more interested in technical quick fixes that focus on efficiency, effectiveness and productivity rather than on quality education that promotes questioning and critical thinking.

Scholars argue that environmental education should consider both human consciousness and political action and should encourage individuals to be autonomous, independent critical and creative thinkers. Also, it should enable students to take responsibility for their own actions and to participate in the social and political re-construction of new realities.

Education policies and strategies for advancing sustainability need to be developed by individual systems and institutions so that they remain locally relevant and culturally appropriate. Guidelines and criteria for environmental ethics and sustainability are reflected in the Earth Charter which calls for us to act and conduct our research in ways that; respect Earth and life in all its diversity; care for the community of life with understanding, compassion and love; build democratic societies that are just, sustainable, participatory and peaceful; and secure earth's bounty and beauty for present and future generations.

In sum, what is needed in the twenty-first century is a new paradigm of eco-cosmic education that is focused on education for society and eco-space, since our modern culture dissipates immense amount of energies to move people and goods from one place to another as argued by Orr (1992). Also, we need an education for cultural diversity and citizenship which celebrates diversity and adds value to life.

## References

Afsaruddin, A. (2005). *The Philosophy of Islamic Education*, in Bekim Agai, *Fethullah Gulen and His Movement in Islamic Ethics of Education-Critique* (2002). *Middle Eastern Studies*, 11 (2002), 41.

Berry, T. (1988). *The Dream of the Earth*. San Francisco: Sierra Club Books.

Bloom, A. (1987). *The Closing of the American Mind*. New York: Simon and Schuster.

Bowers, C.A. (1993). *Critical Essays on Education, Modernity, and the Recovery of the Ecological Imperative*. New York: Teachers College/Colombia Press.

Cobb, E. (1977). *The Ecology of Imagination in Childhood*. New York: Columbia University Press.

Griffin, S. (1995). *The Eros of Everday Life*. New York: Doubleday.

Hargrove, K. and Smith, M. (2005). *The Natural Advantage of Nations: Business Opportunities, Innovation and Governance in 21st Century*. Earth-Scan: James and James Publishing.

Lessem, R. and Palsule, S. (1997). *Managing in Four Worlds*. Oxford: Blackwell.

Lessem, R. and Schieffer, A. (2009). *Transformation Management: Towards the Integral Enterprise*. Farnham: Gower Publishing.

Orr, David W. (1992). *Ecological Literacy: Education and the Transition to a Postmodern World*. Albany, NY: State University of New York Press.

O'Sullivan, E. (1999). *Transformative Learning: Educational Vision for the Twenty-First Century*. London: Zed Books.

Ramzi, Abdul Qader H. (1994). 'Islamic Education in the Understanding of Present Day Muslim Educationists'. PhD thesis, University of Durham, UK.

Wackernagel, M. and Rees, W. (1996). *Our Ecological Footprint: Reducing Human Impact on the Earth*. Gabriola Island, BC: New Society Publishers.

WCSD. (1987). *Report of the World Commission on Environment and Development*. Oxford University Press.

Van den Bor, W., Holen, P., Wals, A. and Filho, W. (2000). *Integrating Concepts of Sustainability into Education for Agriculture and Rural Development*. Frankfurt: Peter Land.

# Epilogue

Sustainable development in the twenty-first century needs to harness both the technological and cultural wealth of nations. This epilogue will highlight the importance of a set of dimensions that need to be mainstreamed in a new discourse for sustainability that is rooted in culture and ecology. The world since 2008 has been preoccupied with economic and financial problems. The global stock markets lost more than US$30 trillion and pensions lost 15 per cent of their value in 2008, commodity prices are fluctuating wildly, food prices are increasing and unemployment is rapidly approaching 9 per cent globally. While the state of the global economy deserves the attention it is receiving, another crisis is going virtually unnoticed: the global decline in ecosystems and the biodiversity. The economic crisis can eventually recover, but the loss of biodiversity which represents our natural capital and life-support systems may be irreversible. It should be noted that policy makers should be mindful that implications of the degradation of ecosystems are likely to undermine the basis for economic recovery. An important tool for addressing these linked problems is information and communications technology.

The wave of democracy in the Middle East or Arab awakening in 2011 was induced by ICT and social media where requests for good governance (*adl*), new heightened consciousness (*ihsan*), intact social capital (*arham*) and a fight against corruption (*fasad*) were all evident from the voices of youth in the public domain. All these requests constitute the DNA for sustainability.

## Investing in Our Natural Capital

Realising the global challenges including poverty, climate change, HIV-AIDS and biodiversity loss, the world needs a stronger appreciation of the sustainability principles along with sound ecosystem management to build a support system for economics. The climate change will compromise economic development and it is imperative to enhance the ecosystem resilience and to invest in nature as part of a transition to a green economy.

All communities of life (*ummam*) including plants, animals and micro-organisms live together in ecosystems which provide sustainable streams of benefits to people, known as 'ecosystem services'. These include providing food and timber, ensuring regular supplies of freshwater, maintaining a healthy climate, pollinating crops, preventing soil erosion, regulating diseases and pests, minimising the impact of extreme natural events and cycling nutrients through natural systems to enable our economies to flourish.

Our impact on Earth's resources is entirely out of proportion to our size, and we cannot increase these demands indefinitely. The current ecological challenges are the result of a mode of development that is as old as civilisation. McNealy (2009) argued that prehistoric societies were stable and enduring: they evolved a sustainable relationship with their environment. Only the energy of the sun entered the nature-human system, and only the heat radiated into space left it – everything else was cycles and recycled within it. This is no longer the case today. We are operating at the outer limit of the planet's capacity to sustain life. The Earth is a finite system, with finite space, resources and regenerative potentials, and we are now exceeding the effective range of these limits. Each minute 21 hectares of tropical forest are lost, 50 tons of fertile soil are blown off and 12,000 tons of carbon dioxide are added to the atmosphere. Each hour 685 hectares of productive dry land become desert, and each day 250,000 tons of sulphuric acid fall as acid rain in the northern hemisphere.

In terms of trade, some 40 per cent of world trade is based on biological products or processes, and the increasing dependence of many countries on imports of food and other biological resources underlines this important contribution biodiversity makes to economies. In essence, biodiversity also affects national security. Conflicts over water, fisheries and other shared resources are endemic in many parts of the world. Natural resources also help feed some conflicts. For example, conflicts in Sudan and Palestine are being fought over water and land rights and other natural resources that help to provide livelihood and human security for local people.

McNealy (2009) documented the research tools made available by Google and other search engines which are helping to accelerate research in highly complex fields, such as genomics and genetic engineering, and helping scientists to better understand the full wealth of species and ecosystems on our planet. For example, the 'Encyclopedia of Life' (www.eol.org) is an open-access system that intends to provide information on all of the known species on our planet. ICT is also essential in reaching out to the public and contribute to what is called digital democracy, green advocacy or civic activism as seen in the waves of democracy in the Middle East and North Africa. Social networking sites and blogs also enable the public to organise themselves around key conservation issues, perhaps acting as a watchdog or providing a weighty voice for or against certain developments. Public awareness campaigns can also be affected through such Web2.0 applications. The new information and communications technologies that are constantly being improved are essential to enabling the conservation of the living wealth of our planet, an essential foundation for a sustainable future.

## Sustainability and Spirituality

Hossein (1968) argued that the lack of acceptance of the spiritual dimension of the ecological crisis will soon lead to the destruction of the environment. In reality, this is rooted in an externalisation of the humanity's inner soul. The actions of humans are responsible for this ecological crisis. Thus, the most important contribution to the global discourse on the environmental issue is the restoration of a spiritual vision of nature. Reflecting on the main environmental problems, such as, the destruction of natural habitats (mainly through deforestation), reduction of wild foods, loss of biodiversity, erosion of soil, depletion of natural photosynthetic resources, introduction by humans of toxins and alien species, artificially-induced climate change and overpopulation, we see that all are triggered by human behaviour. If we scrutinise the factors historically linking the collapse of past societies, it is clear that the root cause is the inability of man to live harmoniously and respectfully with the basic laws of Nature.

According to Diamond (2002), the eight main factors contributing to societal collapse are the following: deforestation and habitat destruction; soil problems such as erosion; Salinisation and soil fertility losses; water management problems; over-hunting and over-fishing; introduction of foreign species; human overpopulation; and increased per-capita impact of humans on the environment. Diamond added that another four new factors may contribute to the weakening and collapse of present and future societies: human-induced climate change; build-up of toxic chemicals in the environment; energy shortages; and full human utilisation of the earth's photosynthetic capacity.

## Development for Human Dignity and Freedom

It is important to realise that, in order for sustainable development to work well and ensure the development of human civilisation, it requires shifts of paradigm from individual-centred development to development that emphasises the harmonious relationships of the individual with society, nature and the Creator. In this context, the concept of human rights needs to be assessed. There is the need to reintroduce the concept of a human in a holistic framework addressing his relationships with other humans, society, nature and the Creator. Hence, spiritual values and the pursuit of social well-being at a high level of development take precedence.

In the Brundtland Report (1987), 'Our common future', sustainable development was defined as a process of change in which the exploitation of resources, the direction of investments, the orientation of technological development, and institutional change are all in harmony and enhance both current and future potential to meet human needs and aspirations.

Religious values in the spiritual dimension can provide guidance for sustainable living, as the essence of religion is not only about God and rituals, but about a relationship with the environment. Religion is important for people's personal development, as it provides a code of conduct of how human beings should conduct themselves on the shared planet.

## Islam as a Transformative Worldview

Islam also stresses that God has not created anything in vain, or without wisdom, value and purpose. Humans have a mission and mandate to build a sustainable human civilisation that respects the value of every single human being. The Quran clearly states that to kill one person is to kill all humanity. The Quran says: 'Whoever killed a human being, except as a punishment for murder or wicked crimes, should be looked upon as though he had killed all mankind; and whoever saved a human life should be regarded as though he had saved all mankind' (al-Maidah:32).

Human beings have been giving the responsibility to manage life on earth, both for themselves and for creatures that inhabit the earth. In a way, human beings are in charge of the world, and of everything which God has created in it. Thus, it is vital for the security and survival of the human species to maintain the code found in nature and in the laws that govern life on earth. This code defines the environment as a sacred 'gift' given by God.

If we view nature as a reality that also possesses spiritual significance, then our sense of responsibility toward nature must be conceived in broader and more fundamental terms. Any act of negligence on the part of human beings represents a danger to and prejudice against other beings. All this is to ensure that we can grow in harmony with nature. Thus, we have to accept its norms and its rhythms rather than seeking to dominate, overcome or overwhelm it. The future sustainability of humankind and civilisation rests very much on human values and ethics and hence spirituality becomes central to development. A deep transformation of our understanding of nature and the human state and the nature of our relationship with God and the natural environment is necessary. This implies a radical change in our worldview and development models. Being ethical and respectful towards nature should guide development strategies. People organisation and societies need to be inspired in order to apply this concept. The prosperity enjoyed by human beings is a result of harmonious relations between mankind and nature.

## Sustainability as a Pursuit of Good Life

Humans are viewed as trustees and stewards who are responsible to respect the natural laws and ensure justice (*adl*) and sustainability (*tayebah*) approaches to harness natural resources. All human endeavours and acts are forms of worship of God. There is no disconnect between the spiritual and the secular or this life and Hereafter. This unity of time and belief inspires the human to celebrate the diversity of life and to proceed continually in his (her) pursuit to discover, understand, live and enjoy this world without having any feeling of guilt, provided he (she) seeks to live within the Islamic code of conduct.

Islam requires humans to maintain a balance between the attachment and pursuit for material things and the pursuit of the Hereafter. This notion of living lightly on earth (*zuhd*) is a key ingredient in Islam, since it provides a self-organising mechanism to restrain the human from all forms of over-consumption and overuse of resources. This worldview ensures environmental stewardship and respect for the concept of the carrying capacity of our natural systems. Besides, every generation should show consideration for the future generations in the use of resources. At the global level all nations should exercise transformational leadership and ensure environmental justice (*adl*) and *tayebah* development for all nations and species.

The Islamic worldview and perspective of the origin and the unity of humanity are simple and clear. Islam views all human beings as children of Adam. As human beings, they are all equal and are part of a global family who should know each other and share knowledge. Thus, the present day situation in which the poor countries are heavily indebted to the rich countries is not in conformity with the Islamic vision. Social, economic and environmental justice are universal human ethics that must be respected by all. The Islamic economic model is based on communal equity and encourages individual innovation (*ijtihad*) but with certain checks and balances to define the limits and degree of government invention that would prevent the building up of concentration of economic power.

Islam teaches that there is a purpose for this creation and humans are accountable. Humans have responsibility and trust (*amanah*) as the vicegerent of God and they are accountable to God for all actions on the Day of Judgement Thus, Islam prescribes a strong system of accountability at all levels. This is true at the international level as in the case of the climate change debate. The present situation in which certain powerful nations and global corporations are not accountable to anyone in this world is not congruent with the Islamic worldview. Islam envisages a world in which everyone with authority is accountable for his actions. Also, Islam teaches that all species, human and natural resources must be safeguarded against waste, depletion and destruction.

Islamic civilisation and culture redefine the notion of good life (*hayat tayebah*) as reflected in the notions like *zuhd* which means sufficiency and living lightly on earth and *ihsan* which means inner beauty and excellence. The Western life styles and standard of living and consumption patterns produce high ecological footprints in terms of consumption of food, energy and goods. Through global trade, we are outsourcing development and environmental costs across borders to India, China and other parts of the world. The scale and intensity of ecological degradation (which Islam refers to as *fasad*) in the last five decades is unsurpassed in the history of humanity.

There is a need for a macro-shift in our worldviews, a rethinking of the fundamentals of the Western economic model to ensure a humanistic and sustainable model that resonate with culture and ensures balance (*mizan*), social equity (*adl*) and respects harmony between nature, people and markets.

Above all, what is needed is a new and fresh look at Islam as a source of global peace, prosperity, inspiration and restoration of the natural and equilibrium (*fitra*) between society, markets and nature.

The paradox of having poverty within wealth in the Western model is attributed to the illusion that the media promotes which conveys the message that happiness is a function of material possessions and accumulation. In Islam, happiness is a reflection of peace of mind (*alnafs al mutma'innah*), which is possible to attain only if an individual's life is in harmony with his inner nature. This happens when both the spiritual and the material urges are adequately satisfied. Since the material and the spiritual are not separate identities, the desired satisfaction takes place only when a spiritual dimension is injected into all material pursuits to give them meaning and purpose.

It is probably not possible to satisfy the needs of all members of society, unless all wasteful and inessential uses of resources are eliminated or minimised and all socio-economic institutions that promote inequities are reformed. This in turn is not possible if individuals take into account their own individual preferences and financial ability. Every individual therefore needs to be made aware of the social priorities in resource use and to be motivated to behave in conformity with these priorities. Humans need to be concerned about the well-being of others while striving for their own well-being.

What could be more conducive to the creation of such a discipline than a moral system given by the creator of the Universe Himself, combined with accountability before Him? Within the framework of such a discipline, material possessions do not command a value for their own sake. They are of value as long as they fulfil the objective of their creation as defined by the value system. Such an attitude creates a voluntary restraint in the use of scarce resources that minimises unnecessary consumption and over-exploitation of resources. Such a moral system makes it possible to satisfy the needs of all by living lightly on earth and by realising that we can attain prosperity without growth. This in turn will result in social cohesion and solidarity where all members of the community feel empowered by the sense of belonging, not their belongings.

In the absence of a moral dimension, material possessions become an end in itself. Satisfaction then does not remain a function of need fulfilment but of much more than that, of vying with others. Conspicuous consumption creates only temporary satisfaction. Without any meaning and purpose of life, fashions and models only exchange one kind of emptiness for another.

Everyone is constantly busy acquiring the necessary resources, leaving little time to fulfil obligations towards family and community. The pressures on the individual expand beyond his or her ability to bear and peace of mind suffers. The entire machinery of production becomes directly or indirectly directed toward the satisfaction of a maximum amount of wants. This is supported by banking policies which encourage people to live beyond their means. Claims on resources, therefore multiply and imbalances increase and those unable to keep pace with this struggle fall behind. This will lead to dissatisfaction, social tensions and human alienation.

Realisation of the intent of laws (*maqasid*) requires different priority setting. This includes the realisation that public goods need to be shared in an equitable manner that will achieve public interest (*maslaha*) through fair trade and *hima* (protected areas) system schemes. Islam views humans as having a purposive existence which is to create an ethical social order on earth that is just and humanitarian. Islam's social philosophy is based on the perspective of human intent, the satisfaction of needs and wants and the enjoyment of things, as well as on the primacy of individual and collective responsibility, all within the guidelines given by Islamic values. Islam argues that all people are part of one large human family, hence they are equal and should be treated as such. The diversity of mankind is itself a divinely created phenomenon for the purposes of social learning.

Islam constitutes the principle of a median community (*ummah wassat*) as a platform of commonality based on faith, values and ethics. It envisions the social order embodying several *ummahs* living in peace and harmony. It suggests mutual cooperation for private and public good through social commitment, social solidarity and altruism. It diffuses collective responsibilities among all citizens. Therefore, it becomes the task of all members of society to contribute toward the establishment and maintenance of the ethical social order and trust funds (*waqf*) so as to maximise socio-economic welfare as well as the opportunities for self-development and personal growth for the largest possible number of people.

## Green Activism and Innovation

To address the market failures as seen in climate change, poverty and the financial crisis, I proposed a model which consists of three components Green Jihad, Ijtihad and Zuhd (Green JIZ). I envisioned four strategies to address market failures including climate change and poverty through a transformative responsible development that is characterised as 'local-centred and green along with having a quality education and Islamic finance models'. This model, called Green JIZ, represents a holistic response to climate change from an Islamic perspective. Green Jihad is about harnessing the civil society activism to save nature and people's right in a free, safe and healthy living. Green Ijtihad is about unlocking the potential of human innovation to improve human well-being. Green Zuhd is about living lightly on earth and to avoid and limit waste, over-consumption, overuse and over-exploitation of resources. Muslims, as a median community among all nations (*ummah wasat* ), should take responsibility and transcend the consumer culture and to develop models of renewable energy, clean production, fair trade, *hima, ihyaa ard mawat* and localised production which in turn will lead to less carbon emissions and minimise risks and potential disasters of climate change. In essence, the stagnation in the world of notions, ideas and dialogue with the 'other', enhances the imagined clash of civilisations and the so-called phenomenon of Islamophobia. These misconceptions are the human-made 'fires' (both in forests and the world of ideas) destroy the wealth of our forests which are in reality our pharmacy, playground, class room and source of inspiration.

## Mecca City as a Global Forum for Dialogue

Good life can be manifested and embodied in a good city. I propose Mecca as a model for an eco-city which seeks to manifest good life (*Hayat Tayebah*) and the purposeful efforts to establish a model for the built environment (*Imran* and *Imaratu Al-ard*) that produces benefits (*manafie*) beyond space and time. It will be illuminating to transform Mecca as a city that unifies all three global fora (economic, social and environmental) and unify a human discourse with a new narrative and a story of a city embodies unity (*tawhid*) of good life. The essence of pilgrimage (*Haj*), besides the spiritual dimension, is to share the wisdom and best practices and to address the current risks, threats and challenges worldwide. The same can be said about Jerusalem, as a city which Prophet Mohammad (pbuh) led all prophets in a prayer at Al-Aqsa mosque in Jerusalem, which shows, from an Islamic worldview, that Islam is not a new religion but a continuum for all monotheistic religions.

The notion of benefits (*manafei*), as stated in the context of Prophet Abraham's prayer (peace be upon him), is a generic term that encompasses human well-being, livelihood, socio-economic development and human-centred development. Benefits also encompass human dignity and the nurturing of human mind, soul and well-being. Also, living the experience of Mecca should be a transformational experience that contributed to the enlightenment of the civil movement in the 1960s and is expected to play a new role of the twenty-first century to address current global challenges and to inspire the global community (*ummah*) to shoulder a human responsibility and to embody a global visions and mandate that transcends national boundaries.

Realising the global challenges from climate change, pollution, over-consumption, biodiversity loss and poverty, Mecca can be the stage to demonstrate how a transition to a low-carbon economy and contribute to new ideas of green economy like protected area (*hima*) and trust funds (*waqf*). Mecca, like other cities in the Middle East and North Africa, is rich in solar energy and if this renewable energy is well-harnessed in the built environment, auto-industry and ICT can be a model for achieving prosperity without being addicted to fossil oil.

Harmony, balance, governance, human dignity and reconciliation between human and nature are key ingredients for good life. The rich historical experience of pilgrimage is a story of social cohesion and human empathy, all of which are the cornerstones for a good life and a good city. Living for few days in Mecca as a good city (*balad tayyeb*) encompasses good practices, good food (prophet food), unity of appearance in white clothes and unity in remembrance of Allah.

## Education for Sustainability

Holistic education that addresses the unity (*tawhid*) of humans and knowledge is important in transforming the current mode of development. Holistic education helps foster an open spirit of inquiry in which faith and reason lead toward higher consciousness and inner beauty (*ihsan*). Hence, to educate people holistically is to let people know, understand and to respect the interdependence of all things and the equality of all species in the sustaining their lives on earth.

There should be an increased consciousness and awareness among all walks of life over the welfare and fate of the earth. They would insist, as the old African saying goes, that 'the world was not bequeathed to us by our parents but rather entrusted to us by our children'. The development of science and technology that is based on the teachings of religious and cultural values must be mainstreamed at all levels of society. Thus, holistic education can serve to bring together both knowledge and values. In essence, the prosperity enjoyed by human beings is a result of harmonious relations between humankind and nature. In order to ensure a sustainable human civilisation, people need to have a set of rules and values that respects the harmony and 'natural state' (*fitra*). We need to learn the basic lessons from the collapse of ancient civilisations which was attributed to combined effects of environmental damage, population growth, unsustainable agriculture, climate change and warfare. It is imperative to understand that progress and prosperity of early civilisations were founded on the harmonious relationship between human and environment and we in the twenty-first century are to be mindful of this basic principle to sustain our human civilisation.

## References

Diamond, Jared. (2005). *Collapse: How Societies Choose to Fail and Survive*. London: Penguin Books.

Hossein, N. (1968). *Man and Nature: The Spiritual Crisis in Modern Man*. London: Allen & Unwin.

McNealy, Jeff. (2009). 'ICT for a Global Sustainable Future'. International Conference of European Commission, Brussels 22–23 January, 2009.

The Brudtland Report (1987). UN Report – Our Common Future. Oxford: Oxford University Press.

# Index